GANDER PUFFING

Navigating the World's Absurd Realities

By Mark Olson

Table of Contents

Introduction

gander noun

informal
look; glance; observe
//take a *gander*

puff verb

puffed; **puffing**; **puffs**

transitive verb
1: to emit, propel, blow, or expel by or as if by puffs
2: to praise extravagantly and usually with exaggeration

ganderpuffing gerund

1: To observe the world, particularly through travel, while noting ironies, misconceptions, mischaracterizations, oversimplifications, and

exaggerations

LIVING ON THE EDGE:
ABLE ARCHER 83

The Cold War was a time of immense uncertainty. A half-century ideological contest of wills culminating in an arms race that delivered humanity the tools to destroy itself many times over. Imagine living on that geopolitical edge? Bomb drills were routine in public schools! These days, despite pandemics, it appears the biggest fear the Gen-Z crowd has is amassing enough likes on their latest self-indulgent Instagram post or Tik-Tok dance off. A world consumed in conflagration is far off the radar. Perhaps we're witnesses to a different kind of societal breakdown. So, what if an exercise meant to prepare for war almost started one? Until recently, President Ronald Reagan's, March 1983, Strategic Defense Initiative (SDI) sat in the trash bin of good ideas. Mocked as "Star Wars," the proposed missile defense shield is as misunderstood today as during its conception. While SDI failed to pan out as expected, it created a structure that did enable some modern breakthroughs. SDI wasn't conjured in a vacuum either. Its origins are rooted in perspectives codified into Cold War doctrine, gleaned from fiction, and reinforced by conflicts scattered across ideological frontlines. Yet, one exercise proved so terrifying it taught a sitting President the limits of nuclear stalemates and the benefits of open discourse, even amongst adversaries.

Popular culture parallels are useful in this requiem. In the 1980s, two films tapped into Cold War hysteria. In 1983, *WarGames* introduced us to a nerdy Matthew Broderick who somehow hacks into North American Aerospace Defense Command (NORAD) with a dial-up connection. He unwittingly challenges the WOPR (War Operation Planned Response) – a defense application designed to address human error by taking the man out of the loop – to a game of Thermonuclear War. Movie-goers learned that sometimes the only way to win the game is not to play at all. The true lesson: A nuclear pissing match has no winners.

James Cameron's 1984 classic, *The Terminator*, gave audiences a leather-clad, killer combat robot rocking Ray-Bans, leather, and a bad accent. In that epic, the real antagonist, Skynet – a neural net-based artificial intelligence system – is activated to navigate the Cold War's brinkmanship and eliminate the same human error feared in *WarGames*. Skynet's subsequent "Judgement Day" left the world in shambles. Looking back, it's undeniable that the Cold War environment, during production, deserves a spot in the credits. After all, what is science fiction, but social commentary wrapped in a spacesuit?

It's no surprise both movies arrived when they did. These movies may now seem kooky or even antiquated. Seemingly, the spectre of Armageddon has faded, at least in those forms. Though outwardly anti-nuclear, there are buried, less-structured messages in apocalyptic cinema: The importance of mutual understanding.

Errors can unleash a cataclysm. A single rogue missile, careless operator, mistaken radar blip, or misinterpreted radio report could be deadly. If an end to nuclear weapons was impractical – and during this period of Cold War relations, it was – what other option was available to military brass? With nuclear weapons, you cannot accept risks, nor rest on your laurels. Off-screen, it took one event to sear that message into President Reagan's brain.

When Reagan entered office, he brought a new attitude to the Oval Office. Moscow entrenched themselves too. The two sides barely talked except when one event, Able Archer 83, altered the status quo. An event so scary that many, even the stern-faced calm, cool, and collected commies occupying the Kremlin, were ready to light themselves on fire and leap from their offices into vats of vodka. Though the Cuban Missile Crisis may be the low-water mark for U.S. – Soviet Relations, 1983 was uniquely troubling due to the comparative might of nuclear power projection capabilities.

By this time, the nuclear build-up yielded an unparalleled arsenal of warheads and gave us wonderful instruments of modern carnage such as the MIRV or Multiple Independently Targetable Re-entry Vehicle. What's better than one nuclear warhead? Try six, or even a dozen or more in one missile. Instead of puny, ordinary ballistic missiles that could only target one city, one missile could pepper the globe in mushroom clouds like a sawed-off shotgun.

It remains a mystery how the world survived November 1983. Able Archer 83 was the codename for a command post exercise, or simulation, carried out that November by the North Atlantic Treaty Organization (NATO). Command post refers to headquarters, meaning this was a top-level command and control simulation. What were they simulating? Escalation from DEFCON 5 all the way to DEFCON 1 (i.e., all-out nuclear war referred to a 'Cocked Pistol'). Command-level exercises are not unique. Training for the worst comes with the territory. For comparison, during the Cuban Missile Crisis, NORAD went to DEFCON 2, termed FAST PACE (ready to engage in 6 hours).

This exercise was slightly different. The Belgium-based Supreme Headquarters Allied Powers Europe (SHAPE) added new elements that piqued the interest of eavesdropping Soviets. There was a unique format for coded communications, periods of radio silence, a planned headquarters shift, covert airlifts of almost 20k soldiers, and, most importantly, the participation from heads of government (remember that last one).

This period was a mess. Jimmy Carter's feckless leadership had calcified wounds between the two rivals. The Iranian Revolution delivered a humiliating roundhouse to the gut. Meanwhile, El Salvador was "draining the sea" of insurgents by adopting scorched earth tactics in the countryside. Stagflation sunk the American economy. The list goes on.

Once in office, Reagan ordered unprecedented military growth and called out the 'Evil Empire.' Yet, actions cut more than words, and, despite America's problems, the Soviets were in their own hurt locker. The U.S. Army replaced the Pershing Ia missiles with advanced Pershing IIs (in 1983) throughout Europe in response to Soviet SS-20 deployment. The Soviets saw these missiles as first-strike weapons meant to bypass the constraints posed by "Mutually Assured Destruction" or MAD. They were believed capable of destroying underground silos and bunkers. Soviet misadventures in Afghanistan increasingly mirrored

America's calamity in Vietnam (Afghanistan 2.0 shows how much history rhymes). Additionally, Cuba, their staunch comrade, was floundering economically and draining Soviet funds. A pro-Eastern bloc regime in Angola struggled in the fight against a U.S.-backed insurgency. Lastly, Nicaragua's Marxist government faced opposition from Contras, who earned a *friend* in Reagan (see Iran-Contra Affair). The world was falling apart in 1983 and hit critical mass in November.

Enter RYaN. Who's Ryan? RYaN – a Russian acronym for nuclear missile attack – was an intelligence operation. Back in 1981, when Soviet leader Leonid Brezhnev met with KGB Chairman, Yuri Andropov, the head spy hinted that America planned to nuke Russia. Naturally, Brezhnev experienced a pucker factor and increased funding to KGB services. What resulted was the largest, most comprehensive peacetime intelligence operation in Soviet history. KGB operatives working abroad were tasked to closely watch anyone who would decide on launching a nuclear attack, the technicians and servicemen who would implement an attack, and any facility where a launch could originate. If you're imagining a plethora of spies, double-agents, sleeper cells, and seductresses occupying local Air Force watering holes, you're probably not far off. Details remain scarce but the scenario provides much food for the imagination.

The true goal of Operation RYaN was to identify the first intent of a nuclear attack and pre-empt it. This should sound scary. Remember, MAD relied on both nations seeking to avoid confrontation because any victory would be pyrrhic. Who wants to rule a scorched radioactive wasteland? Reagan even referred to MAD as a "Suicide Pact." The fact that the Soviets came to believe a pre-emptive strike was a necessity shows how sour relations had gotten. This wasn't Reagan's fault either, despite the pleasure many get lobbing verbal grenades his way, almost as much as they revel in giving him zero credit for the USSR's collapse. Truth is, Reagan's rhetoric made an impression, but Soviet paranoia preceded "the Great Communicator." Both Brezhnev and Andropov were old school, full-fledged believers. They took everything Reagan said literally and held a deep scorn for the West. They were zealots.

Thus, by 1983, RYaN was a mature program reporting on the policies and suspected intent of American decision-makers. What agents observed shocked the Kremlin. From 1981-1983, the U.S. military executed Psychological Operations or PSYOPs aimed at testing Soviet reactions and radar systems. Its modus operandi had vessels conduct clandestine naval transits through icy gaps near the North Pole, and Norwegian and Baltic Seas, to get within range of key bases. Bombers would fly straight at Soviet airspace, only to peel off just before entering. The entire situation frazzled the Russians. Of course, RYaN agents knew these near penetrations were devised to assess vulnerabilities and showcase U.S. capabilities during a nuclear war...To some extent. Near penetrations are not unusual but represented a departure from Carter-era policies. Adding fuel to the fire was April 1983's North Pacific Fleet Exercise, which included forty ships, twenty thousand American personnel, and hundreds of aircraft. CIA involvement compelled the U.S. military to provoke a Soviet reaction to gather radar characteristics and other valuable signals. U.S. aircraft also overflew a Russian island in the Kurils. The Soviets responded by passing over the Aleutians.

U.S. actions, while justifiable, instilled zero confidence in a suspicious Soviet leadership who were conditioned to fear the West, saw America preparing for war, and succumbed to Reagan's rhetoric. To compound matters, Andropov assumed Soviet leadership once Brezhnev died. Yes, the one guy convinced that the Americans were committed to launching a sneak attack, and who once stated, "Reagan is inventing new plans on how to unleash a nuclear war in the best way, with the hope of winning it," took the helm of the the communist bloc.

Yet, two events changed everything: The shooting down of Korean Air Lines Flight 007 and a false alarm. On September 1st, 1983 – just a few months before Able Archer – a Soviet Su-15 fighter shot down the airliner heading from New York to Seoul via Anchorage. The aircraft drifted off course and well into Soviet airspace due to navigational missteps. The Soviet pilot took her down with air-to-air missiles. All told, 269 passengers and crew were killed, including a sitting U.S. Congressman, Representative Larry McDonald of Georgia. Wholly ironic, he was also President of the right-wing, anti-communist John Birch Society. Soviet damage control was abysmal. First denying the event, then arguing that the Boeing 747 was a spy plane even though the Soviet pilot witnessed blinking lights and knew it was civilian. Then again, they feared even civilian planes would be converted to military use, were a strike to occur. The Soviets also claimed the Korean Airliner was a deliberate provocation. Six hours after the downing, South Korea mistakenly issued a statement that the aircraft landed safe and sound in Russia. Alas, they were misinformed by the reliably unreliable Kremlin officials. The debacle brought relations to a new public low. The attempted Soviet cover-up had been inept, and hatred for the USSR intensified. Two weeks later, the Soviets found the flight recorders but kept them concealed until 1993. One 'benefit' – if it's proper to use such a word of this horrific tragedy – was that the Reagan Administration allowed worldwide access to GPS following the disaster.

The second event brought danger even closer. On September 26, 1983 – the same month the airliner was shot down – the Soviet orbital missile early warning system (SPRN) codenamed Oko, saw something. What did it see? The system reported a lone ballistic missile barrelling from the U.S. in the upper atmosphere. Imagine the Soviet strategic command that night. Frantic pounding on keyboards, communications circuits flooded with panic-filled reports. Amidst the chaos, Lieutenant Colonel Stanislav Petrov harnessed his logic. As in the film, *WarGames* – released the same year – when Dr. Stephen Falken – the man who created WOPR, saw the screen full of incoming and outgoing missiles, he stated, "General, what you see on these screens up here is a fantasy; a computer-enhanced hallucination. Those blips are not real missiles. They're phantoms," Petrov also saw how illogical it all was. Why would the Americans fire a single missile? It made no sense. In a split-second decision, he dismissed the report as a false alarm. There, in their control room, they waited for an impact. The end of the world. He'd seen previous malfunctions and reasoned correctly this blip was nothing more than a computer-enhanced hallucination. But later, four more blips appeared as additional ICBM launches. He dismissed those too, wiped sweat from his brow and braced for the shock. No, they weren't ICBMs, but false alarms caused by a rare alignment of sunlight on high-altitude clouds beneath the satellite's orbit. However, the Soviets had been ready to strike. Billions had been invested in state-of-the-art tracking equipment, and yet it was tricked by environmental anomalies.

With the setting established, Able Archer 83 commenced. According to SHAPE historian, Gregory Pedlow, the exercise pitted a fictional country, Orange, commencing hostilities in Europe on November 4th. Two days later, chemical weapons entered the fray. Despite simulated skirmishes, Russian invasions of neighbors, and scripted diplomatic responses, this exercise wasn't about conventional fighting. The goal was to test transition procedures to DEFCON 1. Simulating combat heating up, embedded KGB RYaN agents pushed reports to Moscow. Again, they were tasked, perhaps obsessively so, with spotting the warning signs of an American nuclear attack. Yes, right when the Soviets were looking for clues, we gave them one – albeit simulated. Because of the added realism, a suspicion festered that Able Archer was cover for an actual strike. The prolonged radio silences and new codes resonated as well. Why such secrecy if only an exercise? KGB telegrams poured in, painting a picture borne out of paranoia and deteriorated relations.

The thing is KGB protocol required agents to simply report observations and not opinions. What you really had were agents abroad who knew this was a drill but who were divorced from the assessment and analysis arm of Soviet decision-making. This was identified as one of the major flaws in Soviet intelligence operations highlighted during RYaN. Funnel intelligence through the Kremlin pipes and then let 'experts' far removed from the truth on the ground sort it out. This is precisely what happened during Able Archer.

The participation of heads of state exacerbated matters. The "Iron Lady" Margaret Thatcher and West German Chancellor Helmut Kohl played minor roles. On the U.S. side, the President, VP George H.W. Bush, and SecDef Caspar Weinberger were slated to have involvement in the final stages. Rumors of their participation amplified concern amongst RYaN agents. While a first strike seemed ridiculous, new communication procedures and a heightened state of NATO readiness created a cloud of confusion. This happens all the time. More information flows in and the timeline (albeit arbitrary) compresses. Time-sensitivity adds pressure. Demands for clarity are hampered by urgency and overbearing bosses. What was once believed tends to alter, shift. RYaN agents navigating exercise details in real time, began to wonder: Could the exercise truly be a cover? A ruse? A Trojan horse to catch Moscow unprepared, unprotected? What were all the near-airspace penetrations with aircraft about? A pattern emerged that fit neatly into preconceived notions, becoming a self-fulfilling prophecy.

On the morning of 8th November, Supreme Allied Command Europe (SACEUR) requested approval to conduct limited nuclear strikes against specific, fixed Orange targets. Then, as planned, prolonged silence. For what seemed like decades, everyone waited for permission to take the simulated contest to nuclear heights. Giddy, care-free NATO operators might've even joked around to cut the boredom of the typically mundane exercises, left their consoles for the bathroom, or snorted at their frustration that these weren't the real thing. Meanwhile, the Soviets were caked in perspiration, desperately trying to decipher American intent. Locked in on their consoles with maniacal focus and filled with a gut-wrenching terror. Oleg Gordievsky, the famous double agent and highest-ranking KGB defector, made it clear when he said that the agents in the intelligence cycle simply reported and did not analyze information which fed into an immense fear of nuclear aggression. Consider that for a moment. Sitting back waiting for hours and hours. Front row seat to a potential world's demise. It was evening when SACEUR finally got their response...approval cleared the top echelons. Engage targets with nuclear weapons.

On the 9th, SACEUR launched their salvos against Orange. But, as in *Terminator 2* – when the protagonists succeeded in stopping Cyberdyne Systems and de-facto Skynet – Judgment Day never came. Why? Reagan, Caspar Weinberger, and National Security Advisor Robert McFarlane deserve serious credit for one decision. Prior to the exercise start, McFarlane considered the implications of involving Reagan and Weinberger in the decision tree for the exercise. He reasoned correctly that there was a high likelihood that communications issuing nuclear-related orders would be intercepted by Soviet spies and monitoring systems. The risk was not worth taking. He pushed for the removal of the U.S. leadership element and won. A critical decision that averted potential disaster.

Secondly, the actions of RYaN agents proved instrumental. Around the time the request was issued to go nuclear, Moscow sent a frantic "flash" message (meaning highest priority) demanding a final intelligence push to ascertain America's first-strike intentions. Soviets, fearing their only option was a pre-emptive strike, readied their arsenals. The CIA immediately noted Soviet movements to ready strategic bombers. But, according to former CIA analyst Peter Vincent Pry, "this was just the tip of the iceberg...ICBM silos easily readied and difficult to detect...were readied as well." RYaN agents, though, kept throwing reports to Moscow, and it is suspected some became more outspoken, opinionated, pulling the Kremlin from the brink of a nuclear exchange. Yet, it was Lt. Gen Leonard H. Perroots who may have played the largest role. As the CIA flooded him with intelligence on Soviet preparations, he resisted the urge to heighten NATO troop readiness. This decision was a crucial signal to the USSR that the attack was, in fact, a simple peacetime exercise.

On the 11th, Able Archer 83 ended without fanfare, catastrophe, or death. The sun rose, Americans and Soviets went to work, and children went to school. The judgment day – a feared nuclear holocaust – was confirmed as a hallucination: A fantasy conjured from Cold War tensions and nations wielding weapons capable of killing everyone. The biggest scare since the Cuban Missile Crisis might be forgotten by most. However, its sobering legacy lives. The impact was profoundly felt. The fragility of MAD doctrine; a policy crafted in desperation. Logical, sure, but madness masked as strategy. Though still relevant when considering state actors with copious stockpiles, the modern world is fraught with hidden dangers that demand added safeguards.

Reagan, seeing the chaos unfold – airline debacle, false alarm, and Able Archer – rightfully realized that MAD alone could not guarantee safety. The 83-scare resonated with Reagan. He started to see things differently. A movie called, *The Day After*, similarly affected him. It depicted the aftermath of a nuclear attack on Lawrence, Kansas. The latter horrified him and left him greatly depressed. All those red-blooded Americans, wholesome Midwesterners clambering for shelter from the blinding blast and wave of destruction from a menacing mushroom cloud. The irradiated plains, the country's breadbasket torn asunder. The results of Able Archer were equally stunning. Reagan operated from a faulty assumption that everyone knew a first strike was unthinkable. Upon learning how unnerved the exercise made the Soviets, he wrote:

We had many contingency plans for responding to a nuclear attack. But everything would happen so fast that I wondered how much planning or reason could be applied in such a crisis... Six minutes to decide how to respond to a blip on a radar scope and decide whether to unleash Armageddon! How could anyone apply reason at a time like that?

During the Reykjavik Summit from 11-12 October 1986 between Reagan and Gorbachev, the President could not be swayed from his commitment to SDI, despite Gorbachev's proposal to ban all ballistic missiles. Though critics bashed Reagan for missing out on what they deemed a historic opportunity, the summit led to an enormous breakthrough: The Intermediate-Range Nuclear Forces (INF) Treaty. SDI investment continued, despite objections. Reagan's decision then was wise and forward-thinking. Once the Cold War ended, SDI morphed as political resolve for a defensive shield waned.

By 1993, SDI officially came to an end. To some, President Clinton destroyed it. SDI lived on and funding was redirected to focus on missile threats under the guidance of the Ballistic Missile Defense Organization (BMDO). In 2002, it was re-christened the

Missile Defense Agency (MDA). Yes, the agency at the forefront of BMD shares DNA with SDI. Those rumors of SDI's demise were vastly exaggerated. It continues to bear fruit, albeit under another name. It's provided an insurance policy from the manic world of MAD.

As a long-haired, hippie from the "Age of Aquarius," Jeff "Skunk" Baxter is an unlikely pioneer in the missile defense. The founding member of Steely Dan, and road-ridden rhythm guitarist who later joined the Doobie Brothers, always had an interest in technology, especially with music. Conversion fascinated him, like how rappers used turntables to revolutionize sound. Luck and a subscription to an aviation magazine piqued his interest in applying creativity to defense. His white paper discussing how to translate AEGIS shipboard capabilities for BMD earned accolades within the Pentagon. He remains a recognized expert in the blossoming field.

The Cold War is over. Stockpiles remain, warheads rest in silos, strategic bombers await orders in their hangars, and ballistic-capable submarines prowl the deep on call. In place of a singular Soviet foe – Russia, China, North Korea, and, one day, Iran – round out a list of potential adversaries. India and Pakistan (both nuclear powers) continue a decades-long dispute over Kashmir. Afghanistan has fallen again. The risk for miscalculation has intensified, especially with an explosion of non-state terrorist groups and nuanced threats in the cyber domain.

MAD "worked" in a simpler, bipolar world. However, Reagan reasoned that MAD had considerable limitations. In this modern, complex, and seemingly peaceful world, it is easy to toss aside concerns. The East versus West, Capitalist versus Communist divide drew a clear line in the sand. Today, lines are blurred. Enemies and their intentions are less defined. The result is a more chaotic, unpredictable geopolitical space cloaked under a veil of stability.

In this environment, missile defense capabilities are not only prudent, but a necessity. Neither humans nor systems can ever be error-free. Rogue actors can destabilize the globe, and state actors may adopt aggressive policies devoid of reason. Critics might question their utility; however, ballistic missile defense offers critical safeguards. Given that global denuclearization remains elusive and problematic, investment and continued support for anti-BMD technologies is a sound insurance policy. Yet, it isn't everything.

Luck aided operators and decision-makers back in 1983, but luck is fleeting - and it can be either good or bad. Reducing the risks of miscalculation isn't done with fancy radars and sloganeering. Dialogue is necessary to drown out paranoia, bridge ideological gaps, and take situations out of fate's hands. An exercise meant to prepare for the worst almost caused it. Yet, it took that scare to make a Presidential Administration fully contemplate the lurking danger. Sun Tzu said, "know your enemy." Fortunately, Reagan learned his lesson because, once properly introduced, Gorbachev and he made a terrific duo.

Fast forward to Saturday, January 13, 2018. Shortly after 8 am an employee at the Hawaii emergency Management Agency ran an internal test of the emergency missile warning system. A system meant to alert the public without sending it to the public. The operator made a mistake and transmitted it to Hawaiians headed to work. Instead of selecting "Test Missile Alert", he selected "Missile Alert." Residents received a message on their phones: "Ballistic Missile Threat Inbound to Hawaii. Seek Immediate Shelter. This is not a drill." Suffice to say, a surge of panic swept the islands. For 38 gripping minutes, a terrified public said their last goodbyes, cried, prayed, and may have enjoyed one last romp in the sack with a newfound love. In the end, the simple error was corrected. There was no Judgment Day...this time.

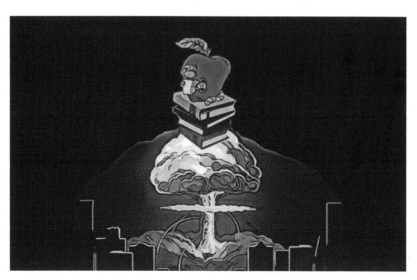

CHECKMATE! RUSSIA'S ART OF THE LONG GAME

If revenge is best served cold, Garry Kasparov would be wise to keep his retinue of bodyguards employed and bottled water in stock. His unwillingness to mince words placed a red, fat target on his back stretching from the Kremlin's heights. It isn't everyday someone regarded as the history's greatest chess savant becomes *persona non grata*, but these are strange times. In 2007, "reformed" former KGB general, Oleg Kalugin, estimated that one day Kasparov would join the exclusive club of critics assassinated with Vladimir Putin's blessing. Lucky man! Despite the danger, Kasparov isn't just bunkered in New York, nor have threats *exiled* his Russian whit. Common mishaps are brushed off as fouled attempts on his life. "Lame assassination attempt, Putin is desperate," he sniped on Twitter after a taxi driver's abrupt slamming of the brakes sent him to the hospital with a head wound. Yet, there's a seriousness behind the entertainment. As a student of chess, he sees pawns inching into position and bishops zipping towards objectives. More than anything, he understands the strategic art of the long game. Experience has taught him patience, assessing the risk-reward, and predicting the adversary's next move. It's an intricate dance between cat and mouse. With Putin's popularity down, poisonings are up. It's time to reassess the long game Russia's been playing ever since its death was greatly exaggerated at the dawn of the Cold War.

The Russian National Tourist Office has an entire page devoted to the origins of Russia's chess obsession. It is home to 11 world chess champions, by far the most. Ivan "the Terrible" purportedly died while playing chess. Meanwhile, Peter the Great marched off to war with a board at the ready and choice opponent in his cohort. Famed members of the intelligentsia dabbled in the game, ingraining it into high culture. However, it was under the Soviet Union that chess became the national pastime and staple of communist rule. Authorities made chess compulsory to test the acumen of would-be soldiers. Moreover, the Soviets won a lot. Winning is sure to gain converts and they decimated rivals on the global stage to a comical degree.

While *Operation Typhoon's* two German pincers closed in on Moscow, Russians held their coveted chess tournaments. As "Black" players held their lines against determined "White" attackers in hardened auditoriums and arenas, Soviets mobilized frontline units and reserves into defensive belts. Russian patience was awarded when counterattacks clawed the capital back and dashed dreams of a thousand-year Reich.

Their Cold War nemesis glorified another pastime: Baseball. The dichotomy is stark. Then again, that's the point. Whereas the exploits of "boys of summer" encapsulate American innocence and optimism in their purest forms, Russians have a conflicted relationship with the traumas of the past and hopes for tomorrow. Consider that serfs cast off the yoke of boyars (the aristocracy) only to see defeat snatched from the jaws of victory. To summarize, the intelligentsia came around flaunting new ideas and it worked! Kind of. They ditched the old system, but the Tsar decided to repay the boyars for confiscated land by saddling serfs with massive loans. Serfdom by another name. Thus, rabblerousers got together to burn the system down with an ideology imported from the west. The Tsar was toppled, and communism proceeded to kill millions through poor management, starvation, and political purges. Not clear enough? Let's consider the renowned Russian short story, *The Overcoat*, by Nikolai Gogol.

The main character, Akaky, is a ridiculed, downtrodden, and pathetically endearing man who labors at a menial job in St. Petersburg. For some ghastly reason he becomes obsessed with purchasing an overcoat. He pours money he doesn't have to design the crème de la crème. Attending a party in the overcoat, he feels good about himself for the first time. On his way home ruffians beat him up and steal his coat. Authorities, who couldn't care less because this is Russia, berated him for wasting their time on trivialities. He ends up dying (from the cold). The story ends with his ghost embarking on a crime spree, swiping overcoats from unsuspecting victims. Tragedy meets irony, that is Russia!

I almost forgot. Russians are always being invaded and they're culturally ostracized too. Rarely invited to the European parties, Russia has a deep inferiority complex. Never trusted, sometimes useful, and more often the doormat for some God-Emperor's imperial aspirations. They ignore the whole "Evil Empire" period, forgetting why people think they're untrustworthy assholes. Instead, they wallow in self-perceived victimhood...Bullied by

Euro-snobs and ugly Americans at the playground. Heavy stuff!

So, Russian fascination with a game of strategy, deception, defense, patience, and heart-wrenching defeat totally adds up. Russia represents an "otherness" in global politics. They're only friends are creeps and sadists (you know who they are). To survive Russia believes it must be cunning, ruthless, methodical. Surgical... Play chess in a world of checkers.

On March 4th, 2018, Yulia Skripal was visiting her double-agent father, Sergei, in Salisbury. Who could have imagined the cathedral city in Wiltshire, England, home to a modest 40,000 residents, would spark international controversy, condemnation, and the expulsion of diplomats? Yet, this event wasn't by chance: The poisoning of Yulia and Sergei had Russian fingerprints. Kasparov perked up.

It wasn't surprising it coincided with Putin's reelection. For anyone keeping track, since 1999 he's been Prime Minister two times and President four, including his current reign. Then again, victory is assured when your chief rival, Alexei Navalny, is barred from competing. The Wall Street Journal described Navalny in 2012 as, "the man [Putin] fears most." The anti-corruption opposition leader was the catalyst for anti-Putin protests through 2011-12. Then fraud charges materialized, followed by a harsh sentence the European Court of Human Rights challenged. Russia relented to a five-year suspended sentence. However, Putin got a *checkmate*. The government Navalny calls "full of crooks and thieves" placed levies before the tide of change.

As a founder of "Other Russia," Kasparov is equally perturbed. Attempts to get on ballots have been obstructed. Before jetting to New York, authorities arrested Kasparov twice and prevented the renting of meeting halls for Other Russia supporters.

Coincidentally, an official meeting hall is a prerequisite for electoral campaigning. It's no wonder Kasparov has chosen to stay in New York since 2013. The poisonings were the same message Russia's been sending since the Soviet Union's death wails.

Until the early 90s, few knew the poison used existed. It hails from a family of the most potent nerve agents ever created. The infamous Novichok Agents are 5-8 times more deadly than VX. For those unaware, VX was the doomsday weapon featured in the film, *The Rock*, and killed thousands of Kurds in northern Iraq. If anything helps illustrate the psyche of Putin's Russia today, and the Soviet mentality prior, it is Novichok Agents.

I don't recommend experimentation (i.e. huffing them in your grandma's basement while you play Xbox). Nerve agents are organophosphate acetylcholinesterase inhibitors. In layman's terms, nerve agents prevent the normal breakdown of acetylcholine, a neurotransmitter. Concentration increases force muscle contraction followed by respiratory and cardiac arrest. Death results from heart failure or suffocation from fluid secretions in the lungs. Difficult of administer and timely treatment exists; however, lasting nerve damage is likely regardless.

The conventional narrative is that the USSR's collapse banished Russia into the geopolitical wilderness. Democracy replaced tyranny, NATO's eastward expansion created a protective envelope for ex-Soviet satellites, and the EU delivered progress to stunted neighbors through economic liberalism. Meanwhile, the Soviet arsenal rotted along piers or was sold piecemeal for pennies on the dollar to warlords and crazed dictators. It's a fun story pushed by the victors in classrooms full of impressionable children. Everyone loves a happy ending. The truth is worse than the lullabies.

Frozen conflicts scar geographic chokepoints and nibble at the edges, predominantly along ethnic lines. They erode sovereignty and complicate viable pathways towards peace. Under the de facto control of unrecognized entities, they're visual reminders of a messy divorce: "Traps" around the board.

Russia's post-Cold War actions mirror a strategic withdrawal, or *gambit*, during which they sacrificed vulnerable stakes in Europe while shoring up relations with former Soviet Socialist Republics through interlocking military and economic agreements. Prior to dissolution, the Soviet Union consisted of 15 states divided into five regions. The Eastern region included Russia, Ukraine, Belarus, and Moldova. Central Asia included Uzbekistan, Kazakhstan, Kyrgyzstan, Tajikistan, and Turkmenistan. The Transcaucasia region consisted of Georgia, Azerbaijan, and Armenia. The Baltics comprised Lithuania, Latvia, and Estonia. So, what really happened after independence?

To illustrate Russian *moves* it's easiest to go from strongest to weakest ties. Belarus is smack dab between three NATO members – Latvia, Lithuania, and Poland – Ukraine (NATO prospect), and Russia. In 1999, coincidentally the year Poland joined NATO, the Union State of Russia and Belarus was formed to integrate both countries, while preserving independence. They are lockstep in foreign relations and operate in concert to suppress dissent. Russia maintains an active military presence for joint training, early warning radar detection, and submarine communications. As always, agreements on tax policy require further fleshing out.

The Eurasian Economic Union (EAEU), established in 2015, evolved through a series of bilateral treaties as a hedge against EU and Chinese encroachment. After the "color revolutions" during Putin's first term as President, Russia applied "hegemonic bilateralism" to pressure Belarus, Armenia, Kazakhstan, and

Kyrgyzstan to form a single market with over 180 million people and GDP of $5 trillion. Although, EAEU mimics the EU's framework, it is comparatively weak. Russia remains unenthusiastic about crafting a rules-based system to strengthen supranational institutions at the expense of sovereignty, especially its own. Thus, ambitious plans for a common currency or other enhancements have stalled. It provides little economic utility for any member. Rather, EAEU is a power-based structure designed by Russia to exert foreign policy control without the hassle of governance. Getting embroiled in domestic squabbles is low on Russia's list of priorities. Instead, Russia is solidified as gatekeeper to Eurasia, symbolically rises in global stature, and sacrifices little in the process. Kowtowing to the Kremlin's strategic aims is a pittance compared to remaining in Putin's good graces. Uzbekistan is on track for full membership in upcoming years. Speaking of Uzbekistan:

Nukus, Uzbekistan is a remote area in a remote county in a remote region with two claims to fame. The first is the Nukus Museum of Art. Stalin's systematic erasing of Russian and Uzbek modern art, and imprisonment of creators, the survival of pieces a miracle. Apparently, Nukus was beyond Stalin's reach. The second is the Red Army's Chemical Research Institute. Evidence suggests the rare Novichok Agents were born there. In 2002, the U.S. Department of Defense dismantled the facility in a joint effort with Uzbek authorities, but stockpiles shifted hands well prior.

The Collective Security Treaty Organization (CSTO) is a NATO-like military alliance consisting of every EAEU nation, plus Tajikistan (Serbia and Afghanistan gained observer status in 2013). CSTO was formed in 1994 to replace the dissolved Warsaw Pact and deter foreign aggression. It originally contained Azerbaijan, Georgia, and Uzbekistan; however, all three withdrew in 1999 (Uzbekistan reentered in 2006, left again in 2012). Ukraine, the Baltic States, and Turkmenistan have consistently rejected membership. Although not on par with NATO, Russia has practical reasons for its maintenance and expansion. It symbolically codifies Russia as a regional hegemon while forming buffers zones to counter terrorism and stifle narcotics trafficking. Tajikistan borders Afghanistan and China and, including Kyrgyzstan and Kazakhstan, forms a defensive ring along China's entire border with Russia. CSTO's bylaws prevent members from joining other military alliances. This means Russia can stiff-arm would-be suitors, especially China. However, CSTO is really Russia's military sales medium to trade and transfer military equipment and training to members transitioning from Soviet standards to modern ones. Yet, Putin has bold ambitions to transform CSTO into a multipolar alternative to U.S. dominance. Iran repeatedly resurfaces as a candidate. With America's exodus from Afghanistan, the Syrian Civil War becoming a stage for "Great Power" proxy wars, and China's Belt Road Initiative carving out infrastructure deals, Russia is keen to hold the line.

The Commonwealth of Independent States (CIS) was created in 1991 to successfully transition Soviet Republics towards independence. When the Soviet Union fell, 15 new nations didn't magically appear. Aspirants first declared sovereignty and international recognition by UN members followed. Currently, CIS includes every Soviet Republic except for Ukraine, The Baltic States - Estonia, Latvia, Lithuania – Georgia, and Turkmenistan.

Ukraine never joined since semi-statehood was granted under Stalin. Whereas, the Baltic States had general recognition prior to official collapse, everyone else had to wait. Georgia withdrew in response to the 2008's Russo-Georgian War and Turkmenistan never ratified the treaty. All CIS members, except Azerbaijan, are also participants in the CIS Free Trade Area (CISFTA). CISFTA, while important, is vulnerable to the shifting winds of Russia's foreign policy choices. To many, CIS is an obsolete appendage that means little and does less.

Well, that's not entirely true. CIS is useful in one major way: Understanding who's "In" and who's "Out" of the Russian sphere and why. These overlapping organizations are Russia's "tell." For instance:

Uzbekistan offered U.S. forces access to Karshi-Khanabad Air Base (or K2) to support post-9/11 operations in Afghanistan. In 2005 the 416th Air Expeditionary Group was forced to vacate. The U.S. cited the Uzbek President Islam Karimov's disturbing crackdown of anti-government dissidents, a quid pro quo of a renewed lease for turning a blind eye, and Russian pressure.

From 2001 to 2014, the U.S. Air Force's 376th Air Expeditionary used Kyrgyzstan's Transit Center at Manas to fight global terrorism. Russia and China (to a lesser extent) stirred up local animosity against U.S. presence and sparked a rent war. Kyrgyz Parliament demanded a threefold increase. The U.S. took flight fearing further entrenchment in the nation's crooked practices.

Since the end of the Cold War, NATO and EU expanded to 30 members and 27, respectively. This process choked Russia's maneuvering space, pinning them to fewer tiles. In Europe, "White" captured their Soviet era pawns and encircled defenses in the Balkans. Former Yugoslavian nations have either joined the West, or are candidates to do so, even Serbia. While some nations might decide to forgo NATO membership, or vice versa, membership in either organization culls Russian influence. Ukraine also aspires to escape Putin's reach. Even Georgia, far off in the Caucasus Region, sees NATO and EU membership as a matter of survival (formal EU application is expected by 2024).

Provoked, Putin laid *traps* in Ukraine and Georgia, a *block* in Moldova, and got a *checkmate* in Azerbaijan. Yet, each case follows a common script.

Tap local resources for disgruntled leaders, useful idiots, intellectuals, and an emotional public to sow internal dissent. Use mercenaries to nurture separatist forces and broaden fringe movements through intimidation, terrorism, appeals to ethnic groups, and media manipulation. Undermine opposition power bases. Respond to opposition responses with fabrications and exaggerations. If appropriate, apply sanctions based on constructed narratives or justify the deployment of peacekeepers to reduce tensions. When all else fails, invade, or launch cyber-attacks. You can always justify invasion for the sake of innocent children anyway.

Nowhere is this clearer than when examining the GUAM Organization for Democracy and Economic Development (formally GUUAM). Geographically dispersed, they're united by a collective axe to grind. Georgia, Ukraine, Azerbaijan, and Moldova developed this body in 1997 to strategically integrate relations. Perennial fence-sitter, Uzbekistan, joined in 1999 and withdrew in 2005. Frozen conflicts and Russian-backed escalation are the norm for each nation, and boy do they all rhyme.

In Ukraine, pro-West candidate Viktor Yushchenko stunned the Kremlin by winning the 2004 presidential election against

Prime Minister Viktor Yanukovych. The election was messy, including repeated runoffs due to widespread fraud on behalf of his pro-Russian opponent. Subsequent events sparked the Orange Revolution. Afterwards he was poisoned by a rare and potent dioxin, leaving him alive but permanently disfigured. During his tenure he pursued EU membership. In 2010, Viktor Yanukovych, the guy who probably conspired in his poisoning, ousted him (Note: Trump's 2016 Campaign Chairman, Paul Manafort, advised his campaign). This dashed hopes to break Russia's hold. In 2012, Yanukovych delayed a decision on joining the EU. This sparked the "Euromaidan" moment during which protesters clashed with police and occupied government buildings. Parliament voted 328-0 to relieve Yanukovych, who fled a looming impeachment trial before beseeching Putin. In response, Russians occupied vital bases in Crimea under the auspices of defending the majority rights of ethnic Russians. It is worth noting that Nikita Khrushchev symbolically "gifted" Crimea to Ukraine in 1954. At the time, it was a politically calculated gesture to strengthen unity following Stalin's death. Today, Russia uses it as evidence of Russia's rightful ownership.

Beyond Crimea, separatist groups along the Russian border declared autonomy. Non-uniformed Russians, well-heeled mercenaries, and local militias held off Ukrainian forces while Russia mobilized forces. Russia's invasion ultimately ceased after Putin achieved his aims. Ukraine is weaker, knows its role, EU membership is a pipedream, and Black Sea access is secured. Also, two new breakaway states join a list getting longer: The Donetsk People's Republic and Luhansk People's Republic.

The trap is set. Putin correctly reasoned that, for all the lofty ideals about self-determination and dignity, Ukraine is alone. The mealy-mouthed speeches, celebrations, and glad-handing don't amount to spit. When the rubber met the road, the West proved spineless. Now, any solution is more terrible than the problem. Sanctions will come and go but these de jure autonomous republics are here to stay. Best laid plans paid off. Who cares if they've poisoned their relationship with Europe? They'll always need gas.

But, back to Russia's domestic situation. Nationalist fervor skyrocketed after the confrontation with Ukraine. Putin dubiously won 76% of the vote. So why the poisonings, especially in public? Putin sees domestic and international security as intertwined. Poisonings send two messages. First, he will find you anywhere, anytime. You will be held accountable. Second, poisonings stir nationalist sentiments of unfair targeting by the West. Actions so brazen cannot be true. No, it is the West and their obsession with Russia's subservience. Hence the use of poisons. When it comes to killing, poisoning has a certain allure, a "whodunnit." A plausible deniability. Poisonings can afflict you anywhere: A pinprick, a deep breath, or a bite of a Big Mac. Poisonings are brilliant, overtly covert psychological tools.

National sovereignty can also be poisoned. Georgia's troubles trace back to their late-80s push for independence. Abkhazia and South Ossetia were quasi-autonomous subunits of the Georgian Soviet Socialist Republic under the Soviet Union's convoluted federal system. Though sporadic bouts of ethnic strife existed, the Soviet Union's fracturing opened the floodgates. In its wake, Georgia pressed for independence; whereas Abkhazians and South Ossetians believed a reformed USSR could be cobbled together. Legal squabbles turned violent and Soviet forces intervened. Upon Soviet dissolution, Georgia flexed its muscles to establish sovereignty over the entire region. This sparked two wars: 1991's South Ossetia War and 1992's War in Abkhazia during which thousands perished and even more were dislocated. Russian intervention secured a ceasefire and created two breakaway states:

Republic of South Ossetia and Republic of Abkhazia. An uneasy peace followed under the watchful eye of Russian peacekeepers "occupying" the breakaway states. Naturally, Russia used the occasion to mature ties: Issuing passports to create new "citizens," Importing officials, Investing, and Training paramilitary outfits. 2003's Rose Revolution and rise of pro-West President Mikheil Saakashvili altered everything. The story goes:

Saakashvili launched an anti-smuggling campaign which eventually triggered violent outbreaks manufactured by Russian proxies. Russia banned the import of mineral water and wine (can't make this up). In 2006, Georgia arrested four Russian officials for espionage. Russia closed transportation links and deported migrant workers. On August 7, 2008 Georgian artillery shelled South Ossetian positions and captured South Ossetia's capital. Russia arrived in the nick of time. After four days of heavy bombing and destabilizing cyber-attacks, mechanized forces crippled Georgian military capacity. Russia 1, Georgia 0.

Yet, that shitshow was a sideshow. Ask yourself why a powerful country wastes its time on two sparsely populated, unrecognized separatist states? The answer is always money. Sure, Georgia wanted to join NATO...That's child's play. Georgia was threatening another man's livelihood with Western backing. The Caspian Sea is home to one of the world's largest collections of oil and gas fields. Being landlocked complicates matters. All those juicy resources with nowhere convenient to go. Thus, construction of the Baku-Tbilisi-Ceyhan Pipeline began in 2002 (completed in 2006) was designed to funnel oil and gas from Azerbaijan to Turkey through Georgia. It also bypassed landlocked Armenia due to Turkish involvement in the Nagorno-Karabakh feud between Azerbaijan and Armenia, on behalf of the former. Black Sea transit is longer and costlier. Thus, alternative pathways reduce Russia's leverage over thirsty Europeans.

The trap is set. The 2008 Russo-Georgian War is aptly known as "the pipeline war." Still, petroleum politics is part of a broader Western play to reduce Russian influence through economic, diplomatic, and military means. However, Saakashvili's blunder strengthened Russia's position. It gave them ample justification to double down their support for "victimized" Abkhazians and South Ossetians (and get the West off their lawn). If ownership over the breakaway states was uncertain before, it certainly isn't now. In 2015, Russian troops took a stroll outside the boundaries of South Ossetia, finally stopping near Orchosani, a village of nearly 300 Georgians. For a moment they controlled a short length of pipeline crucial to Georgian survival...Because they could.

In 2013, Saakashvili fled Georgia over charges he claimed were politically motivated. He reentered politics as Governor of Ukraine's Odessa Oblast, serving in that capacity until 2016. Now he heads the Executive Committee of Ukraine's National Reform Council (can't make this up). During a 2014 interview with Al Jazeera, Saakashvili commented, "At one of our last meetings [Putin] told me, 'Your friends in the West promised you lots of nice things, but they never deliver. Well, I don't. I don't promise you nice things at all, but I always deliver.'"

During the 2012 presidential debate Mitt Romney's dire warning about Russia elicited a snarky retort from President Obama: "The 1980s, they're calling to ask for their foreign policy back." The crowd erupted in laughter, headlines cheered the takedown, and know-it-all pundits smirked. Such flippancy from the same man who, over an open mic, pledged more "flexibility" once reelected and called ISIS a "JV Team." Arrogance and underestimation are rife in this land of confusion. Who's still laughing?

Even cultures aren't immune to poisoning. Russia's *block*

in Moldova is least publicized, possibly most dangerous. Here, language and identity are strained by a web of compounding factors. The 1990-1992 Transnistria War spawned the Pridnestrovian Moldavian Republic "Transnistria" – a slender span located along the Moldovan-Ukrainian Dniester River border. It is an unrecognized home to just under 500,000 Moldovans, Russians, and Ukrainians stratified into rough thirds. Moldovans are Romanian, except they aren't. Were part of Romania, yet they weren't. Speak a Romanian dialect, except they don't. It's tricky. Chalk this up to Romania's shaky relationship with war and a Soviet campaign to exterminate nationalism.

Romania spent two years of WWI neutral, joined the Allies to hack their rightful slab off the Austro-Hungarian Empire's decaying carcass, quit after the Bolshevik Revolution, and rejoined the Allies a day before German armistice. Allied victory granted Romania Transylvania and Banat from Hungary, Bukovina from Austria, and Bessarabia (including Moldova) from Russia. "Greater Romania" was forged. For 600,000 casualties her population and land mass doubled!

Enter WWII. The fall of Paris and the pact between Hitler and Stalin put Greater Romania in a vice. Soviets demanded Northern Bukovina and Bessarabia, as they were among the last territorial conquests of Tsarist Russia. Germany advised Romania to accept or risk total occupation. Smelling blood, Hungary demanded Transylvania's return. Bulgaria next snatched Dobruja on the Black Sea. Without options, Romania marched to Moscow as an Axis Power.

After dispatching Hitler's invasion, the Soviet Union conquered the region. Strangely, Stalin never recast Romania as a Soviet Socialist Republic. Romania, virulently opposed to overreach, was the only independent, permanent non-Soviet Warsaw Pact member. He did annex northern Bukovina and Bessarabia, gifting parts to the Ukrainian SSR and using the rest to create the Moldavian SSR (present day Moldova). From 1965-1989 Nicholai Ceausescu led Romania *mostly* on his terms. As nationalism sparked calls to unite common tongues under one communist banner, the Soviets embarked on a meticulous campaign to promote Moldovans as a distinct ethnic group. They went so far as mandating Moldovan be written in Cyrillic vice Latin. In an Orwellian *move*, General Secretary Leonid Brezhnev barraged Ceausescu to alter historical records to remove any reference Moldavian SSR territory was once part of Romania or the population spoke Romanian. The Soviets felt political principles trumped historical truth. When pressed whether he observed ethnic differences during his visit to Moldavian SSR Ceausescu replied, "I did, but they spoke with me in Romanian."

In the early-80s, the Soviet 14th Soviet Guards Army cleverly relocated their headquarters from Moldova's capital, Chisinau to Tiraspol, the largest city in Transnistria. Soviet disintegration opened the doorway for Moldovans to seek reunification with Romania or declare independence. In anticipation, Transnistria separated. Moldovan forces were stymied by separatist militias aided by Soviet 14th Guards Army soldiers, Soviet military defectors, volunteer Cossacks, and local support from ethnic Russian on the east bank of the Dniester River in Ukraine. Strategically defeated, Moldova entered a ceasefire agreement. A tripartite Joint Control Commission (Russia, Moldova, Transnistria) installed the Operational Group of Russian Forces (OGRF) to ensure peace and maintain security. If it were so simple.

The block is placed. The UN, EU, and NATO called for Russia's immediate withdrawal, to no avail. How appropriate that OGRF "peacekeepers" operate from Cobasna Depot – the largest Soviet stockpile in Eastern Europe – where over 20,000 tons of expired ordnance are itching to go ballistic. Russia promised to remove it in 1999...But here we are. Moldovan researchers estimate detonation would rival "atomic bombs from Hiroshima and Nagasaki." Maybe that's hyperbole. What's known is that weapons, once protected in dim, musty concrete tombs, are habitually smuggled from this war-ravaged Soviet vestige. Though support for Romanian reunification has risen in Moldova, so has Russian recognition of breakaway states. Moldova appears frozen in place, blocked from Western aspirations, uniting common ancestors, and wondering the whole time if they'll be the next captured pawn.

Peaceful settlements can be poisoned too. Here Russia earned a *checkmate*. In 2021 the Caucasus Region finally produced good news. Russia brokered a ceasefire that ended six weeks of carnage in Nagorno-Karabakh – the latest spat in the 30-year feud between Armenia and Azerbaijan. It was a necessary, albeit bitter, pill for Armenians to swallow. They were already losing and risked further humiliation. Under the terms, Armenia relinquished territorial gains held since ethnic Armenians declared independence from the newly christened country of Azerbaijan in 1991. The First Nagorno-Karabakh War lasted until 1994, during which the fledgling, separatist Nagorno-Karabakh Republic (now Republic of Artsakh) expanded its territorial holdings including overland access to Armenia. Throughout its duration, Russia supplied arms to both sides to maintain neutrality whilst tipping the scales when circumstances dictated. Left out of the accord was Azerbaijan's ally, Turkey. The NATO ally and western proxy was barred from mobilizing peacekeepers. Russia isn't though. Armenians will execute a phased withdrawal...Russians will fill the vacuum.

Checkmate! If peace can be sustained there's a chance Azerbaijan can be brought back squarely under Russian influence. Naturally, Russian peacekeepers will be on station to provide a guarantee. What this really means is diminished influence for

Turkey and her NATO partners. Also, Armenia's embarrassing loss is bound to stir domestic unrest. I'm sure Putin is eagerly waiting to aid a friend restore order. Moscow now holds ample leverage over both nations. With distractions eliminated, Putin's next move in Georgia should be interesting.

Which leads us to the arduous path forward. Moscow's *moves* horrify critics. But what did the West do apart from "virtue signal" with another round of sanctions? The U.S. is on track to have two operational AEGIS Ashore ballistic missile defense sites in Romania and Poland, deliberately atop old Soviet MiG aircraft bases. Yet, hypersonic missiles could render them obsolete. Additionally, NATO is undergoing an identity crisis and internal politics has led a growing contingent to question the utility of the institution itself. For instance, what is to be done about the ongoing feud between Turkey and Greece over Cyprus? Why is a dictatorship like Turkey in NATO? Should America continue underwriting European security so they can finance lavish social programs? The EU is splitting apart at the seams. Beyond Brexit, there's been a rise in authoritarianism and Russia's played a role stoking vitriol. What is an appropriate response to Russian hacks? On the surface Russia's actions may seem like acts of desperation. They aren't...We've been played. Russian hacks weren't designed to elect President Trump but to sow chaos and poison institutions and public discourse. It has worked! From creating Facebook events to put political rivals in one another's crosshairs to pushing conspiracies, Putin is winning the long game.

There are more questions than answers. Still, avoiding poison requires recognizing the snake. Is anyone still laughing? On 20 August 2020, Navalny was heading to Moscow when a physical ailment forced an emergency landing. He was evacuated to Berlin where experts initially confirmed his illness was a Novichok agent. However, further analysis validated it as an entirely new

Novichok variant. He survived (so far). The West, while outraged, shouldn't hold their breath for justice. Nor can revelations of the snake lurking in the grass be hoped away. While Garry Kasparov mastered chess, so too has Russia and the art of the long game. It's a saga playing out ever since Moscow's, once immeasurable, might turned to rubble. But looks are deceiving. Just as scientists labored in the remoteness of Uzbekistan to craft deadly poisons, Russia has slithered around and poisoned the board. Harriet Tubman said, "Never wound a snake, kill it." Is anyone listening?

ISOLATED: THE UNABOMBER + HERMIT KINGDOMS

For eighteen years, the enigmatic *Unabomber* evaded FBI agents in what constituted the most expensive manhunt in American history. During a six-year hiatus, everyone wrote him off for dead. Analysts were proven wrong when he restarted his seemingly random campaign. The *Unabomber* moniker was coined because his early targets were universities and airlines. Yet, despite 16 bombings that killed 3 and injured 23, he was a ghost known only by a crude artist rendering. In other words, he was a mustached man wearing large sunglasses and a hoodie. Ironically, an original, shelved sketch bore closer resemblance to the mythic villain. The manhunt was tracking a false image both literally and figuratively. It took considerable time for FBI agents to connect the dots and ultimately apprehend Ted Kaczynski and that's when it got interesting. The Unabomber's saga highlights the hidden dangers of isolation. In a lonesome cabin in the woods, Ted developed a perverse worldview. In surprising ways, it's not fanciful to see his descent mirroring the downfall of North Korea on a much larger scale. Isolation has immense consequences, especially when coupled with dangerous ideologies.

Believe it or not, Ted's ideas led to his capture. The FBI was desperate. Absent sufficient leads and haemorrhaging support, they relented to the Unabomber's demand to publish his "manifesto" – *Industrial Society and Its Future* – in the Washington Post, or suffer more bombings. His family recognized his unique word usage, arguments, and general "Ted-ness." His manifesto is brilliantly troubling-- few write like him. Meanwhile, the FBI employed forensic linguistics to zero in. His case was breakthrough in that realm of policework.

On April 3rd, 1996, FBI agents finally captured their man. But he was hardly who they originally thought he'd be...An uneducated airplane mechanic with a limp dick (yes, you read that correctly). Nope, Ted's odd dwelling – a small, homebuilt one-person cabin in Lincoln, Montana (i.e., the middle of nowhere) - only eclipsed his stranger background. This isolated, unkempt, scraggly man was no country bumpkin, but a certified genius who once rubbed shoulders with academic elites at Harvard, Michigan, and Cal Berkeley. He was a mathematical whiz and profound thinker. What happened to him? How could things go so wrong? Better yet, what does this have to do with North Korea?

War redefines boundaries, societies, and ideologies. Therefore, it's hardly shocking that the modern-day Korean peninsula's tale begins with violence. Too often, foreign subjugation imbues a people with a sense of inferiority that gravitates them towards isolation. High school bullies have similar impacts on impressionable youths struggling towards adulthood.

Understanding North Korea today requires an appreciation for how it became the "Hermit Kingdom" to begin with. From 1910 until Japan's surrender on the deck of the battleship Missouri, Japanese colonial overlords held sway in Korea and nearby Manchuria. Naturally, their occupation had an incremental flavor. For Japan, the end of the Tokugawa shogunate, in 1868, ushered in the period known as the *Meiji Restoration*. This era simultaneously restored imperial power and strengthened Japan's position through the fusion of Western technology with Eastern values. It was American Commodore, Matthew C. Perry, that – with modern warships dwarfing their Japanese counterparts in size and capabilities – laid bare Japan's backwardness. When sword-wielding samurais spied colossal steamships, it was clear change was due. Thus, Japan industrialized with pronounced efficiency.

Self-preservation, self-interest, and sensing opportunities to achieve both compelled a new breed of elites to align themselves with Emperor Meiji. Feudal Japan transformed into an oligarchy bent on closing the gap exhibited by Perry's armada. They quickly established trade with the U.S., gleaned vital technical know-how, and set their sights on the Korean peninsula. While I'd love to say I have a Ph.D. in Asian Studies, my knowledge was gleaned via boredom-induced study; this was due to the operational requirements of sentencing my crew to wander the South China Seas. Devoid of urgently needed booze to quell the madness of monotony, the entire crew developed odd extracurricular activities. Remember, isolation has its consequences, although, in this case,

I'd like to think the consequences were reasonably healthy and constructive. Then again, Korean history can be a downer.

While Japan eventually embraced modernization and trade, Korea tended to be even more wary of outsiders. The Great Joseon State was a dynastic kingdom that ruled the Korean Peninsula for about 500 years and adopted an isolationist stance. This certainly makes sense when Koreans constantly feel like a shrimp caught between two whales. Koreans suffered countless invasions and power-plays at the hands of foreigners, particularly China and Japan. Thus, for some 200 years, rulers haunted by insecurity about their security, opted for hermit status. Ironically, those 200 years of near isolation delivered sustained prosperity and advancement. China would later bring Korea under their influence when the might of the Great Joseon State waned. The point is that abuse and trauma have left an indelible mark on the Korean people. It persists today. The "Hermit Kingdom" mentality isn't necessarily a product of communism. It's just as likely to be the persistent harm resulting from Korea's designation as a pawn to regional ambitions. As one-time rebel, ambassador, and political scientist, Toyokichi Iyenaga put it:

Korea is to the Japanese Empire as a spear pointed at its heart. Whatever nation holds this weapon becomes supremely important to Japan. Korea, even in the days of junks, if in the possession of a powerful monarch, must of necessity have been a constant menace to the safety of Nippon; but in this age of steam, when the Korean Strait has been transformed into a mere ribbon of silver, the installment of a strong hostile power in the peninsula would prove the deathblow to the aspirations, if not the very existence, of Japan's empire.

Soon after the Meiji Restoration took root, Joseon-led Korea received an 'imperial decree' announcing Japan's new government. Korea's leaders, squarely aligned with China's Qing Dynasty, refused to recognize Japan's imperial government as on an equal footing with China. This sparked the Ganghwa Island Incident, on September 20th, 1875, that pitted a single Japanese gunboat and marines against a well-defended fort. Japan, recalling past incursions by foreigners, knew encroachment along the island's coast would elicit force. That is exactly what happened. After taking fire, the gunboat *Un'yō* pounded the garrison into submission. Japanese marines then landed ashore to mop up before finally withdrawing. Japan subsequently initiated a blockade under the pretext of demanding an apology. In truth, they sought to open the peninsula to trade and break Korea's subservience to China. They succeeded with the signing of the Japan-Korea Treaty of Amity in 1876. An extremely unequal treaty, it didn't merely permit trade and end Korea's tributary relationship with China; rather, it granted extraterritorial rights. Extraterritorial rights gave Japanese citizens in Korea impunity to commit crimes and delegitimized Korea's legal system.

A chain of events reminiscent of a season of *Game of Thrones* ensued. There were attempted coups, assassinations, multiple dead kings without heirs, boy-kings, savvy queens (Queen Min), puppets (Gojong), usurpers, plenty of backstabbing, and a bit of rape. All the while, China and Japan jockeyed to rule a nation that wanted to be left the hell alone. It reached a boil during the Sino-Japanese War which forever altered Korea's fate. When 1894's Donghak peasant revolution occurred, it offered a suitable pretext for foreign powers to intervene. Panic spread like wildfire and Queen Min beseeched China for aid. This garnered an influx of a few thousand soldiers. Claiming that China's military aid violated some treaty that Gojong signed one day either at gunpoint or in an opium daze, Japan reinforced her stake in Korea with troops of her own. Even though the uprising was quelled in a couple of weeks, forces remained in a bitter standoff. Bored of the impasse, Japan marched on Seoul, captured Gojong, Min, and the entire governing power. Forgive me for skimping on details but you'll thank me later.

Japan maintained pressure, rolling through Pyongyang and decimating Chinese forces retreating across the Yalu River. In hot pursuit, Japan built bridges across the Yalu, punched through perimeter defenses, and gobbled up cities throughout Manchuria. Facing heavy losses at sea and on land, China could do little but sue for peace. The Japanese Imperial Army stopped short of Beijing upon acceptance of the Treaty of Shimonoseki. Thereafter, Chinese influence in Korea ceased. Japan took possession of Taiwan, the Liaodong Peninsula, and the Penghu Islands located in the Strait of Taiwan. They also received war reparations and trade rights along vital Chinese waterways. Doubters took notice. Before the ink dried, Germany, Russia, and France coerced Japan to relinquish their claim over the Liaodong peninsula in exchange for money. In the ultimate betrayal, Russia would later swoop in to lease that land from China, securing a coveted warm water port. Japan's triumph turned into a sour affair, setting the stage for war with a new foe: Russia. Oh, and the European powers used China's weakened state to rape them of further concessions, which, coupled with the trauma of Japanese occupation, helps to explain China's current security-related paranoia. With China out of the picture, Japanese assassins entered Queen Min's chamber, slaughtered her, and desecrated her corpse. The rape (allegedly of her corpse) turned Queen Min into a martyr: A heroine who fought for an independent Korea and – like so many others – died at the hands of imperialists. Read about her. She's quite awesome.

The Japan-Korea Treaty of 1905, combined with direct annexation in 1910, didn't just mean subservience or vassal status; rather, Japan sought utter capitulation and assimilation. To further this goal, authorities issued a plethora of decrees aimed at reducing the counterweight posed by Korea's military. Once diminished, Japan implemented reforms to put policing firmly in the hands of the Empire. Shackled, Koreans spent the next decade under cruel military rule. Dissidence crushed, a flood of Japanese migrants – under the encouragement of leaders hoping to cure their overcrowding problem – took residence and property through land reform programs.

It's commonplace to look beyond the cruel treatment of Koreans under the yoke of the Empire of the Rising Sun. That's ancient history. Right?

In Mokpo, South Korea there is a tunnel flanked by statues of South Korean civilians cleaving the earth with pickaxes as Imperial Japanese soldiers jeer and hurry them along. Faster, harder their faces urge. The broken, exhausted, and defeated Koreans return hollow gazes. That very tunnel, along with hundreds of others, was built by Koreans for their overlords in the runup to WWII. They exist as sobering reminders of Japan's troubled relationship with the Korean People...troubles brought on by capitulation at gunpoint.

What impact has Japan had on Korea's collective psyche?

Old Mokpo has a bank, turned museum that was erected in the pre-war era. Every other dwelling is traditional; conversely, the bank seems snagged from Jack the Ripper's downtown London. On the second floor the weight of Japanese occupation crushes each visitor beneath a tidal wave of corpses. It's a gallery of atrocities. The fluorescent, white room removes all distractions. Death and brutality are the topics and the architect will get proper acknowledgment. Headless women clutching their expired infants, scorched skin, flayed humans, and ever-present allusions to innumerable rapes. Japan didn't merely occupy; they dehumanized and battered a culture to ash.

Questions arise such as, "Where is all the North Korea stuff." Aren't they – with lunatic leaders playing with hairpin triggers – the real enemy? It's easy for outsiders to rationalize an infinite well of forgiveness...blissful forgetfulness with trade and bigger fish to fry. How do the descendants of Hiroshima feel, dispersed and erased Cherokee and Apache tribes, and unshackled Blacks whose inheritance hasn't triumphed over freedom's slow arc? Koreans, while divided by a DMZ, remain united in their distrust and disdain for Japan. Victims are slower to forget and forgive than textbooks that whittle down transcendent moments to concise paragraphs.

South Korea's concern for North Korea hugs the line of ambivalence. In the U.S., this seems shocking when about a million rounds could obliterate Seoul before a resident can finish a sitcom. To many, North Korea is "Chicken Little;" constantly preaching of falling missiles. Yet, the world persists. Life moves on in South Korea and the economy booms. Wealthy South Koreans have no interest – apart from unification groups on the margins – in assuming the massive costs that unification would entail. They see a history rife with injustices committed by Japan, not the Kim Dynasty. They see a Chinese relationship – which despite past transgressions – has been far more cooperative and empathetic to Korean cultural identity. China sees the U.S. standing in the way of her ambitions. China remembers a Japan that put them under the boot (Rape of Nanking, anyone?). The U.S., instead, sees just the threat. It sees missiles tested, hears rhetoric, and reads of human rights abuses. Without a doubt, nuclear weapons in the hands of that disgusting regime is abhorrent; however, solving a problem requires understanding it. This hotspot is not merely about one vile regime. Rather, nation-states are the key actors and reconciling their motivations, qualms, and rivalries is essential. History matters! Translated into *bar speak*:

You have one guy named 'Jim (Japan)' and he not only screwed 'Steve's (S. Korea)' wife but also 'Clint's (China).' Now, Adam (USA) likes everyone and is all about business. Adam does have a strange rivalry going with Clint. Clint thinks Adam resents his recent success. Truth is, Adam is leveraged to the hilt with Clint, his supplier, and doesn't really trust him because he keeps trying to undercut him with side projects. He also gets irked seeing Clint's fancy, E-Class car when just a few years ago he was penniless and cruising the ghetto in a used Pontiac Aztek. In a perfect world, Adam just wants everyone to get over it and form a partnership with him as CEO. Of course, there's one big problem because Clint is simply impossible to talk to and likes doing his own thing. Oh, and there's 'Ned (n. Korea)'...a total scumbag. He played high school baseball with Clint, but over the years he got a little too weird, so Clint distanced himself. Sure, they hang out every once in a while, but it's not the same. Clint's more focused on business these days. Trouble is Ned keeps threatening Steve, a former partner, with lawsuits, bricks in windows, etc. All because his business is failing, and he clings to this fantasy that Steve stole the business to begin with. <u>Okay, solve that problem...and replace bricks with gunfire and lawsuits with nukes.</u>

Still, a history of foreign abuse fails to fully explain how North Korea became so awful. Sure, Karl Marx created quite the mess with his 'little manifesto.' Communism unleashed an economic plague, as evidenced by East-West performance comparisons. Still, how does one quantify institutional impacts on economic well-being?

Angus Maddison attempted to do just that. Before his death, the British economist – specializing in quantitative economics – built a data set to discern the extent governmental policies affected growth. His work continued after his death as the Maddison Project. For those fearful of the horrors of math, a browser search for "North Korea, South Korea, and China GDP History" offers a more

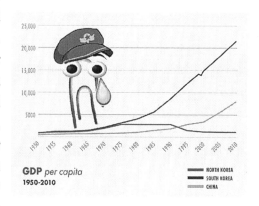

GDP per capita
1950-2010

NORTH KOREA
SOUTH KOREA
CHINA

manageable illustration. In 1950, Gross Domestic Product per capita for each country was roughly the same, with China measuring slightly lower. However, by the mid-sixties, China stayed flat as North and South Korea doubled. Then, in the mid-seventies, North Korea plateaued, while South Korea curved dramatically upward, leaving both communist nations in the dust. By the 1980s, Chinese economic gains – buttressed by President Nixon's 1972 visit – were apparent. Yet, it wasn't until the early 1990s that North Korea and China intersected. As China's economic miracle gained momentum, North Korea nose-dived. Today, North Korean per capita adjusted GDP hovers around 1950s levels and the South Korean economy is almost 37 times larger. Think about that...1950s levels. This chart paints a picture of a nation becoming sick.

Now, economic numbers can be deceiving. Of course, North Korea's GDP per capita in the 1960s was destined to increase. When there's one building left standing after the Korean War, and you build a new one...Poof, there you go. What an economic miracle! Something else was afoot. A cancer metastasized, slowly consuming the patient. It wasn't communism *per se*.

The answers to that question are both simple and extremely complicated: *Juche* and isolation. *Juche*, translated as self-reliance, is the official state ideology and the means to maintain authoritarianism. Based on the premise that man is master of his destiny, a nation must have a strong leader (you can guess who that is). This helps explain the propaganda, children singing songs about the "Dear Leader," and general weirdness. *Juche* isn't just another word for Marxism; rather, it's Korea's spin on it. It rests on the idea that nothing rivals the power of single-hearted unity between the leader, the party, and the masses. They form one single socio-political organism united in both ideology and leadership. The Great Leader is absolute, and the masses do not think for themselves but through the Great Leader, as would an ant colony or alien hive-mind species.

Traditional Marxism focuses societal conflict through the lens of historical materialism and class hierarchies. The Marxist views economic organization, or the mode of production, as the main driver in society. In this sense, a proletariat class of workers suffer oppression at the hands of the ruling class bourgeoisie who extract wealth through exploitation. The mode of production, then, is the source of class-based conflicts and is deemed an inevitable in capitalism. Since, in this view, capitalism is a tool of proletariat oppression it will only lead to a worker's revolt...A class revolution.

Some have likened *Juche* to a strain of Leninism but that's also wrong. Marxism was based on conditions in Europe's advanced and industrialized economies (i.e., where proletariats slaved away under capitalist overlords). The horror! Russia, on the other hand, was agrarian and backward in the early Twentieth Century. Therefore, Vladimir Lenin created what he saw as a practical application of Marxist principles for the socio-economic conditions in Russia. In Russia, the masses were peasants and not a proletariat class (industrial workers). Marx never discussed peasants and Lenin had to adjust theoretical planning to conditions as he found them. He reasoned that the revolution had to incorporate peasants. Chairman Mao did similarly in China. Marx predicted communism could only occur when workers developed a revolutionary consciousness. This would invariably lead to a utopian Dictatorship of the Proletariat. Lenin – gazing at illiterate, drunken peasants – lacked that kind of patience. So, he figured he'd shorten the timetable by creating a revolutionary vanguard...A Dictatorship of the Party. He couldn't wait for industrialization to create this motivated revolutionary working class. That would take forever. Instead, a party of intellectuals would instill such values in the worker bees whether they liked it or not.

Enter Josef Stalin. That tyrant has as much to do with the origins of North Korean strife as anyone except Kim Il-sung. From 1922 to 1953, Stalin ruled the Soviet Union with ruthless efficiency. Stalinism focused on the supremacy of the state over party and class concerns. Since Russia was agrarian, he opted for policies to rapidly industrialize. Instead of seeking a global communist revolution like Leon Trotsky, he wanted to internally strengthen Russia. He wanted socialism in one country. How adorable! Trotsky disagreed, but was exiled and then assassinated in 1940 (sorry, Leon and your permanent revolution). Stalin's other policies focused on political centralization, collectivization of agriculture, and, the big one, creating a cult of personality. Integral to achieving these ends was the eradication of perceived threats through purges. Estimates vary, but unsealed Soviet archives point to roughly 800 thousand executions from 1921-1953 and nearly 2 million from gulag prisons and another 400 thousand from forced resettlement. The numbers game gets dicey, especially when one considers all the deaths resulting from his disastrous policies such as famine. Stalin's death count is somewhere between 9 million and 50 million. What a swell guy.

So, if I told you Kim Il-Sung was a student of Stalin, you'd smell trouble and you'd be right. In the dying embers of World War II, former allies – the Soviet Union and United States – found themselves at ideological odds. The Korean peninsula became the first front. You must remember that towards the end of WWII, Japan's dominion in Korea ended abruptly. As America raced to free Koreans, Stalin fulfilled his pledge (3-months to the day of victory in Europe); declaring war on the Empire of Japan and mobilizing to support liberation efforts. Say what you will about that bastard, he was a man of his word. Japan's surrender created a complicated political situation on the peninsula. Ultimately it was agreed to partition Korea at the 38th parallel; however, it wasn't supposed to end that way. The Soviet Union and the USA failed to reach an accord on the rightful government of a unified Korea. Wartime trust withered amidst conflicting aims. Their politics being like oil and water, the results weren't shocking. The South held elections and became West-aligned, prompting the North to hold their own, and newsflash, they became communist. In 1950, war erupted when the North invaded, with each claiming legitimacy. It's important to note that prior to partition, roughly two-thirds of heavy industry was in the North. Meanwhile, agriculture dominated in the South... almost the numerical reverse. The North's rugged terrain and climate would prove a nagging problem for the communist regime (i.e., it's one thing to industrialize, but a whole other thing to cultivate shitty land).

During this time, the guerrilla leader, Kim Il-sung – a Soviet Red Army trained veteran of bloody campaigns in Manchuria – ascended in stature. As former allies bickered about the future of Korea, he worked to dethrone Cho Man-sik, a Christian nationalist and head of the People's Committee in Pyongyang. The Soviets and Americans agreed to a 5-year trusteeship of the partitioned country. However, Cho Man-sik demanded immediate post-war independence. That put him on the outs and under house arrest. What followed was a series of mergers of disparate political parties, culminating in the creation of the Workers' Party of North Korea. This party would subsequently merge with their southern counterpart to form the Workers' Party of Korea, in 1949, with Kim Il-sung as head dog. An influx of Soviet military hardware and training started flowing in. A Stalinist-style system was implemented. Land distribution, industrialization, and repression followed (the usual).

Naturally, America wouldn't permit communist rule over the Korean Peninsula, and vice-versa. At an impasse, Kim chose force. Though Stalin initially opposed this action, he relented after observing Mao's communist takeover in China. That China offered Kim military support and Stalin had successfully tested a nuclear weapon further diminished concern. Stalin and the commies were feeling "froggy." Upon invading, Kim's battle-hardened soldiers met an ill-equipped, poorly trained opposition. Seoul was captured and pro-West forces were pushed to the Pusan Perimeter. That's when eternal badass, Douglas MacArthur, landed at Inchon, retook Seoul, pushed past the 38th parallel, and barrelled to the Chinese border. Then, in what might be funny if it weren't such a serious scenario, a bunch of screaming Chinese soldiers crossed the Yalu River.

The Chinese swiftly encircled American forces in the Chosin Reservoir. But they hadn't a clue who they were messing with. Immortalized in Marine Corps lore, some 120,000 Chinese learned never to cage a dog, especially a "Devil Dog." For 17 days, about 30,000 Marines and UN personnel fought bravely, mowing down the enemy in droves. Here, renowned Lieutenant Colonel, "Chesty" Puller, exclaimed, "We're surrounded. That simplifies the problem. Now we can attack in any direction!" China's losses remain a source of debate, but some estimate 60,000. Regardless,

UN forces were forced to tactically retreat. The communists would retake Pyongyang and Seoul by early 1951. Although U.S. forces would eventually liberate Seoul once more, for about two years the war became a nasty stalemate. It finally ended with an armistice on July 27, 1953.

The Korean War was over (-ish). Without a peace treaty, an unofficial war continued with both sides claiming victory. To say the south exited the Korean War in better shape than the north is a major understatement. The North was annihilated (thanks to a healthy serving of napalm). Thus, the first "Dear Leader" had a clear playing field to industrialize and rebuild along Stalinist lines. For a decade, he killed off rivals in purges, leaving no opposition to challenge him. He also established a cult of personality to maintain popular support whilst centralizing the governmental apparatus of power. Straight out of Stalin's playbook, he sought to internally strengthen by ridding his state of real and perceived enemies. But times were changing. In 1956, Soviet Leader, Nikita Khrushchev, in a behind-closed-doors speech to Party delegates (but which was rapidly reported widely as he'd intended it to be) unabashedly denounced the legacy of Stalin. This stunned the communist world (like a Republican condemning Ronald Reagan). He specifically called out Stalin, dead Stalin, for creating a tyrannical state in his own image. Now, let's be honest. It's possible Khrushchev merely made this fuss to strengthen his own grip on power. By distancing himself, and better yet, calling out Stalinists still in government, he put them on notice. Nonetheless, whatever his reasons, it did signal an attempt to at least confront the worst injustices of the USSR's past, and it had considerable impact.

In North Korea, Kim Il-sung saw the situation differently. Facing constant dependency on the USSR, self-sufficiency was the key to strength. Sounds good, right? Well, it does when you have arable land, an educated populace, and plentiful resources.

North Korea was devoid of it all, but it didn't matter. Through grit and determination, the regime would look inward and rely on the ingenuity of its people. They'd look to their supreme leader, Kim Il-sung. Over the next decade, the communist party was replaced by a nearly orgasmic reverence for the "Dear Leader." *Juche* went from a philosophy to state-sponsored, mandated ideology. Even a minor slight to perfect leadership was met with swift judgment. Entire families were sent to concentration camps. The implementation of the three-generations rule was conceived; state enemies would sentence their family and the next two generations for their transgressions.

Throughout the 1960s, U.S.-backed South Korea maintained a defensive posture. This led to the fortification of a demilitarized zone along the 38th parallel. Mines, thousands of troops, and razor wire separated foes in a perpetual war fought with rhetoric and erratic fire. Even Chairman Mao grew tired of dealing with Kim, seeing him as incompetent and hardly worth the hassle. All the while, the "Dear Leader" continued eliminating rivals. A police state was born. This was realized by keeping people constantly on edge with claims that the American imperialists were about to attack. His people lived a life of constant mobilization. Mobilization to improve harvests, mining output, lumber, even mobilization strictly to sing his praises in packed arenas (remember it's orgasmic). Mobilization became and remains a part of North Korean life. How do you plan rebellions when your life consists of organizing for the next urgent need? A siege mentality set in with the people.

Back to economics. Yes, North Korea industrialized but food remained a critical problem and industrialization relied on the USSR. That reliance irritated Kim. As he intensified *Juche* practices, he saw dependence on the USSR as an obstacle to real strength. This put North Korea on a path to ruin. By the late-1950s Soviet economic assistance declined as North Korean autarky, or self-sufficiency, accelerated. *Juche* ideology was seeping into every facet of life, isolating the nation from former allies. Increasingly arts and media devoted themselves to celebration of their leader. Post-war economic gains were unsustainable without Soviet assistance from raw materials, food, and technology. That didn't stop several thousand Koreans living in Japan from choosing North Korea to return to instead of South Korea. Many who returned were immediately arrested for exposure to foreign ideas. Talk about your classic backfire.

In the 70s, all hell broke loose as the timing belt snapped on North Korea's economic engine. Apparently, self-sufficiency didn't extend to the accumulation of foreign debt. In what strikes the ideologically pure as hypocritical, North Korea borrowed foreign capital to militarize, at one point devoting 50% of its GDP to military spending. Prior, they relied on the USSR for defense. But this is *Juche* and self-sufficiency is mandatory. Bankrolled by foreigners, an arms race commenced. Kim came to believe North Korea could fund militarization through mineral sales. To do this, North Korea purchased entire plants: petrochemical, textile, concrete, and steel from the developed world. If you're wondering why these nations or companies would engage in such shaky lending, remember that 1960s growth seemed like a good opportunity for a return on investment. Also, recall the lax standards that caused the 2008 housing meltdown. There was even a moment when investing in failed African States was a popular fad. Calmer heads prevail when lighter bank accounts cause money movers to forego the new pad in the Hamptons; or, at least until the next government-sanctioned get-rich-quick scheme overleverages them and subsequently bails them out. Anyways, Kim hoped these investments would deliver ROI and *Juche* would rule the day.

That didn't happen. Instead, the 1973 oil crisis collapsed commodity prices. North Korea suddenly realized no one wanted their crappy steel and cement. So, they defaulted on their loans. Investors learned a painful lesson and steered clear of that steaming pile thereafter. But military spending kept on scraping every dollar to feed a war machine. Precious food was diverted to soldiers, who became the new privileged class. Food emerged as a tool to maintain obedience, punish enemies, and buy allegiance. Not able to buy Western technology, North Korea doubled down on *Juche*. The centrally planned economy couldn't increase output and wasn't efficient. The lack of fuel sent shockwaves through the food distribution system, leading to black markets and corruption. Central planning started robbing the very people who farmed the land of the sustenance to do so. In response, soldiers were sent to guard the fields, but they were easily bribed. With starvation rampant, living on two meals a day became a patriotic virtue! What didn't get spent on the military went towards grandiose displays of opulence. Statues, museums, buildings, the Juche Tower, Nampo Dam, and the notorious Ryugyong Hotel – a 1080 feet high pyramid-shaped hotel which bears the honor of being the tallest unfinished building in the world.

Meanwhile, the world's attention was elsewhere. In the 80s, the threat of nuclear war was ever-present. Soviets in Afghanistan, Iran fighting Iraq, and communist governments in South America were far more pressing than a backward, reclusive regime. People didn't realize the extent either. They were squarely in the Soviet camp, a DMZ separated them from civilization, and all the things we take for granted today didn't exist. There was no Google, Wikipedia, or, yes, Wikileaks inundating the world with information. South Korea, for instance, was becoming an economic power by focusing on computing, not cement. What threat could Kim possibly pose? Hindsight is always 20/20. By the dawn of the information age, the walls were too thick for new ideas to penetrate this brutal regime.

But how did it go from bad to so bad? That answer is simple. When the USSR collapsed, what remained of Soviet aid did too. Without aid, Kim turned to China. Initially, this resulted in food and fuel aid to keep the economy afloat. However, the end of the Cold War altered the landscape. Eastern bloc allies disappeared, and China had other priorities. China made market-based reforms and the U.S. became a crucial trading partner. North Korea was part of the old world - a dead world based on ideological divides. China's support was merely insurance. They feared a North Korean collapse would spill turmoil across their border. Foreign trade was slashed in half, the *Juche* long-yearned for had come. Dysfunctional isolation. A perverse form of self-sufficiency. Anti-Autarky. Out of that isolation, famine devastated the regime. In a period called the Arduous March – since authorities banned the term famine (yes, they actually did) – a million starved to death. An awful period of flooding didn't just ruin harvests, it also destroyed stockpiles the government stored underground. The new leader, Kim Jong-il, used the calamity as an opportunity to reinforce *Juche* ideals...this time with nuclear weapons. Seeing an opportunity to squeeze aid from the U.S. and allies, North Korea embarked on a campaign of provocation to elicit a response.

Throughout the latter half of the 90s and well into the 2000s, Kim Jong-il ramped up military spending, embarked on illegal activities to secure funds, sidestepped international sanctions, and pursued nuclear weapons. All the while, thousands of artillery pieces – within range of Seoul – threatened to flatten the South Korean capital should negotiations fail to meet the North's satisfaction. Throughout this entire time, the regime turned more insular and survival-oriented. Isolation is proven to bear unhealthy fruit. When everyone around you says the same line and sings the same tune, a new worldview is created. The worldview may be irrational, even paranoid, but actions taken within that flawed worldview can still have internal logic. Many say that North Korea is crazy. Kim Jong-Il was crazy like his father, and Un is too. That misses the point entirely. North Korea's actions are extremely rational (almost too calculated, in fact). If one assumes that all actions are predicated on regime survival, the pursuit of nuclear technology shouldn't be surprising.

The reclusive regime, fueled by *Juche* ideology, has conned the entire world. They push up against the line only to walk back at the 11th hour. They now have nuclear weapons and are nearing the capability to miniaturize nuclear weapons, which would enable intercontinental strikes. *Juche* is at the heart of this. History has shown that nuclear-capable powers are unlikely to get attacked and more likely to get a seat at the bargaining table. Should we then be shocked that the current "Dear Leader," has aggressively followed the path his father commenced? Or his father's father? *Juche* is an ideology predicated on isolation. Just as the economy is sick, so are the North Korean people. Abuse and trauma are ingrained in the hearts and minds of Koreans. Opportunistic leaders have capitalized, engineering a police state that exists to maintain its existence. Circular reasoning is precisely the point. Regime survival is all that matters. It's a textbook example of how extreme ideology coupled with isolation is disastrous.

Ted Kaczynski's story is very similar to that of North Korea. The one-day *Unabomber* entered Harvard at the age of sixteen. He was a brilliant kid destined to leave his mark on the world. That mark proved unimaginable. When applying for the Ivy League School, his most enthusiastic endorsement came from the high school counselor who prophetically stated in a letter to Harvard:

I believe Ted has one of the greatest contributions to make to society. He is reflective, sensitive, and deeply conscious of his responsibilities to society.

At Harvard, he participated in the notorious "mind control" experiments of Dr. Henry Murray. A series of experiments – later deemed unethical – during which Ted and 21 others were subjected to abusive attacks on their firmly held beliefs. The experiment assaulted their egos and cherished ideals through stress-filled interrogations. Murray's background in the Office of Strategic Services led many to believe Ted unwittingly participated in the CIA's MK Ultra – a declassified mind control program.

Regardless, Ted graduated and earned a Ph.D. from Michigan. He was a rising star in academia. His mathematical prowess delivered him a teaching gig at Cal Berkeley. Then he disappeared from society. Frustrated by social anxiety and his inability to gain the acceptance he yearned for, he moved to the wilderness of Montana. There, he cultivated an anti-technology, Neo-Luddite ideology. In severe isolation, his resolve strengthened. There were no counterarguments to provide guardrails. For nearly two decades, he struck the establishment with bombs. When his

Manifesto, the same one that led to his capture, appeared on the front page of the *Washington Post*, many academics were struck by the genius, rational logic, and prophetic nature of his words. And yet, they were simultaneously horrified that they did have such a response. How could someone so logical commit such violent acts? From his Manifesto:

> *When a new item of technology is introduced as an option that an individual can accept or not as he chooses, it does not necessarily REMAIN optional. In many cases the new technology changes society in such a way that people eventually find themselves FORCED to use it.*

Cell phones, anyone? His writings, while fascinating, are stained with the blood of his innocent, needless victims. No, despite the *Unabomber* and North Korea's rational thought processes, both maintain a perverse worldview that has been crafted in seclusion. Sophistry, the thought process that seems logical, but is ultimately too hermetically sealed to be truly intelligent, is the fatal flaw of North Korea and the Unabomber. In both cases, it produced an attitude that was essentially devoid of morality. One that justifies errant bombings and murder to voice an anti-technology message, and another subjecting a nation to unspeakable atrocities to maintain control. Yes, isolation and ideology have a nasty habit of turning individuals and regimes into monsters. Just as America learned during the manhunt for the FBI's most wanted man, so has it learned in dealing with a reclusive hermit kingdom.

SOCIABLE SYRUP: WHEN PEPSI RULED THE WAVES

I t was a muggy day in Sokolniki Park. Just a cab ride northwest from Moscow's famous Red Square. Sokolniki, derived from "sokol" or "falcon," served as sovereign hunting grounds in Tsarist Russia. There, generations of Tsars, beginning with Alexis I, galloped through the wilderness blanketed in birches, spruces, and pines. Falcons perched on soft, regal hands wrapped in leather. The whole place represented power. It was an enclave where elites escaped the shackles of court life to enjoy simple pleasures while plotting, as do politicians and lobbyists, over a round of golf. Over time, Russian leaders added personality to the park. Peter the Great brought European-style order by clearing areas and adding pathways. Tsar Nicholas II contributed a maze of alleys. By the late 1800s, coinciding with the waning might of the monarchical system, it opened to the public. Yet, it was under the reign of the Soviet Politburo that it finally emerged as a real park like one in New York or any other Western metropolis (except it was full of Soviet crap such as scowling guards, unsafe rides, and questionable food). With all that history being a hot spot for the upper echelon of society, what better place for PepsiCo to execute an ingenious plan for soft drink domination?

See, for quite some time, C-Suite executives at PepsiCo had been hatching a grand scheme, even consulting (aka lobbying) Dwight D. Eisenhower's Vice President, Richard Milhous Nixon. The latter, ever the conspirator, forged a close relationship with Donald M. Kendall – WWII bomber pilot turned salesman and marketing executive. From then on, PepsiCo had a place at the White House's table and Nixon's ear. Who could have known that a meeting in July 1959 between Nixon and a sweating Nikita Khrushchev would lead to PepsiCo's ascension as a military power, brandishing real weaponry in the "Cola War" that followed?

The American National Exhibition was meant to forge cultural empathy between East and West. To support this effort, an architectural firm designed the "typical" American house. Constructed on those former royal lands, it served as capitalism's counterargument to the Soviet Union's New York exhibit from earlier that year. The Soviets used their display to laud the technological virtues of communism. Off the heels of Sputnik, the ground-breaking 1957 satellite launch that scared the pants off the American public, Soviet ingenuity was omnipresent. Music and agricultural machinery were also prominent aspects of this whole propaganda ploy. Let's not get it sideways, though; Americans *dished* out a heavy dose of propaganda too.

Still, the entire exchange remains puzzling. What's with communism's obsession with agriculture? For something that's been around for thousands of years, they still seem enthralled by it. Wow, corn harvesting. How riveting! This warrants an explanation. When Khrushchev returned to the Ukraine after WWII, he witnessed utter devastation. About one in six Ukrainians had died during the war. Imagine that! Now, add to that the terrible harvests and rampant starvation, and you'll begin to understand the leader's obsession with corn. He even sought to develop a corn belt rivalling Iowa, going so far as inviting an Iowan farmer and a pioneer in hybrid seed corn, Roswell Garst, to visit the USSR as a consultant of sorts. Garst gave pointers such as not planting in desolate, lifeless places like Siberia, but Khrushchev wanted corn. Corn everywhere! Had dating apps existed back then, Khrushchev's profile would read, "I like corn and space. Any other subjects bore me and will be utterly, completely ignored. I will bury those conversations." Of course, the profile picture would be him frowning, ear of corn in one hand, shoe in the other.

In all seriousness, Khrushchev took a liking to Garst. His chilly disposition matched his own. Their exchanges were an incessant tit-for-tat. When Cold War politics came up, the Soviet Premier snapped, "You know, for a peasant, you're a damned poor horse trader." Garst travelled the globe advocating modern agricultural methods, including the Soviet Union six times. During Khrushchev's 1959 twelve-day U.S. tour, he demanded to add a stop in Coons Rapids, Iowa to meet his old friend. He was the only individual the leader visited besides the President. Some considered Garst a traitor and Soviet stooge. His daughter, Liz, believes he "represented the first thaw in the Cold War."

Highlighted technologies illuminate each side's propaganda strategy, domestically and abroad. The Soviets promoted math, science, rocketry, and harvesting equipment. Meanwhile, America heralded the dawn of the dishwasher and toaster age. All hail consumerism, repent, or we'll give you the washboard. One must appreciate the humor. The Soviet focus on Outer Space and farming was a clever way to signal to international and domestic audiences that they were interested in great and noble achievements. Americans, on the other hand, sought to showcase everything the proletariat was missing out on while huddled in their cramped, concrete, dimly lit studio apartments. In other words, "Great job with the satellite, you bunch of nerds. Now try to build a car. A real car and not one powered by a 5hp lawnmower motor."

The typical American house was the site of the famous *Kitchen Debate*. It created the perfect opportunity for PepsiCo to get their massive plug. Here's how it happened. American and Soviet media were filming the entire meet-and-greet between the General Secretary of the Central Committee of the Communist Party of the Soviet Union, Nikita Khrushchev (try saying that three times fast!) and "Dick" Nixon. The idea was for each country to simultaneously televise the exchange to ensure no funny business (though American networks jumped the gun). Both men stood in the exhibit's kitchen as Dick explained how this home mirrored the average house in California. When Nixon pointed at the dishwasher, lauding how it helped the housewives, Khrushchev brushed it off, saying, "We have such things... Your capitalistic attitude toward women does not occur under Communism."

After extolling how any Soviet citizen can get a newly built house without a dollar to their name, unlike America, he mockingly suggested that workers failed to properly finish the exhibit. He went on:

This is what America is capable of? How long has she existed? 300 years? We haven't quite reached 42 years and in another 7 years, we'll be at [America's level]... As we pass you by, we'll wave 'hi'...and then if you want, we'll stop and say, 'please come along behind us.'

Cue the comical exchange of Khrushchev waving his hand, grinning ear to ear while Nixon could only muster a bewildered, forced smirk. The barbs continued back and forth, with both parties maintaining composure without giving quarter. Nixon emphasized the importance of a free exchange of ideas, not fear of them. Of course, this received a sharp retort that Soviets feared nothing. Eventually, they agreed to translate the full text of the exchange to each other's nations, and then they departed.

Although the *Kitchen Debate* garnered all the attention, what happened before is of particular interest. Outside the house, Khrushchev was having a rough go of things. Hot and sweaty, Nixon coaxed him over to a Pepsi stand helmed by marketing savant, Mr. Kendall. When offered the choice between a bottled Pepsi from the great State of New York or the sweet, syrupy concoction from local water, Khrushchev took the latter. Known as the first skeptical sip of Pepsi, the picture was a marketing boon. Kendall was under strict orders to get a damn Pepsi in his hands and would've been in trouble had he failed.

The best part is that Khrushchev tried the American-made Pepsi and immediately rejected it, proclaiming, "Drink the Pepsi-Cola made in Moscow. It is much better than the Pepsi made in the U.S.!" Don Draper couldn't pull a coup like this in his wildest dreams, especially when Pepsi's slogan at the time was: "The Sociables prefer Pepsi." Think about it for a moment. Sour, dour Khrushchev hates everyone and everything, except a nice, cold Pepsi.

It took a while, but, in 1972, Pepsi finally capitalized on the photo-op with Kendall at the helm as the CEO. In the "Great Stolichnaya for Syrup Barter (as I like to call it)," Pepsi agreed to manufacture in Russia in exchange for marketing and importing Soviet vodka. Essentially, they took vodka instead of greenbacks. Yes, you can thank Pepsi for the vodka concoctions in the Red Solo Cups of drunken coeds making bad decisions in Cancun, Mexico. Where would we be without that?

With that agreement, PepsiCo became the first American consumer product in the Soviet Union. Let there be no mistake, though - Soviet Pepsi wasn't great. However, as the only game in town, it quickly became a Soviet staple. In fact, it became so popular it was said that the quickest way to get a nice Russian gal in the sack was a bottle of Pepsi. Forget tiramisu, champagne, and Barry White... Pepsi was the aphrodisiac. The same can't be so easily said in the U.S. Oddly, Pepsi came to be viewed by the Soviets as, well, Soviet. It wasn't until the end of the Cold War that other options, like Coca-Cola, arrived. By that time, PepsiCo had developed a vast distribution network across over 22 million square kilometers – one-sixth of Earth's inhabited landmass.

In 1989, problems arose; both sides needed to renegotiate the terms as the deal was set to expire. Soviets were "Jonesing" for more Pepsi, so an even crazier contract was reached. *The Infamous Syrup for Subs and Vodka Switcheroo*, estimated at $3 billion, was the largest trade in history between an American company and the USSR. Once again, the Soviets couldn't pay, and this time, vodka wasn't enough to close the gap. Let's clarify! PepsiCo taking vodka was supposed to reduce exposure to roubles. Outside the Soviet Union and often within, roubles were useless. Any investors wanted either stable currency or material goods. With Russian currency out of the question, ships emerged as a suitable substitute.

Why? Simple. Mikhail Gorbachev assumed leadership during a brutal time. Plagued by a stagnant economy, waning confidence, and severe shortages, Gorbachev knew the Soviet system had gone rotten. The centrally planned economy was failing the consumer needs and tastes. It's impossible to plan and provide for nearly 300 million people. That's where free-market capitalism comes into play. To further stoke the problem, the Soviet-Afghan War was bleeding them dry. It necessitated a colossal military buildup that siphoned resources from economic restructuring. U.S. stinger missiles aided that cause. Gorbachev, eager to end shortages and improve distribution, viewed a renewed deal with Pepsi as a critical test of leadership. Which is a weirdly true statement. Should it be successful, other Western companies could also find success in a marketplace marked by missteps. Gorbachev, with his dual policies of *glasnost* (openness) and *perestroika* (restructuring), sought to save the USSR through urgent reforms. In the end, he likely brought the inevitable demise even sooner.

On April 9, 1990, the USSR and PepsiCo finalized their deal; they added 17 submarines, a cruiser, a frigate, a destroyer, and a few oil tankers to their books. The ruthless negotiators at PepsiCo even nabbed an incredible discount on the subs, $150,000 a pop. The CIA had to be involved through a shadowy subsidiary. The whole saga deserves a film franchise, directed by Jerry Bruckheimer and starring Nicholas Cage.

Suddenly, the soft drink giant positioned itself as a maritime power commanding the sixth-most diesel submarines in the world. While Coca-Cola had the Christmas polar bears and, "His Airness," Michael Jordan, PepsiCo possessed true might: Soviet might (and Michael Jackson)! PepsiCo would ultimately scrap the ships to reimburse costs. Yet, for a few days, the cola company, like Great Britain before her, triumphantly ruled the waves.

The balance briefly tipped as the *Cola War* slogged onward. Relishing the moment, Donald Kendall told President George H.W. Bush's National Security Advisor, "We're disarming the Soviet Union faster than you are." The victory proved short-lived. When the USSR collapsed, Pepsi's connection with the Soviet past turned into a liability amongst consumers who wanted a true American soft drink (not Soviet crap or New Coke). So, PepsiCo diversified from her cola-centric roots, ceding market share, while the rebranded Coca-Cola Classic swooped in to satisfy proletarian thirsts. Yes, PepsiCo may have won a Cold War battle but lost the vitally important *Cola War*.

Yet, it was a photo-op that spurred a measure of disarmament. One eager marketeer executing a zany idea, slightly opened a closed part of the world. That would never have happened had other zany marketeers (or propagandists) decided against creating a cultural exchange in the first place. Though the bitter rivals were driven by ideological one-upmanship, the outcome of that fateful day was clearly uncertain. Still, isn't that how exchanges are with those at odds? In a world beset by grief and misery, engagement offers a glimmer of hope. Engagement allows the chance for progress. The alternative is fear, resentment, and miscalculation. To me, that isn't a road worth taking. Heck, a farmer in Iowa managed to crack Khrushchev's cold, cantankerous exterior. That speaks volumes.

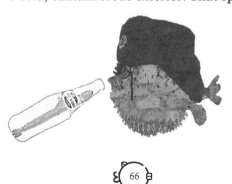

HOOKED: ROMANIA'S CULT OF PERSONALITY

Romania was a dark, cold place during the 1980s. While Americans enjoyed a decade of excess – greed, Hulk Hogan, coke-fueled parties, and power ballads – Romanians suffered chronic food shortages, brutal crackdowns, and the nebulous fear of being on the receiving end of a firing squad. For children, the trauma was unimaginable. See, to stave off a demographic crisis, Romania's authoritarian government hatched a diabolical scheme. In 1967 they effectively outlawed abortion and contraception and boy did it work. The average number of children per mother rose from 1.9 to 3.7 a year later. For those bracing for a diatribe concerning the efficacy of pro-choice and pro-life policies, rest assured that topic falls squarely outside the scope of this saga. In short, women were coerced to have children to bolster the stability of a failed communist state without the institutions to ensure the mothers bearing said children could support them in any practical way (whew). Romania's social engineering proved once again how ineffectual governments are at doing anything except killing people (usually their own people through incompetence) and writing huge checks. Soon, orphanages were so packed that malnourished children were spilling out onto the streets. "Caretakers" either poorly trained, psychopathic, overwhelmed by the scale, or a combination of all three, did what jerks do. They took it out on the innocent children (oh no, this won't come back to haunt them). Physical and sexual abuses were rampant. Estimates vary, but it is believed some 15-20k children died due to deprivation. However, deprivation isn't so terrible when the victims lack perspective. Instead, it took an ill-conceived plan to air a television show about oil tycoons in Texas to drive the message home how crummy Romanians had it. An over-the-top drama helped galvanize the populace against a cult of personality to prove "soft" power has real power.

From 1965 to 1989, Romanian President, Nicolae Ceausescu, used repression and fear to maintain tight control over his people. Originally reform-minded, his reign succumbed to the power of the Stalinist 'The Dark Side.' Isn't that how it always works? Good intentions yield promises of reform...5-year plans, 10-year plans, and timelines dependent on dictatorial whims plans. Just ask that horse. Not Mr. Ed! That horse, Boxer, from George Orwell's *Animal Farm*. Napoleon the pig, and resident buffoon, worked him to the ground rebuilding a bigger, better windmill after the last one collapsed due to Napoleon's poor planning (and Snowball banishment). Boxer's loyal labor earned him a ticket to the glue factory. Napoleon was a pig, which is appropriate. He was also an ass!

As expected, Ceausescu's economic policies resulted in shortages in energy, food, and other crucial goods. Hell, what's communism without that? Again, communism and agriculture. It's farming; why so difficult? Though the population starved, he routinely exported critical foodstuffs to pay off foreign debts. Propaganda on a par with Italy's pre-eminent fascist, Benito Mussolini, buttressed the rotten regime. In fact, his self-marketing itch was inspired by Mao's Communist China and Kim Il Sung. Seeing all the colorful signs of solidarity, he envisioned a new Romania -- one that bowed at his altar. He distrusted would-be rivals hiding in the shadowy corridors of power; therefore, key positions were held by family members. It was socialism in one family (now that's a bumper sticker). But at the core was bitter disdain for Western culture's corruption, immorality, and gluttony.

Despite Romania being a Warsaw Pact member, Ceausescu often sparred the Moscow. A resolute nationalist, he struck a unique balance between independence and Eastern solidarity. When allies severed relations with Israel in response to their pre-emptive attack on Egypt during the Six-Day War, he had the gumption to maintain them. Romania also dared to attend the 1984 Olympics in Los Angeles. His individualism and defense of culture endeared him to many Romanians. Of course, gauging the popularity of a tyrant is a fool's errand and misses the point of authoritarian rule. Smile, or you'll get the boot!

But it was propaganda that saturated the tyrannical milieu. Ceausescu's cult of personality had few parallels besides those used for inspiration. Ceausescu claimed dual titles, Conducator (*leader*) and Geniul din Carpați (*The Genius of the Carpathians*). He was everything to everyone. If communism was the symphony, he was the conductor. He went so far as to have a regal sceptre made to elevate his majesty, prompting renowned painter, Salvador Dali, to send a sarcastic congratulatory telegram. Ever mindful of the need to strengthen his grip on the masses, he looked westward. What could possibly go wrong?

So, one day an advisor persuaded him that CBS's drama, *Dallas*, sufficiently demonstrated the ills of capitalism. The piggishness, lust, and backstabbing offered the perfect counter to the West's claims of moral superiority. By purchasing the entire run of the series, he'd prove just how awful America is (or so he thought). My parents and just about everyone else were lured each week to Southfork Ranch to figure out what that bastard J.R. Ewing would do next. Who would the anti-hero screw next? It was a phenomenal show. People tuned in to see what drama the heirs of Ewing Oil would encounter. *Dallas* confirmed all the stereotypes that Texans wore proudly: big hats, big hair, big cars, and big personalities. At the time, *Dallas* was a ratings monster during an era when you didn't have a million options. There wasn't Netflix, YouTube, or bundle packages forcing you to pay for Disney even when you have no kids or interest in *iCarly* and *Hannah Montana* (that's a deep cut). *Dallas* began in 1978 as an instant hit. From 1980 to 1985, *Dallas* was either 1 or 2 in ratings, averaging 22.8 million weekly viewers. The last episode, airing in 1991, garnered an impossible 33 million viewers (11th all-time).

This popularity led to a major change. Suddenly, capitalism was the bee's knees, the cat's meow, and, combined with Oliver Stone's *Wall Street*, a vehicle for salvation from socialism's bankrupt promises. As Gordon Gekko said in Stone's film,

The point is, ladies and gentlemen, that greed, for lack of a better word, is good. Greed is right. Greed works. Greed clarifies, cuts through, and captures the essence of the evolutionary spirit.

J.R. Ewing (*Dallas*) and Gordon Gekko (*Wall Street*) emerged as spokesmen for a new breed of unapologetic top-earners. Dallas, the city, captured the world's imagination. A destination where anyone could strike it rich with grit and a dose of luck. Even college football was not immune to the luxury Dallas offered. ESPN's 30 for 30 documentary, *Pony Excess,* showcased how greed caught Southern Methodist University's (SMU) in an extraordinary scandal. Seeking to win like Texas A&M and the Longhorns, the SMU Mustangs began to recruit top football athletes. It worked. They nabbed Eric Dickerson amongst other top prospects, culminating in multiple NCAA titles. Eric Dickerson would go on to wear sweet goggles in the NFL and set the game's single season rushing record at 2,105 yds in 1984, a record that still stands.

Prior to Dickerson and the impressive recruiting class, SMU was a joke. How was the sudden turnaround possible? Simply put, it wasn't. It seems competition extended from the football field to the boardrooms. SMU alumni, infuriated at getting constantly bombarded with "hook em" chants by obsessive Texas fans wearing boots with suits, donated bigly. Boosters, in a complicated scheme, paid college athletes and were quite good at it. That is, until they got caught, forcing the NCAA (after multiple attempts to reign the university in) to kill the football program with the notorious "death penalty." But the lesson was clear, in Dallas, money talked and could purchase new realities. Television's Dallas proved truer to life too. Romanians toiling away for gruel sandwiches took notice and became equally hooked.

Soon, they started to drink the capitalist Kool-Aid. If faced with a choice between watching wealthy Texans and cleavage, or propaganda about grain production and no cleavage, the sane go for the former. Kidding aside, *Dallas* had a tangible impact on the socio-economic attitudes in Romania. The show's reach slipped behind the vaunted Iron Curtain. Romanians gobbled up the content and reporting at the time indicated it was having an effect. Maligned citizens wondered if they deserved Cadillacs, mansions, and swimming pools. Instead of a Cadillac, for instance, East Germans waited multiple years for a Trabant made of duroplast, a plastic conceived via a union with recycled cotton waste and idiocy.

Sure, *Dallas* was just a show. However, the adage 'ignorance is bliss' holds merit. When Romanians saw their relative deprivation included a complete lack of ten-gallon hats, they started to ask dangerous questions like, 'Why?' Freedom is a drug. One taste fundamentally alters expectations. Freedom from poverty, hunger, violence, and fear. Pop culture continues to serve as a powerful medium to expose people to new ideas dangerous to parochial status quos, especially ones based on subjugation.

In 1989, Romanians overthrew Ceausescu in a violent upheaval. In a dual twist of irony, he not only met his downfall at the opposite end of his firing squad but also got to witness another episode of *Dallas*, one of the first foreign programs aired on the newly liberated Romanian TV, albeit this time in a ghostly form. Oddly enough, post-Ceausescu Romania elected several former Socialist leaders to political office. You see, the cult of personality was so strong that many didn't identify the Ceausescu regime with socialism, so much as with Ceausescu himself.

Larry Hagman, the actor who played J.R. Ewing, isn't afraid to take credit for toppling Ceausescu stating, "They wanted all that stuff they didn't even know was out there." The truth is more nuanced. Tensions were already building as the police state adopted harsher modes of oppression. Economic paralysis gripped the region and the Soviet Union's collapse shocked the socialist establishment. Invincible tyrants fell like dominoes.

Meanwhile, protests in Timisoara soaked troubles in kerosine and left over one-thousand dead. He has a point though. Unlikely catalysts arise and coalesce whenever people are pushed beyond the brink. They felt repression and Dallas showed deprivation.

A few years later, reports surfaced of an oddity constructed in remote Slobozia. Ilie Alexandru, dubbed the J.R. of Romania, constructed an exact copy of Southfork Ranch. Millions flocked to see an America that only existed on television screens. The 60 rooms, stables, pool, and luxurious ambience is managed some 2,000 townspeople, or one-seventh of Slobozia's workforce. Alexandru wears J.R.'s iconic hat, bolo ties, and the exact shit-eating grin. His ranch is the jewel of Hermes Vacation Park promised to soon feature a replica of the Eiffel Tower. Meanwhile wages were back to pre-1989 levels and inflation was rising.

Hungarian historian George Handlery put it best when he said, "Revolutions are not so much the product of brutal oppression but of frustrated hopes." Communist Romania discovered this truism when their leader decided to offer the populace a glimpse of what they were missing. Awareness of one's relative deprivation develops social-economic conditions suitable for political instability. When those suffering have no medium to voice grievances, pressure will build. It must find an outlet.

Today, Slobozia's Southfork Ranch lies dormant. Once immaculate, the white façade has dulled to a gray. Mr. Alexandru did build that Eiffel Tower he boasted about in the 90s. Now the rusty eye-sore scrambles above split concrete and shrubbery. You can spare your wallet and view both on Google Earth. He later was implicated for tax evasion and embezzlement, or so they say. I'm not sure where Romania's J.R. Ewing is or what he's thinking. If I had

to guess it'd be, "Such high hopes, what went wrong?"

For the people of Pata Rât, everyday survival is a miracle. Located within Romania's 4th largest city, Cluj-Napoca, four settlements congregate around a landfill to form Europe's largest "trash ghetto." Romania has many more. The Indo-Aryan 'Roma' people have no choice. Government-backed evictions sentence them scrape a living off leftovers and repurposed waste. For the EU, it's an example of environmental racism too close for comfort. A European Commission took Romania to court over conditions and won. Awareness has brought some respite; however, little has changed. Pata Rât is still their home but most sarcastically call it 'Dallas.'

Although Romania joined the EU in 2007, they're still searching for Dallas. Those expecting riches overnight must look to the horizon. Still, the economy is growing, and poverty is dropping. Some foresee Romania, with its top-tier digital infrastructure, becoming the next tech-startup hub for the EU. American military presence has brought security and investment, especially since AEGIS Ashore came online in Deveselu. Yet, this wasn't the dream advertised. Meanwhile, Romanians have rekindled their love affair with Ceausescu too. Despite his wickedness and brutality, he's still admired. One poll found that about 60% have good opinion of him.

In 2016, Film director Sherng-Lee Huang collaborated on a low-budget, surrealist exposition of communism, capitalism, and art. *Hotel Dallas* had Patrick Duffy reprise his role, except this time from Mr. Alexandru's defunct tourist attraction. Regarding the show's legacy, Huang says, "If you look at the brand of corrupt crony capitalism embodied by J.R. in the show, it's very much the kind of capitalism running things in Romanian now....So the legacy of *Dallas* is a complicated thing."

Friends Like These: Sinking the Rainbow Warrior

Former First Lady, Ladybird Johnson, planted an indelible mark on America's landscape. While history books remember her as President Lyndon Baines Johnson's wife, countless Texans have experienced the beauty she spread. Traveling through Texas Hill Country - a belt north of Austin spanning past San Antonio - sightseers bear witness to a breathtaking smattering of yuccas and prickly pears atop rugged hills of granite and limestone. Flanking the highways, there's also a kaleidoscope of flora. Wildflowers stretch beyond the horizon, magically arriving as superblooms, only to vanish beneath the Texas-sized, starry night. Ladybird, frustrated by unsightly billboards and litter, pressed for highway beautification. She wasn't alone. Rachel Carson's 1962 book, *Silent Spring*, received broad acclaim for exposing the hidden dangers of the pesticide, DDT. Her work captivated Americans and is credited with spawning modern environmentalism. Heck, a professional wrestler named his finishing maneuver the DDT because of its deadly reputation. From the 1970s onward, planet stewardship gained popularity. The Environmental Protection Agency was founded, Earth Day created, recycling mainstreamed, peak oil predicted (incorrectly), global warming entered the lexicon, anti-nuclear attitudes developed, and anti-littering campaigns flourished. The Texas Department of Transportation addressed the latter by hiring advertisers, Mike Blair and Tim McClure, to craft a zippy anti-littering slogan. Soon, "Don't Mess with Texas" appeared on bumper stickers, T-shirts, and in country music lyrics. The simple government initiative transformed into a cherished battle cry that succinctly captured the bravado of the Lone Star State. Coincidently, over 7k miles away on a former British colonial possession, an idealistic cadre of anti-nuclear and whaling activists also didn't want to be *messed with*. In response, the French government hatched a conspiratorial sneak attack. Strangely, the first international terrorist attack against New Zealand (NZ) came from devilish Frenchmen. C'mon, with friends like these, who needs enemies?

While deployed to Naples, Italy, augmenting *depleted* forces in the Global War on Terrorism's *ever-important* Italian Theater, I met a New Zealander who had a serious axe to grind with France. How I managed to snag a sweet gig in Italy is surely an odd story. President Obama's drawdown in Iraq and Afghanistan resulted in the cancellation of two prior assignments to serve as an Individual Augmentee, or IA, in both places. IA positions were created to staff traditional Army and Marine Corps billets. Facing severe fatigue and manpower shortages, the Navy was tasked to close the gaps. Why Italy then? Well, it seems the Navy took advantage of alternative budgetary channels, using Overseas Contingency Funding to shore up pet projects such as Ballistic Missile Defense. While my comrades sucked sand, I horsed down slices of pizza and gallons of wine. Boozing in Florence, three-day weekends every other week, and a Mercedes rental car. No, life is not fair.

The full story of how I ended up in Italy is doozy. Twice in a row my overseas deployments were cancelled a week before heading to Fort Jackson, South Carolina for training. The "yoyoing" left me mentally spent. The officer, whose lovely task was sending on expenses-paid vacations to the "bomby" Middle East, reached out. "I'm sorry we keep jerking you around. Pick a deployment from these ten options or I'll take your name out of the hat." To which I responded, "what exactly does taking my name out of the hat mean." "Oh that just means you'll be the first person I assign next time I need a short-fused IA assignment," he responded. Sensing a supremely shitty job in my future, I begrudgingly chose Naples because an administrative issue precluded the one I wanted: Liaison to Special Operations Command in Pakistan. Do the calendar math and you'll discover that I might've supported the team isolated the location of Osama Bin Laden. Instead of getting to take credit for the actions of the others, I settled for Italy.

In Italy I made a new friend, John. He was from NZ but served as an officer in the U.S. Navy (unsure how that happened). One day we were discussing all the amazing places we intended to travel to when I gauged his interest in France. His response shocked me.

"Screw France. Those guys attacked us," he snorted.

"What do you mean, they attacked us?" I queried.

"They attacked New Zealand!"

"Like a crazy Frenchmen hopped up on hallucinogenic perfume killed some Kiwis?"

"No, the French government attacked the Rainbow Warrior in Auckland."

"Like a former government employee?"

Now exasperated, he described the tragedy in meticulous detail. That's when I fully realized why older Kiwis despise all things French and why US-NZ relations have been frosty. That's right! The country's first international terrorist attack was committed by Frenchmen...government Frenchmen. The sabotage, as the French claim, killed one peacenik whose only crime was his enthusiasm for dolphin-safe tuna, keeping whales (like Willy) free, and generally not wanting the French Polynesian Islands to turn into an irradiated retelling of *Lord of the Flies*. Francophiles should brace themselves because this story is supremely f'd up.

It's hard to imagine, but there was a time when testing nukes was all the rage. When J. Robert Oppenheimer – American theoretical physicist and "father of the Atomic bomb" – uttered the famous words, "Now I am become Death, the destroyer of worlds" after detonating the first A-bomb on July 16, 1945 in New Mexico, it seemed only he fully understood the Pandora's box mankind opened. After the dual nuking of Nagasaki and Hiroshima, everyone raced to not just build their own shiny, new nukes, but test them in remote locales, pushing the limits of explosive power to churn out more potential megadeaths. Yes, when talking about nuclear death tolls, scientists labored to assess the hellish aftermath and came up with megadeaths to tabulate the symphony of destruction posed by nuclear war. Metallica's second-rate cousin takes their name from a term coined by strategic thinkers pondering the aftermath of thermonuclear annihilation.

Herman Kahn wrote in, *On Thermonuclear War*:

It was difficult for people to distinguish in the early 1950s between 2 million deaths and 100 million deaths. Today, after a decade of pondering these problems, we can make such distinctions perhaps all too clearly. Most of the decision makers and planners who have been facing the prospects of a thermonuclear war would find it difficult to distinguish between zero and two million deaths and very easy to distinguish between two million and a hundred million deaths.

Khan later wonders if, in a post-apocalyptic world, the survivors might envy the dead? The nuclear arms race drifted far into the realm of batshittery. According to the Arms Control Association estimates, a total of 2,056 global tests occurred since that box opened. The U.S. leads the way with 1030, Russia 715, France 210, UK 45, China 45, India 3, Pakistan 2, and North Korea 6. The Comprehensive Nuclear-Test-Ban Treaty (CTBT), adopted by the United Nations General Assembly in 1996, made nuclear testing the path to pariah. A catastrophic environmental and human toll finally compelled major nuclear powers to cease the madness and choose a better way. Although not technically in force, since eight nations have yet to ratify it, all nuclear powers except for India, Pakistan, and North Korea are, at least, signatories and abide by the terms.

17 states, including the U.S., are signatories yet to ratify the treaty. Why hasn't the US ratified it? Good question! Congressional concerns range from America's continued ability to validate their arsenal's operability to having an out in case circumstances necessitate a return to testing. Ratification also lacks a substantial constituency since the U.S. already abides by the terms. Besides, our rugged individualism lives on amongst Americans not inclined to commit to Euro-things such as the UN crap and soccer.

Since adoption, sub-critical or cold tests – producing no yield because critical mass of fissile material is not achieved – have gained popularity and acceptance as the only allowable test or simulation allowed under the ban. The CTBT is a very good thing. Live nuclear tests have battered the planet. Radiation has an annoying habit of sticking around for decades, contaminating soil, water, and fish...Fish who might just migrate into your freezer. Permitting only sub-critical tests is sufficient for advanced nuclear powers but is the bane of emerging ones. Therefore, North Korea continues testing despite others abandoning the practice. Their weapons program, predicated on trial and error, lacks the technical know-how to manage these simulations. Live testing also advances ballistic technology required to achieve long-range striking ability. If you read this as being able to hit a Starbucks in Seattle, you're on the right track.

On a lighter note, we can thank nuclear testing for the creation of the bikini swimsuit. On July 5, 1946, a French fashion designer named Louis Réard introduced a new garment to the public. He called it the bikini in hopes it would create an "explosive commercial and cultural reaction." See, a few days earlier, the U.S. conducted a massive nuclear detonation over the Bikini Atoll. Sure, the environmental and human impact was terrible, but the bikini is awesome. It's rightfully earned the moniker "atom bomb of fashion." Let's consider it a draw.

It's important to realize that, while testing is not okay today, it wasn't until the 80s that anti-testing movements gained significant traction, and NZ led the charge. For NZ, the 210 French tests started the drama. How did Operation Satanic go down? Yes, that was its name. Well, France was at its wit's end. Pesky environmentalists from Greenpeace had repeatedly disrupted nuclear testing efforts off Mururoa. Politics in NZ also changed dramatically in the runup to France's *satanic* attack. In 1985, after decades of festering, anti-nuclear sentiment reached its apex

with the Labour Party winning the 1984 elections and the newly elected Prime Minister, David Lange, barring nuclear weapons or nuclear-powered ships from operating in and around the country. NZ became the first nuclear-free zone. This posed two problems: France enjoyed peppering the vicinity with radioactive fallout and NZ's opposition to nuclear technology put them on the wrong side of the ANZUS Treaty. The treaty was a 1951 three-way defensive pact binding the U.S., Australia, and New Zealand to protect each other from communism or other terrors.

The Reagan Administration was concerned about the newfound anti-nuclear craze. Who the heck did NZ think they were? As a direct challenge, Reagan ordered the *USS Buchanan*, a guided-missile destroyer, to make a port visit. The idea being that if NZ refused entry, the U.S. could put shine on this upstart government, forcing them to buckle under diplomatic pressure. This is where Cold War semantics set in. See, *USS Buchanan* was neither nuclear-powered nor equipped with nuclear weapons. This shouldn't be a problem, right? The trouble was that America maintained a policy of neither confirming nor denying nuclear capabilities on anything. This ploy was done to aggravate Soviet war planning with the idea being to prevent them from ruling out any American military asset from delivering a dose of megadeaths to Soviet metropolises. Despite NZ being a staunch ally, our fearless leaders refused to budge. NZ didn't either.

Part of it had to do with dubious experiments done at the dawn of the nuclear age. At one point, the U.S. Navy experimented with nuclear depth charges with ships like *USS Buchanan*. Imagine a sub is down deep. You can throw normal explosive depth charges designed to detonate at differing depths or nuke them. Nuking was cooler than "The Fonz," so why not! As Nelson Muntz from *The Simpsons* once said, when Lisa asked him about his "Nuke the Whales" poster, he shrugged then responded, "You gotta nuke something." The U.S. refused to divulge the vessel's nuclear disposition. Ultimately, NZ denied *USS Buchanan* entry to Auckland Harbor, a perceived slight from a tiny island nation to the greatest power in the history of great powers. So, NZ doesn't like nukes. Who cares? Can't we all just get along? The real world is not Oprah...No, we cannot!

As for France, they took it far worse. Disrupted nuclear tests by cooky environmentalists were infuriating. Every time they tried to clear the test range, the *Rainbow Warrior* – a 130-ft Greenpeace Organization Trawler adorned with rainbow striping against a black hull – arrived to delay, and, in some cases, cancel the test. You can't, no matter how much you want to, start testing nukes when civilians are in the kill radius. What is France to do, lodge a complaint, pick another location, or stop testing altogether? Heck no! They had a better plan that would put that bitch to the bottom and wreck the ANZUS Treaty in the process...Making this operation high on the "Prickdom Scale."

According to Greenpeace, they are an independent organization that uses peaceful protest, creative communication, and non-violent confrontation to expose and solve global environmental problems. To be honest, my opinion is mixed. Greenpeace was formed in 1971 to halt nuclear testing off the coast of Alaska. From there they became a provocative thorn in the side of other nuclear powers and whalers...Some called them terrorists. Greenpeace played an important role banning whaling in 1986. Yet, it was events in NZ that forever changed the organization, gained converts, and set the conditions for a nuclear testing ban. Controversial as they are, time vindicated their position on both issues.

Transiting under a bridge enroute to the Portland Rose Festival, we spotted dozens of Greenpeace radicals protesting the military's use of depleted uranium rounds (DU). The Navy claimed they were safe to handle but might've fibbed. In Fallujah, where depleted uranium tank rounds were fired aplenty, cancer rates skyrocketed. The Phalanx Close-in Weapon System (CIWS) aboard my ship was designed to turn threats into Swiss cheese courtesy of DU rounds. Today, the Veterans Affairs Administration has a voluntary, ongoing study to monitor the effects of exposure. The risks of asbestos were once downplayed too. Conveniently, the CIWS now fires tungsten rounds.

France hatched a plan to snuff out these environmentalists. On July 10, 1985, the action branch of the French Defense Ministry, the Directorate General for External Security (DGSE), executed *Operation Satanic*. It was greenlit by the French Defense Minister himself. Posing as married Swiss tourists – because nothing says peaceful like being Swiss - two French agents toured *Rainbow Warrior*, moored in Auckland Harbor, to scout the location. Greenpeace planned to send their vessel to the French Polynesian Islands to frustrate another round of tests, but fate had another idea. Christine Cabon, under the alias Frederique Bonlieu, arrived six weeks earlier, volunteering as a staunch environmentalist and French aristocrat. A crucial cog, she monitored communications, gathered maps, technical drawings, and itineraries to aid the conspirators.

Afterwards, Cabon would vanish, only to resurface 32 years later in a small French village. The stage was set, but even France couldn't imagine what would go down. There were three initial options: Sabotage *Rainbow Warrior* while at sea, contaminate the fuel system with a bacterium, or attack her while harbored. The third option was deemed most practical and least risky.

They'd done their homework. Blueprints revealed the perfect areas to strike. In the pitch of night, three agents – including two combat divers – arrived in a Zodiac. The divers made their watery trek to the rainbow-striped ebony hull. Colonel Jean Luc Kister, the team lead and one of the two divers that night, claims the sabotage attack was devised to cripple the vessel, not kill anyone, or sink it. Instead, it turned bloody via a series of errors prone to happen when explosives enter the mix. Berthed at Marsden Wharf, the divers attached two limpet mines: One near the engine room and a smaller by the keel. What happened next proved horrifying. At 11:38 pm, the first bomb detonated, ripping a two-square-meter hole. Rapid flooding of the engine room ensued.

Meanwhile, the crew were aboard celebrating a birthday party (because of course). The agents had hoped it'd be an empty ship (because of course it wasn't). The first bomb was supposed to get people off the ship while the second would keep people from coming back aboard. Unfortunately, they misjudged the power of that first mine. Within seconds the vessel began listing and the crew did not react as intended. There was no prompt evacuation. Who would think they'd been bombed? Some departed, others investigated. That's when Portuguese-Dutch photographer, Fernando Pereira, headed below decks to collect his camera equipment. When the second explosion, at 11:45 erupted at the keel, he was trapped below and succumbed to drowning. Topside, Captain Peter Willcox was thrown overboard. Four minutes later, the "sabotage" designed to cripple *Rainbow Warrior* had sunk it. The symbol of anti-nuclear sentiment became a victim of terrorist attack by the French government.

Jean Luc Kister's team scattered. However, Kister and his diver-colleague didn't depart NZ right away. As NZ authorities sifted through the wreckage to gather pertinent details, Kister enjoyed the week skiing. He then climbed aboard a commercial airliner with a falsified passport. By then, he knew a public relations disaster was looming. NZ Police captured two other agents red-handed. I imagine they spotted them wearing berets, eating crepes, and reciting poetry. Naturally, France denied any wrongdoing; however, further bombshells chronicled the extent of French involvement. When the two agents pleaded guilty, all hell broke loose. The NZ Prime Minister called it an act of terrorism. But France stood firm arguing, "The French does not deal with its opponents in such ways." What followed was a massive inquiry. More perpetrators were nabbed. A neighborhood watch group helped bust Captain Dominque Prieur and Commander Alain Mafart. Three more were located by Australian police sailing the *Ouvea* near Norfolk Island. However, when Australian law prevented detainment, a French submarine snatched them up and *Ouvea* was scuttled. With the cloud of confusion lifted, it was clear France was squarely behind the attack, prompting NZ to call this act a criminal breach of international law.

Prieur and Mafart pled guilty to manslaughter and were sentenced to 10 years. France then did the unthinkable: Demand extradition under the threat of an economic embargo. No one really jumped in to back up NZ. In fact, it found itself alone. NZ feared that an embargo would collapse their export-dependent economy. A month later, media outlets reported that French President Mitterrand had approved the bombing, sabotage, or accidental killing. The backlash was swift. Defense Minister, Charles Hernu, resigned. The head of the DGSE, Admiral Lacoste, was fired. Remarkably, Prime Minister Laurent Fabius, in a 200-word statement, admitted to a full-scale cover-up. Yet, the culprits mostly went unpunished.

In recent years, Colonel Jean Luc Kister emerged from the shadows to answer for his part in the operation. Appearing before BBC, he apologized for the "accidental" killing of Fernando. Expressing deep regret but doubling down on the Nuremburg Defense. Sorry bud. But true leaders always have a choice; very few people were satisfied by his confession. Fernando's daughter viewed the "accidental" killing comment as a callous attempt to distance himself from what she believed to be a clear-cut case of murder.

Roughly a year later, France and NZ struck a deal; France would pay a meager indemnity to NZ and apologize. France got their conspirators back but reneged on plans to detain them for 3 years on Hao Atoll, a French base. Mafart returned to France for medical treatment and was subsequently released. Prieur, on the other hand, resumed military service and earned promotion to Colonel. This breach of the agreement sparked outrage, prompting the UN Secretary-General to award increased reparations and establish a NZ - France Friendship Fund. Friendship? What a farce.

Only under extreme pressure did France pay a meager $8.16m to Greenpeace and an insulting $2m to Fernando Pereira's family - separated amongst his parents, spouse, and two children. The real issue is that the operation that sunk a civilian vessel, killed an innocent family man, and embarrassed an ally remains merely a "serious error" from the French point of view, nothing more. That will forever be the ultimate insult.

If the goal was silencing the anti-nuclear protest movement, the opposite happened. NZ stood firm on their nuclear free policy. A rare feat in politics. As mentioned, NZ's allies didn't exactly rush to her aid. One bombed her and threatened an embargo, the UK was basically mute, and America was just petty. The U.S. suspended its responsibility to defend NZ as part of the ANZUS Treaty in 1986. America and Australia would protect one another, Australia would continue protecting NZ and vice-versa, but the U.S. would not hold NZ under its protective envelope. Talk about a confusing alliance.

Though one can agree with many of Reagan's foreign policy initiatives, this was wrong. Differences over nuclear policy needn't disrupt our two countries' military relationship, but it did. For over thirty years, relations were cold despite significant areas of commonality. Until recently, a port visit to NZ was the white buffalo! Prior to 2012, if you went to the U.S. Embassy in NZ's website, you'd find an interesting disclaimer commenting that relations suffered from NZ's position on nuclear matters (i.e., it's NZ's fault). That is the epitome of petty.

If you were a New Zealander, how would you feel? Would you suddenly disregard the environmental damage other foreign powers did to your backyard? Would you forgive and forget France's blatant act of terrorism? Would you back down on your principles and allow American ships to visit under the neither confirm nor deny policy when NZ is a signatory to "Five Eyes," or FVEY? FVEY is an intelligence-sharing agreement that includes the U.S., the UK, Canada, Australia, and NZ.

The Cold War is over, and times have changed. In 2012,

President Obama lifted a ban on visits by NZ warships and NZ participated in the multinational Rim of the Pacific (RIMPAC) exercise. The petty remark on the embassy's website was removed. Though NZ's policy remains in place, in the modern post-Cold War world, we've finally discovered that capitalizing on areas of agreement is far more important than focusing on differences.

Thirty-three years after the ban, *USS Sampson*, a modern guided-missile destroyer, was selected to visit Auckland as a guest of NZ Prime Minister, John Key. Satisfied the vessel was nuclear-free, she made her trek. Then disaster struck in the form of a 7.5-7.8 magnitude earthquake. *USS Sampson* – along with ships from Australia, Canada, Japan, and Singapore – were redirected to render humanitarian assistance to quake-ravaged Kiwis. NZ also sent its military. Finally, Americans and New Zealanders worked as brethren to assist fellow humans in need. It was about time.

As a tribute, *Rainbow Warrior* was gifted to the sea as an artificial reef and marine life sanctuary. Divers still flock to reflect in tranquil silence. There's no yelling or crying down there, just whispers. As each day passes the seabed consumes her. Currents flatten and shear sections. In a decade no sign will remain. There's hope that NZ's relations with France and the U.S. can mirror this transformation process. But whispers will remain. Greenpeace used reparations to construct *Rainbow Warrior II* and continues to use the namesake. So, in a way, her legacy sails onward.

COMING TOGETHER: THE BRITISH IGNITION

The mid-1960s was a golden age for music aficionados. Bands like the Beatles, the Rolling Stones, and the Who burst onto the American music scene, utterly dominating American pop charts. But they weren't alone. The Dave Clarke Five, The Yardbirds, The Kinks, and The Animals also achieved significant mainstream success. It was a British Invasion. These days, British musical exploits are all too familiar. A second invasion during the 1980s brought us Boy George moaning "Karma Chameleon," Sting and the Police, the always erotic Duran Duran, the suicidal sounds of the Cure, a sneering Billy Idol, Depeche Mode, and the awesomeness of David Bowie. Americans love UK pop so much, they gleefully suffered a resurgence in the 90s. Remember the Spice Girls? British music is a staple. As essential as peanut buttle, waistlines, and a gas guzzling SUV. America and their former colonial overlord always maintained deep ties. However, Beatlemania fundamentally changed the relationship, making British music, oddly, part of *Americana*. Fashion, television, and film were also infected with the bug. Beyond Sean Connery debuting James Bond to moviegoers in 1962, four of the decade's Oscars for Best Picture went to British films. It even extended to auto racing, where Carroll Shelby, a former racer and Texas chicken farmer, linked up with the Brits not only to build arguably the greatest sports car in history, the Shelby Cobra, but also bested Ferrari on the track during the 24-hours of Le Mans. History proves that when Americans and Brits, "Come Together," greatness often results.

On February 7, 1964, the Beatles touched down at the newly christened JFK airport, kicking-off a Beatlemania. The timing was ideal. America had a serious case of the blues: JFK's assassination, civil rights turmoil, aftermath of Cuban missile crisis, and escalation in Vietnam. The Beatles' blues-inspired rhythm helped cure it. The Beatles owe part of their success to a) having talent, and b) being in the right place at the right time.

The band's arrival was greeted by a massive audience, eager for something fresh. Soon, other Brits made their trek across the pond, adding momentum. But the new sound wasn't fully original; bands such as the Beatles were heavily influenced by Black artists from the decade before. Liverpool, being a port town, lent itself to all types of contraband (music included). Brit rockers, especially the Beatles and the Rolling Stones, blended blues riffs – made famous amongst White crowds by Johnny Cash, Elvis, and Jerry Lee Lewis – with upbeat melodies. Instead of gravitating to those mainstream "White" acts of the 50s, though, British imports were obsessed with the originators: Chuck Berry, B.B. King, Muddy Waters, Howlin' Wolf, and Little Richard. Alas, these trailblazers largely didn't get their due during segregation's high watermark. The 1964 concert film called the *T.A.M.I.* (Teenage Music International) featured a young James Brown dazzling the audience. The Rolling Stones, who had the go-home act right after Brown, later said that "having Brown go before them was the biggest mistake of their careers since there was no way they could top him." Earlier, it was Mick Jagger who demanded Brown be able to perform. Jim Crow be damned! From a cultural standpoint, the British Invasion helped create opportunities for Black performers to shine by highlighting their influence and routinely showcasing them. All these artists needed was an opportunity, a platform, and patrons.

British influence wasn't limited to music. For America, Carroll Shelby's ascendance to racing immortality would not have been possible without the Brits. No, without them, his racing career would be a tiny footnote. There'd be no Shelby Cobra, the Ford Mustang would still be a secretary's car, and Le Mans would still be dominated by Ferrari. Oh, and the Dodge Viper wouldn't exist either. Shelby is the epitome of badass. It is rare to find something that captures the builder's essence. The Shelby Cobra represents automotive perfection. A small, agile car fitted with a monstrous V8. Menacing, yet understated. The Cobra arose from an Anglo-American marriage. Yes, the most impressive, pined for (most go for upwards of $1 million), and "truly American" sports car ever produced has British and American DNA. How and why did this happen?

Shelby always had a passion for speed. During WWII he served as a test pilot for the US Army Air Corps and afterwards became an oil roughneck and, yes, a chicken farmer. He gravitated to cars as did many former WWII pilots. Heck, hot rodding was created by adrenaline junkie veterans in the post-war era. The same goes for motorcycle gangs, from the Boozefighters to the Hell's Angels. While chicken farming was interesting, it couldn't compete with racing.

As an amateur, he raced a buddy's British MG TC along with a Cad-Allard. While they handled beautifully, Shelby felt they were missing a spark. This early experience made him wonder what the combination of an Anglo-roadster with an American V-8 could do. Unlike their American counterparts, British autos were understated cruisers perfect for navigating narrow cobblestone roads and winding countryside. In other words, Grey Poupon-eating, sophisticated gentlemen sporting leather racing gloves and riding caps above their high brows. In America, vast highways, rugged individualism, and uncouth sensibilities created an appetite for an aggressive and muscular breed of automobile.

Shelby's racing chops got him noticed immediately, placing him in the cockpits of Aston Martins and Austin Healeys for Brit teams. In fact, while driving a heavily modified Austin Healey 100S, he set sixteen speed records at Bonneville Salt Flats. By 1957, he was a two-time *Sports Illustrated* Driver of the Year. He was a serious up-and-comer destined for the heights of stardom as an automotive driver, especially when he won the 1959 24 Hours of Le Mans in an Aston Martin DBR1. The guy who gave him that big break to race in Le Mans, the world's most prestigious race, was Englishman John Wyer.

Shelby, a cardiologist's worst nightmare, often popped nitroglycerin tablets between turns to ease chronic chest pains. His dreams were dashed when that bum ticker prompted an early retirement. No longer a driver, he figured if he "couldn't race 'em, he'd build 'em." After setting up a high-performance driving school, he got a big idea. At Le Mans back in 1959, he grew impressed with a British GT called the AC Ace. He reckoned that with a decent power plant, puny straight six, it could turn heads. Around 1960, Shelby approached England's John Cooper (creator of the Mini Cooper) about building a production sports car for America. An overstretched Cooper couldn't support additional production runs. However, he introduced Shelby to his friend Charles Hurlock. The same man who created the AC Ace that captured Shelby's attention in the first place.

In September 1961, Shelby wrote to Charles Hurlock in hopes of modifying an AC Bristol roadster to accept a V8. As luck would have it, AC had just lost an engine deal. This opened the door for a partnership so long as the right engine could be found. Chevrolet balked, fearing a threat to their vaunted Corvette, and told him to pound sand. Ford, on the other hand, hooked him up with two 3.6L Windsor 221 cubic inch small block engines. With engines, Shelby and AC went to work, adding further modifications to the rear differential, brakes, steering, and beefing up the small block to a 4.3L 260-cubic inch. Ford's backing and Shelby's relationship with AC Motors created a world-beater, especially when they later upgraded the engine to a 289-c3. Still, Shelby needed a name. Feeling restless one night, he awoke and scrawled five letters on to a scrap of paper: C-O-B-R-A. An icon was born.

Although Cobras sliced through the ranks on the American circuit, Shelby knew aerodynamic limitations prevented them from realistically competing in European endurance races. Le Mans was the crown and, there, Ferrari was king, winning six of seven titles from 1958 to 1964. That lone loss came from Shelby and his Aston Martin.

Meanwhile, a feud was brewing. In 1965, Henry Ford II, the CEO of Ford, married an Italian socialite Maria Cristina Vettore Austin. During courtship, and *not at all* trying to impress her, Ford attempted to purchase a 50-percent stake in Ferrari for $10 million. The part pleasure, part business deal proved embarrassing. In 1963, Ford was a pen stroke away from securing the racing giant when Enzo Ferrari rebuffed him. An infuriated Ford vowed revenge. Imagine what a disaster Ferrari would be today had deal gone through though. A Ford Taurus badged with a prancing horse? Gross!

Ego bruised, Ford determined that if he "couldn't buy 'em, they'd beat 'em." So, in 1964, while still courting his Italian bombshell, he authorized the development of the Ford GT40. A car specifically designed to conquer Europe while flipping Enzo Ferrari "the bird." Yet, initially this rivalry was as lopsided as contests between the Packers and my beloved Bears. Ferrari was kicking their teeth in. Unable to suffer continued embarrassment, Ford beseeched Shelby for help.

On a chilly day in December 1964, the first Ford GT40 arrived via Trans World Airlines. Shelby's team was tasked to prepare it for the 1965 racing season. Test drivers, American Bob Bondurant and Englishman Ken Miles, would manage a continuous testing program to upgrade and analyze every future GT40. John Wyer had been responsible the prior year, but GT40s performed poorly. In fact, Wyer spent the bulk of his time correcting Ford's over-engineering and clinging to his sanity. As with the Cobra, the GT40 was based on a British-designed Lola MK6, conjured by Eric Broadley. After a nudge from Ford, the Brits passed the reins to Shelby's team for "Americanizing." Shelby's team had carte blanche to cut or alter necessary to make it faster. Whereas Wyer was a bit more restrained in the modification game, Shelby was an aggressive risk-taker.

The results were astounding, nabbing a victory at Daytona in its inaugural race. But it was at Le Mans where the GT40 shined. In 1966, a year after Shelby went to work, Ford stunned the world by finishing first, second, and third. Between drivers and co-drivers of those three cars, you had two Americans, three Kiwis, and one Brit. The clean sweep was a game-changer. America had arrived and proven itself against the best. GT40s repeated in 1967, finishing first and fourth with Ferraris sandwiched in between.

If 1966 was a good year for Anglo-American racing, Anglo-American rivalries in music would be the genesis of two of the most influential records of all time. In 1965, the Beatles released *Rubber Soul*, an artistic statement infused with pop, soul, and folk music. This record expressed the increased maturity and complexity of the band as musicians, not just pop stars. Since they'd stopped touring, they poured their hearts and souls into the project. Following its release, Brian Wilson of the Beach Boys was caught between panic and hero-worship. He lauded the individual songs and the way they blended, but also feared his own band couldn't compete. Inspired, Wilson immediately went to work on an entirely new set of songs to make his own, personal statement. He desperately wanted to be taken seriously. He would be!

In May 1966, the same year GT40s killed it on the track, *Pet Sounds* was released to mixed reviews. Fans and critics who expected songs about bikinis, cars, and surfing were confused and disappointed. At least, they were upon initial listening. However, the power of songs like "God Only Knows" and "Wouldn't It Be Nice" eventually converted the detractors. The album established the Beach Boys as true evolving artists. Paul McCartney, when asked, called  *Pet Sounds* his favorite album ever. John Lennon was equally impressed. In 1967, while GT40s were crushing competition on the international circuit, the Beatles issued their response and *Sgt. Pepper's Lonely Hearts Club Band* was released to rave reviews. Both *Pet Sounds* and that response would become two of the most influential and best-selling albums of all time and set the bar for musical creativity.

More importantly, the British Invasion paid so much homage to Black originators that racial lines started to blur. Marginalized Black talents garnered more airplay. This created the conditions for Berry Gordy's "Motown" music scene. By the time Motown really ramped up, an America mired in racial strife, welcomed them. Consider that Gordy's label gave us Otis Redding, Smokey Robinson, Marvin Gaye, The Supremes, The Temptations, and

Aretha Franklin...In short succession. How big was it? Motown produced 79 Top Ten Billboard Hot 100 records from 1960-1969. That big!

On the raceway, Ford decided to scuttle operations and cease international racing to focus on NASCAR. In a twist of irony, Ford handed the keys to the GT40s to John Wyer, the man who gave Shelby his big break in the first place. Wyer went on to win Le Mans two more times for an even four in a row. What about Ferrari? Welp, Enzo tucked his tail and fled sportscar racing entirely, opting to focus on Formula One. Although they've decimated foes there, Ferrari's no longer scream down the Mulsanne Straight.

America had the talent but ultimately needed a little British ignition. That's because both nations share a special bond across the pond. A collective ingenuity. They've fought together. Bled together. Worked on existential challenges together. America's Navy is modelled after the Brits. The *USS Churchill's* navigator is always a UK exchange officer. They have special intelligence sharing agreements. They're NATO partners. American courts borrow Common Law traditions. Yet, it goes beyond geopolitics and democratic ideals. It's also complementary. Without the blues pioneers from the American South, the Beatles and the Rolling Stones wouldn't exist. Without the Beatles, it's doubtful The Beach Boys would've transcended the shackles of their genre to become musical legends. Additionally, Motown might've garnered a muted response, never to be embraced by audiences unwilling or unable to see past skin tone. Can anyone truly imagine living in a world without Smokey Robinson, Marvin Gaye, The Temptations or Aretha Franklin? The boundaries are limitless when these two nations "Come Together."

KOREAN WAVES,
BUTTER BATTLES,
& BS

All eyes were on North Korea during the opening ceremony of the 2018 Winter Olympics in Pyeongchang, South Korea. Kim Jong-un's sister, Kim Yo-jong, spearheaded an unprecedented delegation and became the most senior member of the family to visit their sworn enemy to the south. As fate, or design, would have it, she sat behind then Vice President Mike Pence. Amidst the Trump Administration's attempt to reset relations with the reclusive regime, the media couldn't resist its urge to editorialize. It was an all-out charm offensive. As usual, the media lapped it up. Glee-filled youths singing and mesmerizing displays of synchronized solidarity. Knowing full well of South Koreans obsession with beauty, North Koreans brought an entourage of smooth-skinned bombshells in crimson, form fitting military attire reminiscent of flight attendants for Pan Am. Don't forget the cheerleaders in their red, fur-trimmed peacoats. Are you seeing a pattern here? The media circus rivalled Tim

Tebow's arrival to the "Big Apple." Utter bullshit. Those deluded by peaceful spectacles of pure propaganda overlook, or at the very least downplay, despotic realities. Time and again, South Korea has been duped. The world has been duped. The *Dear Leader's* sister was an overnight sensation, despite being a puppeteer in strategic communications. From the outside, it's difficult to see through the sleek veneer. However, these odd tit-for-tats have characterized the peninsula's half-century culture war. Across Korea's Demilitarized Zone (DMZ), a butter battle takes place. However, there's a swell brewing in the heart of Seoul. It's created a mighty wave that threatens to flood the ramparts.

My favorite Dr. Seuss story is *The Butter Battle Book*. Most adore *The Cat in the Hat*, *Green Eggs and Ham*, or *The Lorax*. To each their own. Written in 1984, Dr. Seuss jumped into the anti-war movement in an unconventional way. The Yooks and the Zooks live on opposite sides of a long, winding wall. Besides physical barriers, the proper way to spread butter on bread generates ferocious enmity. Butter side up or butter side down? Here's how it all went down.

The arms race starts when a Zook patrolman slingshots and ruins a Yooks *Tough-Tufted Prickly Snick-Berry Switch*. The nerve! The Yooks get to work, crafting a *Triple-Sling Jigger* – three slingshots in one (a modern miracle). The Zooks counter with a *Jigger-Rock Snatchem*. This goes back and forth – each time, the Yooks are bested by the technological achievements of their rival. That is until they develop the weapon of all weapons, the *Bitsy Big-Boy Boomeroo*. A small weapon so powerful it can kill them all. The book ends with each side possessing their own *Boomeroo* as the narrator asks, "Who's gonna drop it? Will you, or will he?" The cliffhanger is analogous to the nuclear arms race during the Cold War.

Dr. Seuss' story faced criticism and even censorship! Now, the book is not without its faults. The biggest one is that of moral ambivalence. This runs counter to consensus opinion that the Soviets were the baddies. Yet, his book more accurately mirrors the absurdity of North and South Korea's DMZ and a frozen conflict since WWII. With forcible reunification a pipedream, what is the non-fight/fight about?

The 160 nm DMZ arose as a convenient solution to a growing Cold War problem. The peninsula's separation had everything to do with American and Soviet distrust following Japanese expulsion after WWII. Allies in war, enemies in peace. More than a buffer, it offers a visual representation of constant war-footing. A real-life butter battle. Families hacked in half by an arbitrary line on a map. When Korean War hostilities ended, North and South Korea, along with China, the U.S., and UN, agreed to split the peninsula along the 38th parallel. The Armistice Agreement of 27 July 1953 may have ended direct hostilities, but the proxy war drags on. Sporadic outbreaks of violence killed between 500 South Korean soldiers, 250 North Koreans, and even 50 U.S. soldiers between 1953 and 1999. Civilians have been victims as well. North Koreans, sentenced to draconian rule under a delusional regime, remain the biggest victims.

Distrust, misinformation, and myth are the foundations of this warped relationship epitomized by the jagged scar disfiguring the peninsula. Those in the "live and let live" camp need to really brush up on their history. Then again, those whose only knowledge comes from internet jokes miss the crushing reality of this human rights disgrace. Now, all of us have developed our own opinions on North Korea. In many ways our discovery of the regime is intrinsically linked to that internet. Prior to the late-90s, the only people talking about the country were policy wonks up late at night, eating cold pizza, and hammering away at their keyboard on articles no one read. That changed when America went online. Leaked stories opened eyes to the greatest human rights crisis going on today. While ecological disasters, famine, genocides, and civil wars flare up, North Korea is fundamentally different. It is an ongoing plague of injustice. The internet gave us our first glimpse of North Korean craziness precisely at the same time the country was economically left behind. As the world globalized, they grew more isolated.

Even talking about North Korea elicits all types of emotions from fear to mockery. It is nearly impossible to have an honest discussion about the true threat she poses because, for so many years, cyberspace and its related media have created a cottage industry based on poking fun at the reclusive state. Therein lies the biggest obstacle in dealing with North Korea. Rumors, misstatements, and mischaracterizations fuel the country's perception of not just being a joke, but the easiest way to earn a cheap laugh in modern history. A favorite target of internet memes, a simple image search for "North Korea funny" delivers comedy gold. What's better than a picture of Kim Jong-un holding a floppy disk? How about the caption, "With this technology we will bring the United States to its knees." Probably the most widely distributed images come from

satellites. A luminescent globe – portraying human civilization emerging from the dark ages via modern technology – for some hails capitalism's promise to enrich the globe, for others its steady destruction. For everyone, though, it acutely demonstrates North Korea's perpetual backwardness. To the south, their Korean neighbor is aglow. China sparkles too. But not North Korea. Its capital, Pyongyang, is merely a glimmer...A basement light bulb twitching in slow demise. Devoid of electrified radiance, the nation stands apart. With obscene delight, the darkness confirms our suspicions and grant reassurance that no country so underdeveloped can carry out threats against the global order. Certainly, America is safe from this paper tiger, or so we would like to think.

Take the Third Aggression Tunnel, which perfectly showcases North Korea's nuttiness, paranoia, willing suspension of disbelief, brashness, and dishonestly. Back in 1978, South Korea detected unusual noises they believed to be underground explosions along the DMZ. Though an armistice was agreed upon, incredibly, both countries are technically still at war. A reality North Korea loves trumpeting. This global hotspot is arguably the most dangerous border in the entire world.

Which explains North Korea's penchant for digging. After months of searching and counter-digging, South Koreans intercepted the "aggression tunnel." Over a mile long, six and a half feet tall, and nearly seven feet wide; it traversed the DMZ's granite bedrock at a depth of almost 250 ft. North Korea's foray in extracurricular excavation had nothing to do with a sudden interest in geology; rather, they sought a sure-fire way to mobilize forces in the advent of war. Had it been completed, tens of thousands of troops per hour could swarm through to occupy Seoul – South Korea's capital. As expected, the UN promptly chastised North Korea for knowingly violating ceasefire terms. You'd think North Korea, caught red-handed, would apologize and move on. You don't know these tricky fellas. I imagine it played out like this:

UN and the Coalition of Sane Nations (UN&CSN): *Hey, we found this tunnel under the DMZ. You gotta stop this nonsense. This is wrong and dangerous.*

North Korea: *Tunnel? What tunnel?*

UN&CSN: *The one South Korea intercepted. The one you're clearly digging. That tunnel! We all believe it's meant for mobilizing forces.*

North Korea: *That's not a tunnel. That's a coal mine. You've heard of coal, right?*

UN&CSN: *Yes, we understand coal and its many uses. That's not a coal mine.*

North Korea: *I assure you it is. Did you see the walls and how black they are?*

U.S. & CSN: *That's soot. Ya know, carbon residue from the explosives you used. A byproduct of the chemical reaction.*

North Korea: *I'm afraid you're wrong, respectfully, of course. That's certainly coal. Our geologists have confirmed the ample supply of coal there.*

UN Geologist: *Hey, I thought I'd lend my expertise. We've run a series of tests. I can 100% guarantee the geological formation is granite covered with a moderate dusting of amorphous carbon produced by incomplete burning of organic matter. The walls are igneous rock formations...not sedimentary in nature, like coal is.*

North Korea: *Capitalist lies. An American plot against our Dear Leader and our glorious revolution. Agree to disagree!*

North Korea's proclivity for denial (yes, they said it was a coal mine) makes frank, direct conversations impossible, forcing concerned actors to expend time and energy fact-checking and, yes, searching for "aggression tunnels" – of which there are innumerably more. That North Korea maintains a myth of a Western plot bent on invasion and subjugation only adds another layer of complexity. North Korea straddles the line of victim and aggressor, pre-emptive and reactionary, peace-seeking, and warmongering. They navigate their hypocrisy through a system of overreaction, provocation, and carefully crafted messaging. Outside influence is censured and history is rewritten. Dissenting opinion is either crushed by the boot or sapped from the soul. The only greater tragedy than an inability to think critically is losing the desire to do so.

Then there's North Korea's fake town, Kijong-dong, located on the north side of the DMZ. The so-called "Peace Village" consists of human cutouts, vacant buildings, and manicured lawns. Concocted to lure defectors, the presence of a phony town juxtaposed with a real one illustrates an insane level of cross-border tomfoolery. North Korea constructed a fake town! Let that sink in. It gets stranger. This is the sight of the famous "flagpole war." When South Korea erected a 323-foot-tall flagpole, North Korea responded as one might expect a petulant child. They topped it with the 525-foot-tall Panmunjom flagpole – for a time the tallest in the world.

The trouble is there's absolutely nothing funny about North Korea. A nation of 25 million in abject poverty, lacking basic rights, and facing constant fear of reprisal from a government that doesn't just punish the perpetrator in a network of concentration camps, but three generations worth. Yes, concentration camps still exist. Prisoners, mostly innocent on account of the three generations' rule, suffer torture, rape, and dehumanization. No one is safe. North Korea has a history of detaining foreigners, kidnapping

South Koreans and Japanese citizens – including a South Korean director and his wife Kim Jong Il tasked with building a vibrant film industry. For six years – from 1977 to 1983 – North Korea kidnapped at least thirteen Japanese citizens, in Japan! Other abuses include forced marriages, murder, links to terrorism, and identity theft. Cyber-attacks, prevalent in recent years, fleece the globe for millions. In response to a silly 2014 film, *The Interview*, featuring Seth Rogen and James Franco, North Korea hacked Sony. This criminal enterprise scrapes the sludge of global misdeeds.

It's so easy to dismiss North Korea's bold proclamations as crazy and move on. Overreactions are a staple of North Korean politics. A prime example pertains to loudspeakers. Yes, loudspeakers. Imagine for a moment you live in a world where rival nations engage in decibel combat, spraying propaganda from colossal speaker systems. Sounds awesome, sign me up! On the DMZ, it is very real (and not so awesome).

Loudspeakers became a routine discussion point while onboard the carrier, *USS John C Stennis*. After North Korea tested another nuke, the Carrier Strike Group awaited a decision on a Flexible Deterrent Option, or FDO. FDOs are escalation measures designed to reassure allies, deter aggression, and influence desired outcomes. These tools can be diplomatic, political, economic, and military-related. One popular arrow in Commander in Chief's quiver is parking an aircraft carrier in the backyard of a misbehaving nation. It's become so commonplace that ascertaining the closest carrier's location is the sitting President's first question whenever a crisis erupts. So, there we were in the South China Seas – troubled waters and a modern-day flashpoint between Chinese hegemonic aspirations and a U.S.-buoyed international order – awaiting further orders regarding North Korea's most recent provocation.

We soon learned that South Korea had re-activated its noise

campaign. Originally stopped in 2004 as a goodwill gesture, Seoul brought it back, after an 11-year hiatus, when two South Korean soldiers were injured by a landmine. That return was negotiated away. The North's fourth nuclear test, in 2016, pushed the issue. South Korea pumped up the volume. Every day, for two to six hours, South Korea blared propaganda. What propaganda? Historically, overt messaging was selected to challenge the awfulness of North Korea's corrupt system. However, these methods fell out of favor. Saying, "Hey you, yeah you, your country sucks," lacks a certain *je ne sais quoi*. Today, speakers blast the weather, news, soap operas, and even South Korean pop music, called K-pop (aka "The Korean Wave"). Although K-pop is banned in North Korea, it is impossible to contain. One cannot stop a Korean Wave, DMZ be damned! On the surface, this is comical. Pop music and dramas challenging a brutal dictatorship? Yet, it's true. South Korean movies and music, in high demand, are smuggled into the North where black markets peddle them to K-pop crazy North Koreans. Not being a K-pop kinda guy, I had to do some research.

OH MY GOD! What happens when you combine South Koreans, "NSYNC," avant-garde, and visuals causing epileptic seizures? A band of rainbow-haired dudes, singing sort of like girls, and with move's that make Justin Timberlake jealous. Despite its obnoxiousness, these groups rake in millions of views on YouTube from around the world. To put it bluntly, North Korea hates loudspeakers. In a classic North Korean overreaction, Kim Jong-un equated playing K-pop to armed aggression and even an act of war, threatening to fire upon the speakers. He called it "cancerous."

Essentially, playing wannabe "NSYNC" music loud constitutes scorched earth retaliation. Okay, North Korea. You realize this is why you don't have friends. South Korea firmly believes their campaign is working and this belief does, in fact, make sense. Why else would the speakers cause such an uproar? In fact, all evidence points to a transformative effect on average citizens and military personnel. North Korea counters the loudspeakers with her own; however, they lack the same output strength (i.e., they're crap). When heard, North Korea just comes off as an angry old man shouting over his fence, "Stop that party and turn off the K-pop! Our *Dear Leader* is trying to get some sleep...some people around here have to plan an invasion tomorrow." Thus far, North Korea has yet to attack the speakers of doom. At least, not yet.

When Donald Trump entered office, he immediately fired a warning shot across North Korea's bow. Policy analysts were stunned, the media balked, and allies squirmed. War was looming, they predicted. Armageddon was upon us! The trouble is, for decades, establishment figures have debated policy minutiae lathered with "Senate Speak," only to snatch defeat from the jaws of victory. Their expertise says little, means even less. Nothing of substance was accomplished via their foreign policy acumen. Can anyone prove otherwise? Instead, the "Hermit Kingdom" doubled down on rhetoric and provocations. Throughout at least three Administrations - Clinton, Bush, and Obama - the Kim Dynasty advanced their weapons program and consolidated their grip on power. American foreign policy has been an abysmal failure. This is a bipartisan cesspool brought on by mealy-mouthed politicians, weak-handed diplomats, and a feckless international order.

Trump's policy shift arrived at the back end of Obama's ratcheting up of UN-sponsored sanctions. This time with China's tacit approval. The early-2016 nuclear test and subsequent ones proved too brash to ignore. That said, prior administrations were generally a day late and a dollar short. This time, a key difference was that Trump gave North Korea a dose of their own medicine. That scared the piss out of them. The regime, for a moment at least, appeared rattled by Trump's unpredictable volleys. North Korea has grown accustomed to well-articulated strategies full of protocol and faux deference, common in emissary circles. That wasn't Trump's *forte*. Either this was a glimpse of Trump playing 4D chess or a simple byproduct of his penchant to "tweet" about the last thing an advisor mentioned. Others can debate and decide. While decorum is warranted during most encounters with foreign nations, North Korea is a different animal and should be treated accordingly.

Recent UN sanctions pushed for by Obama, and Trump's grandstanding, have changed the conversation. Bullies back down from a bloody nose. North Korea's economy suffered from severe drought recently, manufacturing is down, and sanctions show some positive signs. While recent developments offer a glimmer of hope for long-term solvency, results have yet to materialize. Trump's fire before aiming mentality upended the status quo, culminating in a novel summit and Un's pledge to work toward peninsula disarmament. The reality is more complicated and all too common. That pledge appears little more than a

piece of paper. After all the buzz and Trump's boasts and bellicosity, Un remains entrenched in power. The regime is back to her old tricks. Trump's summit made headlines, but no waves. The *Great Negotiator* ultimately failed to deliver meaningful results, joining a long list of other presidents similarly rebuffed.

For too long, America and her allies have negotiated with the wrong folks. Even in oppressive governments, sowing dissent is crucial for real, long-standing change. While top-level negotiations are appropriate in most cases, North Korea is a clear exception. However, those in the "destabilization camp" are typically sidelined. China, a major stakeholder in this drama, is fearful that regime collapse would spill over, causing internal turmoil. Thus, they begrudgingly work to prop up Un and his criminal enterprise. American foreign policy objectives are ambiguous at best. For starters, America should commit to the swift ending of this horrific regime by focusing on its people. We should be ramping up smuggling operations to black markets. We should be more aggressive in the cyber and psychological operations (or counter-information) game. We need to open the eyes of average citizens. We need to show them the world they're missing out on. While Trump may have applied maximum pressure through sanctions and naughty language, we need maximum pressure against misinformation and disinformation.

North Korea's Olympic charm offensive was carefully crafted to receive goodwill. Has it suddenly reformed like an abusive boyfriend who's off the bottle? Don't fall for it. Policy momentum moves at a snail's pace and, in North Korea's case, fails miserably. It fails because the government clings to power through a system of overt and covert oppression. Fear is its only mandate. America and the world must weaken its pillars of authoritarianism, starting with public beliefs and attitudes.

Korean Wave and other elements of South Korean pop culture are defying literal barriers. One of the biggest stories out of the Olympics revolved around the United Korea Women's Hockey Team. Despite sleeping in separate dorms, traveling on different buses, and being kept under the watchful eye of North Korean supervisors, the unified team bonded. North and South finding common ground in sport and, yes, K-Pop. This is not another "made for TV" feel-good moment, either. Music and other aspects of culture have historically transcended the constraints of politics, gender, race, and creed. Music, and to a greater extent, the arts, nurture commonality. They cut through animosity to forge connections. In the end, humans like what they like. Catchy music is more infectious than any pandemic. While I might loathe hearing "Gangnam Style" 42 times in a row, one can't ignore the beat. Annoying? Possibly. Addictive? Absolutely!

Before this odd mix of North and South Korean girls took to the ice, they loosened up and stretched to K-pop. They found a momentary respite from the drama surrounding them. A normalcy divorced from hate. These were young girls from different countries conditioned to fear their neighbor. When one nation has nukes on the rails and the other a powerful ally/buddy and vibrant economy... things get tricky. Interesting things happen, though, when people set aside politics and, well, loosen up. Even a year ago, the very idea of North Korean girls singing K-pop as they learned the latest dance moves from their enemies to the South would be absurd. Yet, it happened. We can all learn something from the young. At the heart of it, all are people, warts and all. We live in an era where friends blast one another on Facebook over differing stances on political issues and celebrity feuds. We live in echo chambers of our own crafting.

We can all learn that when we approach people as humans, there's a world to discover. Some of us are activists fighting abuses. Some are mired in chronic poverty and cultural strife. Some are teenage girls placed smack-dab in the middle of the potential easing of tensions between long-standing rivals. Nowhere is the former truer than during the Olympics, where mortal enemies took the ice together in hopes of cooling things off. Together these sisters wore jerseys, not of their countries, but a blue, borderless Korean peninsula. Though the border remains in physical form, hope exists that one day the DMZ, the mines, the artillery batteries, and the nukes will be replaced by peace. This butter battle needs to end. If sanctions and "tweets" couldn't do it, perhaps the *sage* wisdom of the Biden Administration's latest initiative will. I highly doubt it, though. We've spent too much time talking to the regime. Tired "establishment" policies are played out. We must exert all efforts to reach the citizenry. Sadly, stuff like K-pop has a higher chance of success than more high-brow, beltway bullshit. A wall erected between East and West Berlin crumbled almost overnight. Sometimes all that's needed is the faintest crack.

VeNi ViDi ViCi: CoD WaRS & MiNerVa ReeFS

For kids growing up in the 80s, television experienced a golden age. What was better? You had the essence of action packed into 30-minute episodic thrillers. David Hasselhoff rocking a perm while he slammed his talking Pontiac Trans Am, K.I.T.T., around hairpin turns. *The Dukes of Hazzard* featuring Daisy Duke (and her brothers) along with a Confederate Flag-emblazoned Dodge Charger. My, how times have changed. Then you had the *A-Team*. A team composed of their leader Hannibal, debonair con-man Face, the insane Murdock, and B.A. Baracus, played by none other than Mr. T. Oh, and they drove a black, windowless van. Confederate Flags and creepy, black vans...Those were the days. But my favorite show was MacGyver. Richard Dean Anderson assumed the role of a quasi-secret agent, originally doing jobs for the U.S. government, even though he was Canadian. Instead of guns, he used his brains and science to get himself out of jams. You see, a childhood accident resulted in the death of a friend from a firearm. Thus, he used mental prowess, a handy Swiss army knife, and extensive knowledge of the periodic table to solve the world's most difficult problems. From sealing a toxic chemical spill with chocolate bars to saving a man's life with a makeshift defibrillator cobbled together from candlesticks, a microphone cord, and a rubber mat, anything was possible for MacGyver. Later, he worked for an organization called the Phoenix Foundation. Not much is known about this entity, but the name always struck me as ominous. The show maintained a secretive aura about their goals; however, if MacGyver worked for them, they couldn't be bad. So, what if the Phoenix Foundation was not only real, but also once owned a slice of paradise in the South Pacific?

Alright, they didn't have a bunch of leather jacket-clad MacGyver's running *aboooot*. However, instead of providing a non-violent law enforcement alternative - combating global crime syndicates, and America's arch-enemies - the Phoenix Foundation was a libertarian front group committed to founding independent enclaves (or micro-nations), while upholding Ayn Randian virtues: Individualism, voluntary association, self-ownership, deregulation, maximum freedom, and other things anti-authority which fill her thousand-page books. As with most "well-intentioned" movements, the principles above were a pile of bullshit sprinkled with snake oil.

Long periods out at sea make the mind wander; especially, on deployments. No women or booze results in unlikely conversations. The first time I heard the term micro-nation, I was standing watch in the Combat Information Center onboard the *USS Mobile Bay*.

We were burning holes in a night steam box near San Clemente Island off the Southern California Coast. A night steam box is a pre-approved latitude and longitude box supposedly free of vessel traffic. The idea is to help the Captain finally get some sleep and prevent frantic midnight calls or, even worse, collisions. The new Weapons Officer and I were solving the world's problems: Discussing the United Nations Convention on the Law of the Sea, the Federal Reserve, conspiracy theories, and other tinfoil hat topics. Eventually, he asked if I'd ever heard of Minerva? Let's clarify: The new Weapons Officer not only replaced me when I moved into the Combat Systems Officer position, but he also became my friend. More importantly, he was a huge libertarian and self-admitted poster child for associated stereotypes:

◇ *Submitted lengthy, citation-filled responses to lightly trafficked blog sites.*
◇ *Endlessly debated the definition of obscure political terms.*
◇ *Spent far too much time discussing the Federal Reserve and silver coins.*
◇ *Strongly believed libertarians were right about everything and, when asked why they never won elections, claimed, "Oh, that's easy. Because we don't like government, or voting, and eat our own for not being pure enough."*

I grew to appreciate his firm conviction that the government generally sucked at everything whilst we served that same sucky government. He did have many solid points. I hadn't a clue about Minerva, but soon, I'd learn a story so unbelievable, it could only be true. Evidence and eyewitness accounts support it too. His synopsis was dissatisfying because follow-on research proved the entire saga far more interesting than originally conveyed. What made the story more relevant was that our discussion occurred around the time the U.S. Navy's Third Fleet was supporting a new Overseas Maritime Security Initiative or OMSI in and around Fiji and Tonga.

The Phoenix Foundation arose from a desire to avoid taxation, along with the drunken pipe dream we've all had: The unquenchable desire to start our own country because everyone else is stupid and we're run by bastards. We can sprinkle in the whole liberty aspect, but the money was at the heart of things. In 1972, a Nevada real estate mogul, Michael Oliver, got together with longtime friends. What started as a hair-brained idea to establish a tax haven soon gained converts: Gullible, naïve believers in the cause against liberty-sucking tyrannical governments. The whole story demonstrated that any idea, regardless of how bad, is music to the ears to the moronic.

The Phoenix Foundation created the Ocean Life Research Foundation using roughly $100,000 in personal funds to create a new society. It would be free of taxation, welfare, subsidies, or any economic interventionism. Ever read *Atlas Shrugged*? Well, in that book, by Ayn Rand, all the great thinkers or movers of society suddenly disappear, leaving the world in chaos. Spoiler alert: They form their own enclave based on these very principles. That fictitious society worked, but you also had all the world's successful people and geniuses living there. In Minerva, this was not the case. No geniuses took the bait, and you'll discover why.

With forty-two cultists in tow, they embarked on a journey to the other side of the world: The South Pacific. That year, they constructed a small platform on one of Minerva's Reefs. Never heard of it? Perhaps Ongo Teleki rings a bell *a la* Tongan. Nope? You wouldn't be the first ones. For 19th Century sailors, these reefs brought dread. Minerva Reefs are two submerged atolls located south of Fiji and Tonga. They gained their namesake when the Australian whaleship, *Minerva*, was wrecked there in 1829. Over the years, many Captains would lose their lives and ships navigating through the shallow waters fraught with invisible dangers. But these libertarians, driven by a zeal for being left the hell alone, weren't afraid. Heck no, amongst their first actions was proudly hoisting the new symbol of Minerva: A golden torch on a field of blue. Every nation, even a micronation, must have a flag. If you have a flag, you're halfway to independent statehood, right?

On 19th January 1972, their inaugural and last President, Morris Davis, proclaimed Minerva's independence stating, "People will be free to do as they damn well please. Nothing will be illegal, so long as it does not infringe on the rights of others. If a citizen wishes to open a tavern, set up gambling, or make pornographic films, the government will not interfere." Wow, this place sounds amazing. A true utopia in a world of crapola. That is, until you remember you're in the South Pacific, thousands of miles from civilization and the "land" you're standing on barely rises above crashing waves for brief periods of the day. That "land" is also inhospitable coral.

Sure, they solved that problem by layering on sand but that didn't make it any more liveable. Tavern? They didn't even have fresh water. Pornographic films? Really? Prior to its establishment, Oliver and his team hoped the economy would include fishing, tourism, and soon, light industry. It's obvious Nick at Nite re-reruns of *Gilligan's Island* rotted their brains. Nope, you cannot jury rig a coconut into a radio no matter *your* "Professorial" credentials. Heck, Ginger and Mary Ann would've been smart enough to avoid this cluster. A guy named Maslov taught us to first focus on the essentials like food, shelter, and electricity. The only liberty people had on this new micronation was to die painful, drawn-out deaths from starvation, dehydration, and boredom. Unless the Tongans killed them first.

And that nearly happened. See, in the modern age, you

can't just put your flag on something and say it's yours. Minervan Independence Day was not greeted fondly by countries in the region, prompting an urgent conference. Australia, New Zealand, Tonga, Fiji, Nauru, Samoa, and the Cook Islands gathered on February 24th to craft a response. As a rule, don't mess with neighborhood housewives, retired war veterans seeking crusades against the dog who digs up his flowerbed and leaves huge deuces, or tiny countries seeking any opportunity to get revenge after centuries of being kicked around by bigger world powers. These folks got together to recognize Tonga's claim over Minerva's "valuable" real estate. On 15th June, Tonga made it official by issuing a bold proclamation no one probably read but which oozed majesty.

PROCLAMATION

His Majesty King Taufa'ahau Tupou IV in Council DOES HEREBY PROCLAIM:

WHEREAS the Reefs known as North Minerva Reef and South Minerva Reef have long served as fishing grounds for the Tongan people and have long been regarded as belonging to the Kingdom of Tonga has now created on these Reefs islands known as Teleki Tokelau and Teleki Tonga; AND WHEREAS it is expedient that we should now confirm the rights of the Kingdom of Tonga to these islands; THEREFORE we do hereby AFFIRM and PROCLAIM that the islands, rocks, reefs, foreshores and waters lying within a radius of twelve miles [19.31 km] thereof are part of our Kingdom of Tonga.

As you might suspect, the libertarian colony wasn't impressed by the rhetoric. Instead of shaking in fear, they doubled down, issuing their own currency, the Minerva Dollar. What do you do if throughout your country's history, other powers have belittled you and invaded you either with Wesleyan Methodist missionaries or influenza, like the one in 1918 brought by Kiwis, which killed an estimated 8% of the population? Sure, Tonga never became a colony. Instead, it became a British Protectorate. However, Tongans had been given precious few opportunities to kick someone's teeth in. When this upstart micronation rebuffed Tonga's rightful claim to partially submerged piles of coral, they put on their clobbering boots. When else would they have an opportunity to take out their frustration on smaller fish to fry?

Tonga sent a mighty armada of speedboats, packed like sardines with big-bodied commandos. This speedboat arsenal may have been launched from one of their three patrol boats, a mechanized landing craft (the same type we used during D-Day to land forces on Normandy Beach in 1944), or her majesty's royal yacht. That certainly registered on the scary scale. On 18th June 1972, the Tongans arrived to impose their claim on about forty-plus doped up libertarians, no doubt encircling an idol of Ayn Rand. The conversation possibly went like this:

> "We're here to enforce her majesty's claim to Teleki Tokelau and Teleki Tonga."

> "Oh, I think you're in the wrong place. This is Minerva. See our flag right there."

> "Minerva is Teleki Tokelau and Teleki Tonga."

> "See that platform and sweet flag. We own it now. But you're welcome to join us for a roundtable discussion about objectivism. Afterwards we're gonna drink salt water and have a lively debate concerning the deleterious effects of quantitative easing and banking cabals."

Then the commandos looked at each other, grunted, and said, "fuck this" before they kicked over the platform like a child's sandcastle. This led to a nearly three-month occupation. Yes, occupation of these reefs. The world recognized Tonga's claim in September during the South Pacific Forum, prompting the Phoenix Foundation to fire Minerva's first president.

What did they expect? Soon after, the forty or so "citizens" made a sorrowful trek back to America (and the real world). Their dreams dashed, they probably had difficulty adjusting to a life of things like rules, clothes, and general society. I mean, how can anything top once colonizing an uninhabitable reef and staring into the faces of angry Tongans? In later years, one colonist suggested that Minerva failed not because it was a bad idea but because they lacked the resolve to fight.

Of course, the Phoenix Foundation didn't learn anything. A year later, they attempted to overtake the island of Abaco in the Bahamas after Bahamian independence created a power vacuum. The Bahamas took exception to the plot and snuffed it out. That wasn't the end of it, either-- in 1980, they attempted to foment a rebellion in Vanuatu, only to be thwarted when the government appealed to Papua New Guinea, who subsequently sent a battalion to stamp it down. Finally, NPR branded the Phoenix Foundation a sinister, right-wing organization. But can you really be sinister if you've failed with every plot? Talk about lowering the bar.

Today, Minerva has once again been reclaimed by the seas. The platform is long gone, its currency defaulted, and, apart from being good fishing grounds, its only other use is as occasional anchorage for yachts awaiting calmer seas en route to Fiji, Tonga, or New Zealand. Aside from wealthy yachtsmen and adventurous scuba divers, things are quiet. Makes you wonder if anyone would have noticed the Minervan colonists had they not opened their yaps.

Yet, for all the silence, disputes remain. In 2005, Fiji made it clear that they did not recognize any maritime water claims by Tonga to the Minerva Reefs under the UNCLOS agreements. In November 2005, Fiji lodged a complaint with the International Seabed Authority concerning Tonga's maritime waters' claims surrounding Minerva. Tonga lodged a counterclaim. Hilariously, the Principality of Minerva lodged their own counterclaim. Guys get a clue. In 2010 the Fijian Navy commenced the "war of the lighthouse," during which they destroyed navigation lights at the entrance to the lagoon, and, in late May 2011, they again destroyed navigational equipment installed by Tongans. In early June 2011, two Royal Tongan Navy ships were sent to the reef to replace the equipment and to reassert Tonga's claim to the territory. Fijian Navy ships in the vicinity reportedly withdrew as the Tongans approached, averting war. That's right. War over the Minerva Reefs. In case you were wondering, relations remain sour and complicated to this day.

Regardless of one's political proclivities, the idea that a group set out to make their own nation is pretty cool. But, as "The Dude" said in *The Big Lebowski*, "this isn't 'Nam; there are rules." You can't just go to any island, reef, or rock and claim it because we live in a civilized world made civil by agreements such as the United Nations Convention on the Law of the Sea. This gives nations certain rights such as 12-nm territorial seas and exclusive economic rights stretching 200-nm from their coastlines. It grants, amongst other things, special rights for exploration and use of marine resources for energy production from water and wind. Imagine if, say, Canada decided to start drilling off our coast. They'd never do that because Canadians are so damn nice, but if they did, it would be madness. Lucky for us, history provides countless examples.

The Cod Wars were waged between the UK and Iceland (both NATO members) from 1949-1976. Whether it was three wars or ten is still debated. For hundreds of years Brits overfished Icelandic waters to feed their cod addition. In 1952, the Icelandic fishing zone was extended from 4 nm to 12 nm from the coast. UK disagreed and sent their Navy, Iceland marshalled 6 patrol boats and threatened to leave NATO, the U.S. intervened, and Iceland won. In 1972, Iceland expanded from 12 nm to 50 nm. UK disagreed and sent their Navy, Iceland sent 5 patrol boats and threatened to leave NATO, the U.S. intervened, and Iceland won. You get the picture. Iceland further extended limits to 200 nm. This series of spats laid the groundwork for the modern Exclusive Economic Zone.

France and Brazil fought a Lobster War from 1961-1963. France argued that spiny lobsters swam while Brazil was convinced, they crawled. If they swam, they were fair game, the French reasoned. Armadas were sortied. Ultimately, they worked out a deal before any lives were lost on account of this absurd debate. Thank UNCLOS. For the record, spiny lobsters crawl!

There are hundreds of ongoing territorial disputes around the globe. Each one has the potential to spill over into military conflict. UNCLOS helps mediate these disagreements as peacefully as possible. America's OMSI mission, referenced earlier, seeks to uphold Tongan and Fijian maritime security. But it is broader than that. America works with The Philippines, Thailand, Vietnam, and many others to strengthen bonds, conduct disaster relief, train militaries, and, yes, reinforce global norms codified in UNCLOS.

This is one of the reasons why China's behavior in the South China Seas, wrongly claiming reefs only to militarize them, is so alarming. It's not just that they're violating the

law, as was decided by the International Court of Justice, but they're also making the world less stable by eroding a framework designed to mediate disputes without arms. In recent years, their buildup has accelerated. Bypassing international norms, China routinely leverages its advantageous economic and military position to thrust weaker states into bilateral agreements at gunpoint. The result is a new South Pacific arms race that increases the chances of conflict. Just because you want something, as those libertarians on Minerva learned, you can't always get it. Perhaps China needs to learn that lesson, too.

Prostitution & Spearmint: Everyone's a Weirdo

"The Sandman," James Fullington, achieved moderate fame during pro-wrestling's *Attitude Era*. Although he began career gimmicked as a cheesy surfer, popular culture was at a crossroads. While wholesomeness during the Reagan Era was pervasive – *Different Strokes*, The Cosbys, Mister Rogers, "Hulk" Hogan, and *G.I. JOE* – the 90s brought forth a counterculture antithetical to both conformity and inauthenticity. *The Simpsons* came to truly reflect the state of the American family, and "What you talkin' bout Willis?" morphed into "Eat my shorts." Meanwhile, cartoonish wrestlers became passé. Even Hulk Hogan stopped saying his prayers and eating his vitamins. Instead, went full "Hollywood" by swapping his trademark yellow and red for the black and white of the New World Order (NWO). Amidst these changes, Eastern Championship Wrestling was baptized in blood-soaked, hardcore wrestling to be christened Extreme Championship Wrestling (ECW). ECW's Sandman, a deranged psychopath, triumphantly raised his signature *Singapore Cane*

before bludgeoning hapless opponents until the ring filled with splinters, shards, and broken bodies. Yet, it was his weapon of choice that proved small things can make a big difference and aptly illustrate that, from wrestling to international relations, everyone is someone else's weirdo.

Wrestling is weird. It is a combat soap opera full of swerves and suspension of disbelief. Though scripted, it is by no means fake. As Diamond Dallas Page once said, "You can't fake gravity." I think it was him...who knows? What is known is that being slammed on an unforgiving mat composed of canvas atop wooden planks can inflict considerable long-term damage. In addition, if wrestling is so fake then why does it bring out barbarous instincts from spectators? At times, "heels" or bad guy wrestlers required police escorts. Riots occurred! Wrestlers have been stabbed by fans! Does that sound fake? Done right, the stories can suck someone in as much, if not more, than any big-budget movie or HBO series. It can elicit true emotions. It can infuriate or sadden, be preposterous or grounded, and instil hope or dismay. Unlike many mediums, wrestling can be anything. It is Disneyland with tights and muscles. A fantasy world conjured for the enjoyment of beer-swilling, raucous fans. A place where your hero, Stone Cold Steve Austin, can beat the holy hell out of his bloodsucking pig of a boss. Real life with the volume turned up.

Now, the National Wrestling Alliance (NWA) was the epitome of "old-school" professional wrestling and was hallmarked by the successes of "Nature Boy" Ric Flair and his Four Horseman, "The American Dream" Dusty Rhodes, and Lou Thesz. It began in 1948 as a governing body to sanction championship bouts within its member promotions. In practice, the NWA was a territory system bestowing regional monopolies. That all changed when Vince McMahon purchased his father's promotion. The World Wrestling Federation (now World Wrestling Entertainment) poached talent and took the fight to rivals' turf. When McMahon couldn't beat them, he bought them. Within a few years, WWF was the dominant brand and NWA was all but dead.

NWA's "official" demise came in 1988 when billionaire media mogul, Ted Turner, purchased World Championship Wrestling (WCW). From its headquarters in Atlanta, WCW leveraged Turner's vast cable network to go head-to-head with the Connecticut-based WWF. This spawned television's infamous *Monday Night Wars*. During this period, wrestling controlled cable ratings and every facet of popular culture. The two promotions created some of the most recognizable personalities and groups of all time – The NWO, Degeneration X, "Stone Cold" Steve Austin, The Rock, Bret "Hitman" Hart, Chris Jericho, The Undertaker, and countless others.

Although wrestling had a "big two," ECW emerged as an alternative to the mainstream. While less polished, ECW made up for its shortcomings with brashness, uber-violence, and headline-grabbing controversies. From flaming tables to thumbtacks, ECW was not for the squeamish. Viewed as "garbage wrestling" by traditionalists, stiff competition on Mondays convinced top-tier brands to embrace more attitude. After all, imitation is the sincerest form of flattery. Thus, wrestling got raunchier.

Still, if there was one persona that most exemplified the edginess destined for duplication, it was Sandman. As ECW pushed the *suitable for programming* envelope, a cult-like atmosphere developed. While the owner, Paul Heyman, might have been their leader, Sandman was the in-ring embodiment. With his beer-filled gut, deep-set eyes, short bleached blond hair, and marred forehead from years of blading in matches, Sandman came across as the crazy uncle who shows up at Christmas, urinates on the tree, and passes out on the presents. He would come into the ring through arena crowds to Metallica's "Enter the Sandman," stand on the announcer's table, and bash his forehead with a Budweiser until it left a bloody welt. His wrestling ability was limited to delivering and receiving vicious strikes from his *Singapore Cane*, tables, ladders, chairs, and whatever else he could get his hands on. Who cared, though? If nothing else, he was different.

Around this time, extreme was pushed to the point of cliche. The Los Angeles Extreme of the Extreme Football League (XFL), the X-Games, Taco Bell's Extreme Nachos, Extreme Kiwi Xplosion Gushers, and Extreme Ghostbusters. Not to forget, you also had Xtreme Pringles badged with the ominous warning: Xtreme flavors inside. Try more than one and your heart might Xplode!!!!

It was within this era of heart-palpitating extremeness that Singapore became a household name for its own brand of extreme corporal punishment. For those unfamiliar, Sandman's *Singapore Cane* is a reference to the highly publicized 1994 caning of American Michael Peter Fay. The 18-year-olds caning sentence for theft and vandalism caused a global uproar. Americans were bewildered by such "barbaric" practices. Meanwhile, President Clinton beseeched Singaporean authorities for clemency. Eventually, Fay was sentenced to *only* four strokes, a fine, four months in prison, and a throbbing back. Before then, Singapore was relatively unknown internationally.

The *Singapore Cane* became the ultimate symbol of ECW's brand of extreme wrestling. As WWF and WCW slugged it out on cable television, they pushed the boundaries of violence and sex appeal to satisfy consumer demand. ECW's fringe success resulted in Sandman's preferred weapon getting co-opted by the "majors" for hardcore matches on Monday nights. The *Singapore Cane* became a mainstay in the wrestling industry. "Stone Cold" Steve Austin and The Rock are good, but both bashing each other with a *Singapore Cane* is far, far better. Today, the moniker persists. Imagine that...A silly cane in a silly "sport" perpetually linked to the nation of Singapore. Small things make a big difference.

Unless you've seen it first-hand, it's impossible to truly appreciate the vastness of the Pacific Ocean. One day, my ship passed Wake Island, located roughly two-thirds of the way between Hawaii and Guam. Though now an unoccupied and unincorporated territory of the U.S., the Empire of Japan captured it during WWII. It is amazing that this tiny sliver of land played a huge part in global affairs.

Looking through binoculars on that haze-filled day, Wake gave off an eerie feeling: A spattering of wooden spikes pretending to be trees jutted from the ground. But beyond that stark profile resides a mesmerizing lagoon of the clearest azure. And on the northern end of the island sits a coral rock carved with the message, "98 U.S. PW 5-10-43." On this tiny atoll in the Pacific, the Japanese executed 98 U.S. prisoners of war and dumped them into a mass grave. One captive survived long enough to scribble a eulogy in the coral before being hunted down and beheaded. Yes, even small places can etch their marks on history.

Lurching closer and closer to Singapore, crew members hoped to dispel rumors regarding our upcoming port call. If sailors loathe two things, it is awful exchange rates and rules. This makes sense when, for the right price in Thailand, you can light someone on fire while they ride you around town in a rickshaw singing "One night in Bangkok." Still, Singapore's tough reputation should make one wonder why the U.S. Navy visits it at all. Prolific author, William Gibson, wrote a scathing editorial in which he called Singapore "Disneyland with the Death Penalty," adding:

There is no slack in Singapore. Imagine an Asian version of Zurich operating as an offshore capsule at the foot of Malaysia;

an affluent microcosm whose citizens inhabit something that feels like, well, Disneyland. Disneyland with the death penalty.

Upon our arrival, a Naval Criminal Investigative Service (NCIS) agent gave the entire crew a brief while boring holes in a group of young, snickering sailors.

The sale of gum is tightly restricted...chewing is frowned upon, too. Plus, littering carries heavy fines...especially gum. Don't spit either. Prostitution is technically legal, but these areas are off-limits. Public intoxication is illegal. Oh, public displays of affection might violate modesty rules. Don't forget religion. Make sure you don't say anything defamatory against religion. Any religion. Don't complain about the rules, either. Basically, keep quiet about Singapore in Singapore.

Still, Singapore holds a special place in my heart as my first time in a foreign country. Honestly, pro wrestling was my first exposure to the nation, though the caning reference didn't resonate then. Singapore was a throwaway name like Siam, on a *Risk* board, or Xanadu in Coleridge's *Kubla Khan*.

In Xanadu did Kubla Khan
A stately pleasure-dome decree:
Where Alph, the sacred river, ran
Through caverns measureless to man
Down to a sunless sea.
So twice five miles of fertile ground
With walls and towers were girdled round:
And there were gardens bright with sinuous rills,
Where blossomed many an incense-bearing tree;
And here were forests ancient as the hills,
Enfolding sunny spots of greenery.

The Southeast Asian island city-state is so small that most maps use a big red dot to denote its location (hence the nickname "Big Red Dot"). Singapore rests at the southern tip of the Malay Peninsula and consists of sixty-three islands. Despite its size, Singapore is wealthy. It operates the world's second busiest port in both total cargo volume and container traffic – an incredible feat for a country of around six million people. Singapore can credit the Strait of Malacca and Singapore Strait for this.

As the keystone in the gate between Middle East and Asian markets, Singapore is possibly the most significant nation in terms of securing global economic stability. At any given time, there are roughly 1,000 vessels in Singapore's port. A ship arrives or departs every 2-3 minutes. It's estimated that over 70,000 vessels transit the strait each year because it is the shortest route to get to Asia from the Middle East. As of 2017, between 85-90% of annual oil shipment flows through Singapore. If the strait were ever blocked about half of the world's fleet would need to reroute around Indonesia. Global prices would surge as markets panic. Chronic shortages would send the industrialized, import-driven economies into a tailspin. For China and Indonesia, two of the fastest growing economies, oil imports would cease, and production would grind to a halt! Consequently, Americans accustomed to everyday low prices would feel the pain of skyrocketing costs. Layoffs would ensue. It would be Armageddon for our way of life. Not surprisingly, the cargo-laden merchant vessels provide a ripe target for piracy.

Visiting Singapore stirs conflicting emotions. On one hand, there are signs everywhere, warning of the dos and don'ts. I even saw a "no humping" sign in one restaurant. Hmm... It's easier to get a prostitute than a pack of chewing gum. Yes, gum is outlawed on account it tarnishes the pristine sidewalks. Fines for violating modesty rules? Then again, Singapore is like no other city. It's straight out of SimCity, that old computer game produced by Maxis in the 1990s.

As city planner, I was a psychopath, erecting massive skylines only to pound them with natural disasters, UFOs, and reptilian monsters. In the aftermath, I'd keep the electricity off and watch abandoned buildings consume the once-thriving metropolis. Screwed up, sure, but far better than killing kittens.

Now, imagine an immensely powerful person with a degree from the London School of Economics and a passion for Confucianism decides to build his own city from scratch. A *real* city. That's exactly what Lee Kuan Yew did as Prime Minister from 1959 to 1990, before bequeathing duties to his son. In your SimCity, would you want any risk of being ousted from power? Of course not! That's why Yew's People's Action Party has won every election since 1959. Unfair elections and media censorship make Singapore a quasi-authoritarian state. Yet, the results are shocking. In one generation, Singapore went from the economic backwoods to power broker. Dense networks of mangrove forests and brackish swamps transformed into one of the world's finest cities. It's fifth highest in the world on the Human Development Index, forty-first in nominal GDP, and tenth in per capita. Singapore went from swampland to skyscrapers. Singapore is an entirely modern creation. Singaporeans didn't exist 100 years ago. Instead, residents were an amalgamation of ethnic groups: Chinese, Malay, Indian, and Eurasian. How'd this happen?

Yew was the catalyst. In 1963, Singapore joined Malaysia. However, the marriage was on the rocks before the honeymoon was over. Racial tensions plagued unity, especially the government's preferential treatment policies for Malay people. Yew, then Singapore's chief minister, advocated for equal treatment under the law. Singapore's multicultural, multi-ethnic population joined his movement. The government also feared Singapore's geographic position would eventually undermine the dominance of Kuala Lumpur as the political and economic center of gravity. Seeing no solution, Malaysian Prime Minister Tunku Abdul Rahman expelled Singapore from the messy union with a vote of 126-0.

In 1965, Yew announced Singaporean independence and went to work. By implementing ideals such as modesty and discipline, he crafted a city-state and people who take their rules seriously. In the carrot and stick world, Singapore chose the stick, or rather, the *Singapore Cane*, to train people. Cooperation and social harmony were placed at the forefront. Meanwhile, violators suffer harsh retribution. The law, any law, has meaning, even to foreigners. Yew's ideology was rooted in fear of foreign dominion. Though history justified his concerns, his autocratic methods haven't been immune to criticism. Being a small, fragile state, Yew capitalized on Singapore's one advantage: Location. Through extensive land reclamation efforts, he created a port system to control the flow of trade through the Strait of Malacca. The result is a mesmerizing city that astounds and confounds. Singapore's culture is one of newness. The future drives the culture. Homes and buildings are routinely demolished to pursue endless modernity. A cab driver even told me that no buildings, except in rare cases, could be over a hundred years old, though I could not fact-check this claim. And even if that story isn't strictly accurate, it still conveys the zeitgeist of the place.

Yew also invented national symbols, such as a merlion with the head of a lion and body of a fish. The merlion signifies Singapore's rise from a fishing village into the "Lion City" Singapore's original name, Singapura, derives from. In this place, humility, narcissism, and aspiration elegantly jockey for control. Every night a 70-ton, ivory merlion spouts water as colorful lasers pierce the night. Behind it, the Marina Bay Sands Hotel, the world's most expensive standalone casino, leaves tourists awestruck.

The U.S. Navy, seeing Singapore as a critical ally in the stability of the world's global trade network, established close ties. Bonds have matured in the fight to extinguish piracy, exemplified by the presence of forward-deployed Littoral Combat Ships. But the weirdness remains. America is friends with yet another country that treats its people in ways that perplex us: Limited freedom of speech, uneven power dynamics, and excessive punishments for the trivial.

Despite modernization and amassed wealth, the 1994 caning episode casts a dark shadow. Ask a casual, travelled American about Singapore, and while they might not know exactly where it is, they'll know the country's tough reputation. That caning left a big red mark on perceptions. After all, Singapore *is* weird. Isn't that the point?

Everyone is someone else's weirdo. You might look at Singapore very negatively. Caning? How cruel! Gum is harder to get than a hooker? How strange. Before getting too judgmental, it's best to lace up someone else's pair of boots. Singaporeans likely see us as weirdos. In America, it's easier to get an AR-15 rifle than a prostitute. Now, I'm not a hooker guy, but the Puritan strain in America's DNA baffles other countries, including Frenchmen in tight speedos. We have immigration policy we don't enforce. In Singapore, the law is the law. The U.S. has a history of re-defining legislation... in Singapore, not so much. This isn't an East-West divide either. Routinely, American video games are banned in former British colonies due to their graphic content. Yet, violent video games don't garner much thought in mainstream America. Sure, a goody-goody raises a fuss every so often, but it never amounts to much. This is 'Merica, not some peacenik sissy land but one for the brave (We'll put a boot in your ass; it's the American way). Except if you show a little nipple on broadcast television. That'll get you the boot. Just ask Janet Jackson.

The truth is every country has unique cultures that arise from unique experiences. Therefore, it's essential to work together despite differences. Working together doesn't mean outright condoning their actions; rather, it means prioritizing the extent those differences should impact relations. Too many people live in a binary world where a single issue, they're passionate about, blinds them from the muddled realities of true existence. Single issues generally aren't. Low prioritization doesn't equate to tacet approval.

Singapore matters. Its location makes it crucial to the health of the global economic system. Our relationship, promoting stability and fighting piracy, makes markets safer, businesses more prosperous, and consumers better off. Yes, even small things and places can make a big difference in an increasingly interconnected world. From Wake Island, to Singapore, to professional wrestling. Little things matter. No one, except perhaps Yew, could've imagined a land of swamps would become one of "milk and honey." Then again, who would've thought that a drunken madman wielding a cane, inspired by corporal punishment in a mysterious SimCity, would give Vince McMahon the right tool to bludgeon his competition in the squared circle?

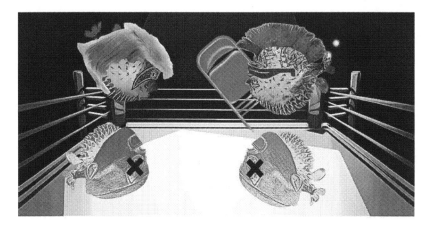

—

UNIFiED:
The Drive Towards
Moderation

Formula One Racing might be the last place to expect social and political change. The sport, viewed by roughly a half-billion people, is dominated by displays of opulence. Here marquee brands like Ferrari, Mercedes, and Rolex mingle with old money and oil money at elite destinations such as Monte Carlo, Barcelona, and Monza. Despite this, developing markets also gravitate toward F1. Places like Kuala Lumpur, Shanghai, and even Manama use the alluring, international platform to showcase their nation's progress, wealth, and rising relevance. Hosting a competitive F1 race is a signal to the rest of the world that they've made it. Unsurprisingly, such symbolism propels tycoons and tyrants to the sport. Like membership to a premier country club, breaking into F1's exclusivity is a point of considerable pride. Let's look at the island nation of Bahrain, something of a petri dish for democracy and capitalism. Here, F1 helps illustrate the ongoing duel between Bahrain's traditional culture and a creeping moderation.

I was stoked. For a few weeks, I'd leave my desk job, providing "beans and bullets," at Commander Naval Surface Forces, Atlantic, to travel back to Bahrain. Though it wasn't Tahiti, $300 per diem and a four-star hotel certainly beat death courtesy of Microsoft PowerPoint. If I ever meet Bill Gates... I'm going to punch him right in his four-eyed face. Your admittedly wonderful product has made my life miserably full of mindless font adjusting to reduce "slide wiggle" for cantankerous Admirals.

At the time, the Bahraini Dinar was worth three times the dollar. Now, 3-1 might have been sore luck for a sailor looking for fun out in town; however, the base had anything an American pinching his pennies desired. As the headquarters of the U.S. Navy's Fifth Fleet, everything was there from McDonald's, Filipino karaoke, and even an A&W Root Beer. When's the last time you enjoyed a root beer float while listening to a Filipino karaoke band singing Journey's "Don't Stop Believin'?"

Since alcohol is tightly controlled, sailors usually opted for booze from the Navy Commissary rather than braving the dry streets of Manama. Yet, the best perk of all was the tax-free pay. See, geography *sentenced* Bahrain to an acutely noxious region of the world. This qualified a *relatively* safe and modern place for a "war zone" entitlement. This meant that if you spent even one day within this "region of death and carnage," your monthly pay was tax-free. Think the government robs you blind? Try going without paying federal taxes for a month and you'll be ready to vote Libertarian. They've since changed the policy to a day-for-day exemption. We can't have nice things.

My naval assignments with Patrol Coastal Crew India brought me to Bahrain many times. For that reason, I'd developed a sense of the culture before, during, and after the Arab Spring. This visit in the aftermath left a profound impression. Upon arriving at Bahrain

International Airport, a sudden strangeness took root. It was much busier than usual. There were more Europeans, business suits, and eye candy. Blondes in Manama, Bahrain...surely you can't be serious? That's when I spotted a giant banner adorning the passage towards customs. It read: "UNIF1ED: One Nation in Celebration." Apart from the clever use of the number 1 to spell F1 (Get it?), the Orwellian slogan left me bemused. "Methinks thou protest too much, Manama;" I channelled Shakespeare while preparing for customs and an exhausting series of armed security checkpoints. Unsurprisingly, this F1 slogan sparked controversy from human rights groups arguing Bahraini leadership sought to exploit the event to undermine their advocacy efforts. Credible reports would suggest that F1 and Bahrain's public relations team operated in concert to obfuscate domestic conditions.

For those in the "why should I care about a 30-mile-long island" camp, location is everything. Formerly under the dominion of our British brethren, Bahrain lies right next to a major artery of the international energy system. With Saudi Arabia to the west, Iraq and Kuwait to the north, Iran to the east, and Qatar to the south, Bahrain is surrounded by the "who's, who" in the Organization for Petroleum Exporting Countries (OPEC). That booger eater who sat next to you in grade school was dead wrong when he said geography was a waste of time. This speck in the Persian Gulf is the melting pot where U.S. military partners — Britain, Australia, Japan, and many more — communicate, coordinate, and conduct missions in support of maritime and regional security efforts. Yes, it's mostly about oil...But oil only scratches the surface.

The Sunni al-Khalifa dynasty has held power since 1783. Although Shiites comprise over 60% of the population, they're relegated to the slums. Disenfranchisement is a flashpoint worsened by the Shiite Iranian neighbor that enjoys fiddling with gasoline. Recent stability convinced the regime to launch a new nation, like an app. Seeking diversification from energy, they lured investment capital through glitzy advertising and eminent domain. Even the slogan 'Pearl of the Gulf' gave way to 'Business Friendly Bahrain' on passports, billboards, and brochures. The dried-up pearling industry no longer represented the Bahrain that image-conscious profiteers sought to showcase. Instead, Bahrain became the freest economy in the Middle East. A place where ideas – like something as ridiculous as F1 in the Middle East – could flourish. Still, someone pays to line the pockets of elites. Shiites, bereft of housing and livelihood, constitute the primary payer and the tab mirrors modern-day serfdom. Such serfdom extends to the influx of migrant workers subject to similar mistreatment. Bahrain is a glimpse into a cyberpunk cityscape of high-tech, low life.

With dwindling oil reserves relative to their OPEC neighbors, the regime prioritized banking, technology, and tourism. Though petroleum still accounts for nearly 80% of exports and 26% of GDP, the financial sector is crowding out energy reliance and generating sizable wealth.

Though overall unemployment is low (~4%), the influx of foreign laborers continues to pinch those who already feel disadvantaged; especially, Shia Muslims. These Bahrainis have long complained of religious discrimination and high unemployment.

Bahrain is ranked 39th out of 169 countries on the United Nations Human Development Index, has a 90% literacy rate, 15 private universities, and even women's suffrage. Though 70% of students in higher education are women, men dominate most leadership positions and female participation in the labor force rests at 35%.

Inadequate housing remains a contentious issue superheated by an incredible transfer of public lands into private hands. Over the past thirty years, 90% of reclaimed coastal lands have gone to private owners. Foreign ownership of land began in 2001, and from 2003 to 2010, an estimated $40 billion in public land transferred to private ventures without suitable payment to the treasury. The poor are priced out, fishermen lose livelihoods, and waiting lists for subsistence swell.

Bahrain doesn't come off as a police state; rather, it's a place where people seem to go to escape theirs. Everywhere, mixed messages fuel an acute tension bubbling like oil beneath the surface. At times, it feels like the whole country wears a mask to project an aura of innocence that hides a darker truth. Despite hosting the forward operating arm of America's efforts to secure freedom and democracy throughout the Gulf, Bahrain is a constitutional monarchy routinely criticized for repressive practices. I'd venture it scores as "mildly authoritarian" on the scale of *Antiquated Regimes Clinging to Power Spectrum*. This is a huge compliment when considering the company. To compound matters, their Saudi neighbor views the country as a progressive tourist attraction. With Bahrain, everything depends on who you ask. During the week, Saudi women even head there to drive and shop for lingerie and fashionable clothes to wear beneath their burkas (read that twice). Reuters once ran an article about a blossoming sex shop industry that was overcoming odds and legality in the conservative region, for married couples at least. One store owner proudly declared, "I don't sell vibrators—this is against Islam. However, other toys such as vibration rings are fine."

One wonders how clerics intellectually grapple with such sticky subjects, but I'm fine with ignorance here. Though overt displays of sexuality remain frowned upon, Arab scholars apparently draw the line when it comes to married couples' bedrooms. Well, except for vibrators, naturally...that, of course, would be terrible! How do they verify customers are married? The honor system? Barcode tattoos? The owner even makes deliveries with her brother if the order is large enough. Imagine a windowless van filled to the brim with instruments of erotic pleasure blazing to Saudi Arabia to comfort a needy housewife.

Since women can't drive in Saudi Arabia, although they've relaxed the rules lately, Bahrain is their de facto driver's education course. Yes, driving, like lingerie, is thriving on the island. I applaud their efforts to stick it to the man, but these women created absolute terror. When a Saudi-plated Lexus darts in front of you without a care in the world, even the staunchest feminist must pause to consider the possibility that some Saudi governmental policies aren't all that foolish. Though it might be hard to accept these changes as significant milestones in gender equality, in this region, change tends to move at a snail's pace. Modern liberalism, accustomed to sweeping transformations, grows impatient. Yet, sometimes undercurrents are far more powerful than waves.

Alcohol, in violation of Islam, can still be found via a hotel loophole. While the women come to drive on weekdays, the men come for drinks and debauchery on the weekends, insisting that Allah can't see them in Bahrain. An omnipotent, omnipresent deity that can't see beyond the King Fahd Causeway? Either that's one long bridge, or these so-called pious visitors are full of baloney. Prostitution is available if you know where to look.

The illusion of control is palpable, even spreading to military personnel in the form of alcohol points. The trick is that each month, a sailor would get a coupon that entitled them to purchase ten points of booze. Non-drinkers became the most popular kids on the playground as four of their points helped a needy drunkard procure an additional handle of Jack Daniels to go along with his other two. If moderation was the objective, this policy succeeded only in lining the pockets of prohibitionists implementing this "bananas" directive. Suffice it to say, this policy succeeded in making everyone substantially drunker and dumber than existence had ever known.

It had been a full three years since I last lived in Bahrain with those PC crews. By April 2012, the Arab Spring, which began in Tunisia in December, 2010 was at its nadir. The movement had already spread throughout the Middle East and North Africa, feeding a narrative that social media was a revolutionary force in the modern age. The Dubai School of Government even issued a report in 2011 that mentioned how nine in ten Egyptians and Tunisians used Facebook to organize and generate awareness of protests. The broad consensus was that social media was having transformative and measurable effects on the pursuit of social justice.

Though the emphasis on social media was criticized, the overall importance of the Arab Spring was clear: A crescent of unrest from Tunisia to Syria toppled archaic and despotic regimes in Tunisia, Egypt, Libya, and Yemen. But two years after the movement began, hope gave way to ambiguity, fear, and pessimism as new leaders cobbled together the remnants of power. Groups like the Muslim Brotherhood gained authority, and, just like the Palestinian Liberation Organization before, suddenly realized governing is a pain in the ass. Media attention seemed to shift from following the loose ends of the Arab Spring in favor of sexier scoops about the economic meltdown in Greece or Miley Cyrus's twerking. Suffice to say, Bahrain was a loose end in the eyes of the media.

Our driver, a Senior Chief Petty Officer from PC Crew Charlie, screamed up to the airport's curb in a beat-up Nissan van. We stacked our olive-colored sea bags into every crevice, and piled in, packed like sardines. Without seatbelts. The Senior Chief zipped onto the highway with reckless abandon toward the tourist district lined with billboards and glitzy hotels that all screamed progress. By the time we arrived at the hotel, I was drained. We were greeted and escorted to the front desk immediately. There, a body attached to a mustached smile welcomed me like his first guest in a decade.

After settling in and ordering Indian curry from room service, I snatched up my computer. I'd decided to fall into the Google and YouTube rabbit hole before bed. You know... the one where you search for "whatshisface" from *The Breakfast Club* and wind up down a path where you've discovered everything about the Brat Pack, Rat Pack, and Frat Pack. After maxing out on pop culture, I turned to researching our little tourist spot. After all, the Arab Spring was not dead in Manama... but things got a bit weird.

SITE BLOCKED

Beneath the dire warning, an explanation quickly noted: *"This website has been blocked for violating regulations and laws of the Kingdom of Bahrain."* No, I wasn't searching for pornography, and Emilio Estevez is not restricted content as far as I know. What *was* controlled was information on human rights in Bahrain. A search for www.bahrainrights.org provided perhaps the best picture of the current situation. At least there was a consolation prize: An embedded link allowed the user to issue an unblock request in a come-hither sort of way. My mind drifted to that scene from *Terminator 2* when the cops surrounded Arnold and the rest of our heroes within the confines of Cyberdyne Systems. Lacking a mini-gun, I decided to err on the side of caution and tapped the print screen key before exiting the site. A picture is worth a thousand words and I wanted to save that image. The host of a major American operating base had successfully stonewalled my attempts to learn more about the protests raging throughout the 30-mile-long nation.

The online encounter with the thought police excited my senses; it provided respite from the doldrums of checklist tracking. I found my other escape in running. Not on a treadmill, but real, outdoor running. To me, it offers a unique visual and authentic experience. Running in Bahrain, unfortunately, is simply unpleasant, lacking any picturesque trails awash with cool ocean breezes. The sun is scorching, so a rational person would run later in the afternoon or evening. Instead, I like to run at noon, during the worst part of the day, when the scorching sun bakes the ground and anything moving across it. There is a joke in the Navy that Surface Warfare Officers are gluttons for punishment, and as time passes, I'm convinced they're right. Hell, back when I served with the PCs, I ran during Ramadan in a long-sleeved shirt and sweatpants, a customary requirement when outdoors during the holiday period. Ramadan happened to fall smack dab during the hottest time of the year. Did I mention you're not allowed to eat or drink in public? Even water. One hundred and ten degrees and no water? Three years later, my runs returned me to the same spots; yet the pace of change was startling.

Dome Café's patrons cover the spectrum of tastes and sensibilities. A thick-bearded, heavyset man wears a traditional white thobe while his three wives are draped in black burkas. Apart from their eyes, the women are figureless, onyx pillars. They don't talk or eat as the stoic man sips his Turkish coffee and takes drags of his cigarette. Nearby, an exotic black-haired woman wears enormous Dolce and Gabbana sunglasses, jeans, and a posh black shirt that reveals a toned midsection. She sips a cappuccino and laughs with her westernized friends. In a corner to their left, a young American, clearly a serviceman, sports a crew cut, tribal patterns, and other American symbols of individualism. He scarfs down an ice cream cone. The contrast is stark, but such is the norm in a country struggling to find itself.

After passing the I, I usually cross around the new buildings, getting lost on streets I once knew, where ornate steeples of modernity rise from the sands, scattering rays of light from crystal facades. Bahrain is one giant construction site interwoven with luxurious hotels. Artificial islands, racetracks, and stunning marinas suck you into the land of possibilities. With money and vision, a desert can be transformed into an oasis. This juxtaposition pulls and pushes. For all this progress holds an embedded artificiality. Why can't America build things like that anymore? The simple truth is that nations cannot be re-designed on computers or sculpted in masonry. Noble visions must take into account the human element.

Nearby were Indian, Bengali, and Pakistani laborers, laying the foundation for the next five-star hotel, and the next one after that. These immigrants flocked to Arab States because of overpopulation, lack of opportunities, and caste systems that prevented upward mobility. They exist merely as visitors in a land whose sweat-filled labor transforms desert lands into international destinations.

Bahrain is a microcosm of global trends: Population bulges providing a cheap labor pool and modernity challenging traditional cultures in unintended and uncontrollable ways. Life is cheap and empathy is in escrow.

There's an angled street called Road No. 4125, which goes through a Shiite community, and leads to Al Manamah's main thoroughfare, "American Alley." It's no more than a quarter mile long. To the right, sand-colored walls create the feeling of traversing a labyrinth. Each morning a visitor can examine a new batch of graffiti coating the walls in reds and blues. Yet, each evening the stains are removed. Expensive solvents aren't used to eliminate these expressions of anger; rather, the rolling of white paint masks the previous day's outbursts. White on sand, an unfinished job. Beneath each layer of crusted paint, sentiments remain, waiting to resurface in the midnight hours. Authorities choose expedience and always have.

A sign outside Asry Shipyard reads, "XXX days since safety mishap." One day I received a call from our Chief Engineer informing me there'd been an explosion at the facility that left five dead. It appears an expatriate welder hit a gas line. The next day the sign read, "0 days since last safety mishap." We drove past--- numb and callous to our fellow man. Besides, there's no shortage of job seekers.

Our first full day in Bahrain was all to ourselves. It was Friday, but Fridays are more like Saturdays in Bahrain. In fact, as late as 2006, weekends, or their equivalent, were Thursdays and Fridays. Yet, international business has a sly way of altering customs when conformity creates cash. With a pen stroke, the Kingdom changed the law to share at least one weekend day with most of the world. Still suffering from the layover, I decided to play that day low-key. Aside from a four-mile run, thirst demanded a beer, or at least one for each mile. Entering the lobby to seek an oasis of spirits, I encountered a backlog at the concierge, courtesy of one pesky guest head to toe in Ferrari apparel.

While they chatted, I snatched a newspaper from a gilded coffee table. The concierge explained, "Pass and transport impossible right now... The racetrack is restricted. All roads closed for now. The only people admitted today were teams trying to qualify... No others." Front-page news informed me of a large demonstration the previous night. Before securing the details, the exasperated man withdrew in dismay. "Can you believe this," he quizzed me in an accent full of shamrocks. After explaining my total and utter aloofness to his problem, he exclaimed, "They're not even sure if the race is going to happen. They might cancel it just like last year!" It seems the pending F1 race had aggravated an already tense populace that saw the Kingdom's "UNIF1ED: One Nation in Celebration" as an utter sham. Protesters demanded cancellation of the Bahrain Grand Prix and security was investigating potential threats. Eventually the Irishman sulked off and I seized my opportunity to ask about that beer. Before I left, I selected an F1 ad from the pile stacked on the reception desk. After a hasty glance, I pocketed it and sped to the hotel's pub, leaving the Irish guy's final words in my tailpipe.

With beer in hand, I recovered the little advertisement tucked away in my khaki shorts. At first glance, there was nothing special about this postcard-sized piece of "propaganda." All typical, it provided the race dates, an event map on the back, and even a glossy image of an impossibly fast race car rounding a bend. It was the description of the race that captured my interest. In a simple paragraph that discussed the origins of the race, something seemed to be missing. I learned that the race started in 2004 as the first Formula One Grand Prix to take place in the Middle East. I also discovered that the Bahrain Grand Prix won recognition as "best organized" that same year. Then it got a tad more interesting. The lines revealed that in 2009, the race delivered roughly $450 million dollars to the Bahraini economy from tourism, tickets sales, and advertising revenues. A little head math...if their economy is approximately $34 billion, this one race equates to 1.3% of the pie. Let's look at this another way. If the U.S. economy was roughly $17 trillion at the time, 1.3% gives you a whopping total of $221 billion. Anyone else know of another three-day event that brings in that kind of dough? The sheer magnitude of the Bahrain Grand Prix, in financial terms, is staggering. Still, it wasn't the money that garnered my attention. Rather, the paragraph made no mention of the 2010 race. Zero mention of the prior year's cancellation. How can that be? Instead, the only comfort I found was the "UNIF1ED" logo centered at the ad's crown. I'd forgotten this was "One Nation in Celebration." Yup, yesterday's realities would not dampen tomorrow's possibilities.

Glancing away from the beer I'd been burning a hole into, I detected a trio of scruffy men in their mid-twenties arrive, wrapped in racing regalia. Out of a curiosity laced with boredom, I introduced myself. When these Brits learned I was an American officer, the inevitable flow of shots followed. It is common knowledge that Yankees, Brits, Aussies, Canucks, and Kiwis are cut from the same cloth...brothers in arms, and, more often, drinking. A few shots later, we drifted onto the subject of the F1 race.

In a strange turn of events, one of them was a driver. Not premier one, like Michael Schumacher, just a regular guy working his way through the maze of motorsports. He was a "privateer," someone unaffiliated with manufacturer-sponsored teams like Ferrari and Mercedes. In many cases, privateers are wealthy entrants competing for the thrill as opposed to earning compensation as a racer. Privately owned teams face steep obstacles, from building and maintaining their own cars to competing on the track against performance industry titans. This privateer made his living taking turns on the circuit. Like a free agent, he was snagged to race for the season. He hoped solid performances would one day land him a position with an established F1 team, not to mention millions of dollars.

All three fully expected F1 President Bernie Ecclestone and the Fédération Internationale de l'Automobile (FIA) to cancel the rest of the event. While hope remained, their eyes expressed misgivings. The surliest one barked his frustration pertaining to costs associated with this looming ambiguity. See, for the dwindling crop of privateer teams, setbacks like canceled races cut them to the bone. Memories of the 2011 mess almost kept the owner from bothering with Bahrain's Grand Prix. Some of the trouble stemmed from how the contract between the FIA and F1 teams, known as the Concorde Agreement, made it tougher and costlier to withdraw from races. To further professionalize the sport and increase commercial viability, this arrangement obligates teams to compete in every race. While providing more stability for broadcasters, and, in turn, advertisers, smaller teams suffered side effects. Now they powerlessly waited on an official verdict from bureaucrats.

Let's back up. What caused all the problems and how deep does the tension and animosity go? While the self-immolation of Tunisian Mohamed Bouazizi sparked the outbreak of the Arab Spring empowering the silent majorities to act, problems in Bahrain that were long obscured nevertheless endured. Still, nothing just happens without warning signs. There are always some canaries in the coal mine. Though difficult to pinpoint a genesis, the Arab Spring was the fulcrum.

Democracy is a great buzzword but can be esoteric at times. Though those demanding a larger slice of the pie routinely called for democratization, innate issues plaguing Bahrain shouldn't be reduced to a singular need or aspiration. On February 14, 2011, the buried finally came to the surface. That day, protests erupted across Shia villages in Bahrain. Fueled by a complicated blend of bitterness and optimism, over 6,000 protesters eventually flooded Bahrain's streets demanding various reforms. Mostly Shia, these protesters specifically called for increased political participation, releasing of political prisoners, respect for human rights, and an end to discrimination against adherents to their faith. February 14th was no accident either. Prior to the uprising, a Facebook page titled "February 14th, Revolution in Bahrain" called for mass protests to commence on the tenth anniversary of the referendum on the National Action Charter (NAS). The NAS was what turned Bahrain into a constitutional monarchy, ending uprisings of the 1990s in the process. This page quickly gained followers and the movement its inertia. Combined with solidarity movements in support of Tunisians and Egyptians, political fervor swept through Shia communities. Here's the kicker, even before these well-advertised protests commenced, the King promised to give 1,000 dinars, or around $2,650, to each Bahraini family. While offered as a gesture of appreciation to the Bahraini people on the anniversary of the NAS, it's quite easy to see this act as pandering at best and bribery at worst. Still, can you blame him? You must understand the panic spreading throughout the Arab world, afflicting regimes large and small with a nice dose of paranoia. At this point, the wave of unrest had yet to afflict the Gulf States. Perhaps he felt his government could somehow establish a breakwater, dissipate the tidal energy brought on by a gathering storm. Besides concerns within his country, it is also likely Saudi leadership applied pressure on their neighbor to cool things down in case marginalized Shiites in Saudi Arabia get emboldened too. As expected, the monetary offer fell on deaf ears.

As the 14th approached, scattered rallies popped within Manama and neighboring villages like blips on radar. Yet, none obtained proper authorization to demonstrate and they ran in strict violation of the Emiri Decree Law No. 18 of 1973 on the Organization of Public Meetings, Rallies and Assemblies. Doesn't that decree even sound ominous? Riot control forces were dispatched throughout Bahrain to quell any disturbances and prevent escalation brought on by the unlawful activity. Spats were reported along with minor injuries, including one sustained when a rubber bullet struck a protester. On the eve of the 14th, police took positions and prepared for round two. The day's events failed to change the regime's perception that Bahrain could and would escape the turmoil encompassing the region. What they would discover is that their quest for free-market prosperity exposed them to its inherent disruptive quality. See, the coexistence of authoritarianism and market-oriented dynamics run contrary. Free markets move towards efficiency and away from restraint, making control elusive. The market establishes the rules and dictates the terms. For Bahrain, the cutthroat reality of the liberal economic forces helped shove frustrations on to the establishment's doorstep.

As promised, February 14, 2011, became a day of protest, or, as reporters christened it, the Day of Rage. Bahrain stirred like an angry hornet's nest as people spilled on to streets in numbers ranging from tens to thousands. While uncoordinated, the frequency, scale, and acceleration of anti-government activity led the Salmaniya Medical Complex (SMC), fearing injuries, to declare a state of emergency. What followed reads like the Wall Street ticker tape chronicling the demise of the real estate bubble:

150 demonstrators in Al Diraz – three hospitalized; 200 in Sanabis – one wounded; 200 on Sheikh Ali Salman Street; 40 demonstrators in Maqsha; 100 demonstrators near Jidhafs; 150 in Karbabad; 140 in Abu-Saiba; 400 in Nabi Saleh – garbage dumpsters set ablaze; 1,000 in Sitra – rocks hurled at police vehicles and personnel.

The intensity of the protests bewildered Bahrain's security apparatus. Unaccustomed to outbreaks of defiance, police aggressively engaged the crowd using tear gas and rubber bullets. You know how it goes; when in doubt, punch someone out. As control slipped, shotguns entered the equation. Note: The use of shotguns for crowd control is a poor idea, just ask the students at Kent State, circa 1970.

At 8 p.m., the exhaustion of tear gas supplies culminated in the death of the movement's first protester, Ali Abdulhadi Mushaima, courtesy of a single shotgun blast to the back. While accounts vary, the official line is that Mr. Almeshaima participated in a demonstration of roughly 800 people in Daih. When protesters attacked eight police officers with rocks and metal rods, police discharged a single shotgun round. Authorities claimed his death was not done with malice since the use of shotguns was a last resort when tear gas was no longer an option. We'll never learn the truth; it's been made opaque by chaos and gun smoke. Police probably did run out of other riot control agents and chose to disperse the crowd by any means necessary. Make no mistake, though, the establishment made an example of him. In the process, they also created a martyr. As history illustrates, all great movements need a martyr, or, as Indira Gandhi once said, "Martyrdom does not end something, it is only a beginning."

News of Day of Rage's first casualty quickly went viral as photos of Almeshaima's body and first-hand accounts barraged social media. Omnipresent internet restrictions couldn't contain the flood of information, especially when bloggers embedded links on YouTube videos and in other feeds to bypass security. In Manama, tech-savvy cyber nerds figured out methods to get around virtual roadblocks. Despite the government's best efforts, they'd discover that supply and demand applies to information too. The cyber domain is a "Thunderdome"...there are no rules.

Near midnight, a large group of protesters marched from the hospital housing Almeshaima's body onto the Gulf Cooperation Council (GCC) Roundabout (aka Pearl Roundabout), testing police barricades and armed sentinels en route. The 15th launched recharged batteries to the streets of Manama. Protests, coalescing in the early morning, left charred dumpsters in their wake. However, it was the funeral procession of their first martyr that galvanized the populace. Astride 2500 mourners, Ameshaima's birdshot-ridden corpse was laid to rest a little after 8:30 am. While angry, saddened supporters stole one last look at the twenty-one-year-old, a second martyr, Fadel Salman Ali Salman Matruk, took a surgically placed shotgun round to the back. The remainder of the day became a walk into bedlam. By mid-afternoon, mourners and a cloud of bitterness occupied the Pearl Roundabout with tents, a projector screen, and a mass of people numbering in the thousands. With darkness falling, King Hamad offered televised condolences for the two deaths and pledged to identify factors surrounding the demonstrations while affirming the public's right to exercise freedom of expression and assembly *in accordance with the law*, that is. I can imagine it now:

Please place your application to assemble in rage at the nearest administrative office and we'll be sure to file it in a timely manner. Verify blocks 1 through 756 are properly filled out, signed, and dated. Thank you for your patience as we try relentlessly to put down this series of unfortunate demonstrations that are preventing our usual ability to timely process applications to assemble in rage, such as yours. We apologize for the inconvenience and wish to also inform you that our administrative offices will remain closed considering recent events.

By Thursday eve, a surprising 12,000 had gathered to mourn, pay respects, or stand in defiance. Though the number would drop to around 1,000 by morning, it was clear the two deaths superheated what had become an undeniable crisis to stability and order. The king took notice and sent his son, Crown Prince Salman bin Hamad bin Al Khalifa, to meet with opposition leaders. For three hours, the Crown Prince listened as they voiced concerns about the Constitution and urged significant reforms. Their appeals were ultimately met with veiled threats against vigilantes threatening the State.

It didn't take long for officials to interpret regal intent. Mere hours later, police battalions descended upon an improvised tent community littering the lawn. This was no ordinary police operation: Strewn into the mix were heavy hitters from government intelligence and Bahraini Defense Forces sporting law enforcement costumes. Well-organized and swiftly executed, within half an hour the clearance operation successfully dispersed the swarm. Yet, as the fearful fled to safety, the cost became transparent. Beneath police boots, tattered tents lay blood-soaked. The writhing bodies of one hundred demonstrators shattered the carefully sculpted image of Bahrain. Somewhere in the carnage, three martyrs were discovered. Three more names – Mahmood Makki Ahmed Abutaki, Ali Mansoor Ahmed Ahmed Khudair, and Ali Ahmed Abdulla Ahmed – ended by three more fatal shotgun blasts.

As I inventory the death toll, filled with so many Ahmed(s) and Ali(s), a foreignness sets in. Like the Vietnam Memorial in Washington, D.C., the names etched in stone are a chronicle of heartbreak. Though nearly as foreign, citizenship and service connect us. But with these three, I'm mystified. Why do I feel so estranged? While I cannot possibly imagine the suffering and pain of either group, my empathy lies with those memorialized in marble. Regarding the fallen Bahrainis, I could reach for a closer bond. Who were they? What did they want? What were they thinking in the final moments? Then searching my soul, I ask, "Would I feel differently if they were named Matthew, Mark, Luke, or John? Would you?

Though both sides wanted to play the role of the victim with security forces and demonstrators each claiming self-defense, the heavy-handedness of the government-imposed evacuation caused them to forfeit the battle over public opinion. The optics couldn't be any worse for the besieged monarchy and the death of a sixth civilian an hour later eliminated all hope of the regime commanding the narrative. How can you spin another shotgun blast to the head of Issa Abdul Hussein Ali Hassan from centimeters away? People will buy all sorts of bullshit, but even the not-so-normal find headshots extreme, barbaric, and unjustified.

With a sixth death logged, something interesting happened; protesters trudged back to the Pearl Roundabout, now cordoned off by armored vehicles from the Bahrain National Guard. They came back. At all angles, people regathered to occupy the intersection once more, leaving Bahrain Defense Force General Command to issue dire warnings. Admonitions failed to sway the rebels. Instead, resistance increased; accounts of violent acts by security forces coupled with rumors of hospitals preventing ambulances from recovering the injured only swelled the ranks of dissidents. Each return met stiffer resistance. With each twist of the security vice, they came back to the Pearl Roundabout. They pressed harder and refused to yield.

Thursday's events changed everything. Memories of 'Bloody Thursday,' would reverberate for years, summoning ghosts of the past. The Pearl Roundabout changed too. No longer an attraction or simple intersection, it simultaneously represented an irresistible symbol of resistance and the unwavering might of the crown. Far removed from the streets of Manama, international media organizations – scouring reports and photos for explanation – understood the Pearl Roundabout as nothing less than the seat of the Gulf's response to the 'Arab Spring.' The Pearl Roundabout, walled off by menacing machinery and sand-colored fatigues, became the backdrop in this contest of wills. Side-by-side images, taken at different times and presented in print, proved damning. On one side, you have peaceful, unarmed civilians joining beneath the shadow of the sun-splashed pearl monument designed to unify, banners flowing, and signs proudly lifted towards the sky. On the other side, barbed wire, barriers, and stone-faced occupiers – oppressors of assembly and free speech and instruments of royal power – obscure a pearl pitched in black. Suddenly the tiny nation was a focal point. If uprisings could happen there, was any Arab country safe? As media poured in from all corners to chronicle the chaos, Saudi Arabia and the remaining Gulf Cooperation Council (GCC) countries – Kuwait, Oman, Qatar, United Arab Emirates – expressed solidarity and support for Bahrain's beleaguered throne.

Now, let's get back to F1. Bernie Ecclestone – commonly addressed by the moniker 'F1 Supremo' – is such an easy villain. The narcissistic billionaire's dominion over motorsport is often characterized as nothing short of fascist. According to the internet – which is always reliable – he once mentioned how women can't be good drivers – referring specifically to Danica Patrick – and should be dressed in white to resemble domestic appliances. There are

Nazi orgy rumors. Oh, and this diminutive mogul – he's goblin-sized – is married to a six-foot Brazilian model. For those who claim you can't buy love with a big bank account, look no further than Bernie. Yet, what makes Bernie so reviled is what he has done  to a once-honored sport. In the pursuit of increased profits, he's courted nefarious company. From meetings with Vladimir Putin about bringing F1 to Sochi to targeting non-traditional Asian and Middle Eastern markets, Bernie has expanded F1, but at a cost. Though his efforts have made F1 a global brand, the damage to the sport's reputation has been a source of consternation.

Under him, F1 pressed forward with its expansionist policy, affording little credence towards the ramifications. Bahrain put F1 directly under a microscope and plunged into a range of issues far exceeding the scope of the motorsport's world. What happens when a sport comes to represent the evils of an oppressive government, inequality, or injustice? As Bernie scrambled to salvage a race predetermined to yield riches, journalists arshalled to document the unique tale of two countries: Privilege and poverty.

On March 14th, the Gulf Cooperation Council, an economic alliance of Gulf States, mobilized thousands of Peninsula Shield Force (PSF) units from Saudi Arabia to snuff out the madness. Conceived in the 80s as a NATO-like entity, PSF swelled to a mechanized force of 40,000 infantry, artillery, and combat support elements. PSF's ill-prepared, tardy response to Iraq's invasion of Kuwait in 1990 certainly was a factor in this buildup. It has become the domestic contingency tool for the maintenance of monarchical stability. Lumbering across the causeway, armored vehicles raced through Manama and secured key urban positions. With helicopter support, the 4,000 PSF-clad Saudis targeted crowds with tear gas and beat others into submission. In the end, another five citizens lay dead, many were tortured, and even more lost hope. In a final insult, the Kingdom ordered the destruction of the Pearl Roundabout. On the 18th, bulldozers reduced the "sacred" sight to rubble and created a square. Fittingly, in the rush to cleanse the spot – as explained by government officials – a migrant worker was killed when a mass of concrete crushed him. His death seemed all too typically tone-deaf. Amal Khalef says it best:

"Squaring the circle is a problem handed down from the Ancient Greeks. It involves taking the curved line of a circle and attempting to draw a perfect square from it; a task that for centuries mathematicians were convinced they could figure out. In the nineteenth century, when the problem was proved unsolvable, the phrase to 'square the circle' came to signify an attempt at the impossible. But in 2011, within days of the most sustained and widely broadcasted protests in Bahrain's recent history, a circle was named a square. The once unassuming Pearl Roundabout or Dowar al Lulu, famous in the international media as the site of the Gulf's answer to the 'Arab Spring', became Bahrain's 'Pearl Square' or Midan al Lulu."

– The Many Afterlives of Lulu: The Story of Bahrain's Pearl Roundabout

Still, the frustrations and anger would metastasize, slicing into Bernie's bottom line and engendering a new emblem of a government gone wrong. Instead of silencing critics, the monument's destruction generated a media frenzy. The racing behemoth approached the situation as one might expect and waited it out. So, rather than an outright cancellation, as critics demanded, the race was postponed. As the next decision date,

May 1st, came and went, organizers received a deadline extension to June 3rd. Protests remained frequent and constant despite the Pearl Roundabout's remodeling. Later, the FIA unanimously voted to hold the Bahrain Grand Prix on 30 October. That decision was short-lived.

Bolstered by increased support from teams, racers, and reporters, the FIA began to back down. A week later, plans to hold the race at the end of the season fell through along with a guaranteed injection of a half-billion dollars to the Bahraini economy. Bahrain's domestic issues transcended the almighty dollar. What makes this so important? I mean, it's only a race; there's always next year. To explore the broader implications of a mere canceled event, one must turn to 2012 and beyond, to where F1's and government oppression remain intrinsically linked.

So, this brings us all the way back to 2012 in that faux-English pub. Later that night, I learned that 2012's race, unlike 2011, would not fall victim to political tension. It would proceed as planned. This might sound like a loss for human rights; however, something was different. Across Bahrain, graffiti bore a resemblance to the toppled Pearl Roundabout. In alleys, on signs, and adorning flyers, the sails and perched pearl became a subversive symbol of an enduring movement. Though invisible to tourists and a government peering through rose-colored glasses, witnesses immortalized in spray paint their memory of the Pearl Roundabout...their Pearl Roundabout. Yet, married with the tributes, onlookers also saw comments chastising F1 and the Bahrain Grand Prix... as if they took on equivalence with despotism and greed. Realizing the stakes, Bahraini security implemented a quasi-martial law. Roadblocks and barriers funneled traffic to the track while denying access from "problem" areas. Even the safety and image-conscious security apparatus couldn't stop the spillover.

Once again, F1 and Bahrain were in the crosshairs of an organized, skeptical media. Bernie Ecclestone assured the world that nothing was happening. In his view, Bahrain remained both peaceful and "UNIF1ED." That same day several thousand attended the funeral of a man killed in a protest weeks earlier. A year later, another martyr. Still, according to F1, I could rest easily. The race would fill the Kingdom's coffers and display the national unity they couldn't present in 2011.

Bahraini youths hurled Molotov cocktails at four mechanics from Force India's team. No injuries occurred, but two members went home. The team beseeched F1 to reevaluate safety measures, even opting out of a practice session in protest. Being a privateer team, F1 rules prevented withdrawal without severe financial repercussions. They sulked back to Bernie and F1. Hours later, a car explosion rocked Manana.

The race had to proceed as scheduled. The stakes were too high to risk another cancellation. Molotov cocktails, car blasts, and angry teams aside, F1 had to come out on top. Yet, the Kingdom's grip on the narrative was flailing.

In 2012, the uneasy marriage between the Crown and the world's premier racing organization staved off disaster. Yes, the Bahrain Grand Prix delivered significant revenue, appearing to stabilize the sport's presence in the Muslim world. In following years, F1 returned, each time doubling down on security and image-conscious marketing to expunge the indelible stains. Instead, F1 remains tied to the legacy of the Pearl Roundabout. The graffiti blotting walls throughout Manama and Sitra eulogize the victims of government oppression. It cannot all be whitewashed away. F1 represents a minorities' callous pursuit of opulence at the expense of the majority.

So, what's the answer? Has anything improved? Here's where things get nuanced and tricky. The government shifted from chaotic crackdowns to institutionalized reprisals. This has reduced visibility of abuses because the legal system routinely targets activists in the shadows. Also, the revocation of citizenship offers an expeditious method to decapitate opposition leadership. While there are far fewer media-jarring headlines, oppression remains an omnipresent tool of the state. While this sounds more depressing than reading Tolstoy, Dostoevsky, Gogol, and all that Russian history that totally explains why Russians have dour faces, there is a silver lining.

The odd truth is that without F1, there'd be no journalists to chronicle the abuses. There'd be no race teams to question the logic of hosting a race in the problematic nation. No race fans devouring reports on the small island's security situation as they assess the risk/reward of traveling. Racing brings eyes to human rights abuses that would otherwise pass unobserved and unappreciated. This also extends to the U.S. military, which – due to its massive presence and command and control structure – must calculate the costs of maintaining residency amidst internal and external condemnation. A contingent of well-intentioned, caring onlookers would certainly dispute this assessment. However, making Bahrain a pariah merely maintains the status quo.

Rather, more engagement is needed. As previously explained, the globalizing influences are already at play. The shift from oil is replacing an insular reliance with one that is international. Supported by tourism and banking, the drive for economic growth continues to open the country's doors. It takes time, but, eventually, substantive changes become necessary. Regardless, once a nation begins to rely on something larger than itself, a possibility for lasting change exists. Just as economics has a way of redefining the weekend, so too can it alter the fortunes of the underprivileged and marginalized. From international investors to the American military, these increasingly important stakeholders garner greater authority, taking on a role as moderating influences. Though efforts may not always be coordinated, sufficient, or successful, the alternative is certain failure.

Thus, the key in changing a regime's attitudes and practices is to figure out unique ways to get them to engage and loosen the controls that define their domestic relationship. Sure, doing so probably results in the accumulation of wealth for the tyrants in the short term. However, it undeniably provides opportunities to present the world with a clearer picture. The implications are huge. Consider Cuba, for instance, and what real good America's embargo against Cuba has done. Are Cubans free?

When he wasn't arguing for the destruction of the Federal Reserve, Ron Paul repeatedly argued for the closure of American bases around the globe. He is not alone; adherents to socialism, pacifism, and isolationism have said much of the same...if only for differing reasons. Such actions, logical on the surface, have a poor track record. Saudi Arabia is another favorite target of human rights organizations. I won't even attempt to defend the regime's innate vileness, but I will question proposals to disengage. Saudi Arabia, unlike Bahrain, is a nation largely immune to international threats. Perhaps if we placed an embargo on Rolex watches, aviator sunglasses, and Lamborghinis, we'd get somewhere. Can you imagine thousands of Saudi princes suddenly realizing their nation is dry of overpriced, unreliable Italian cars? I bet they'd end alcohol prohibition right there and then, if only to deal with the panic.

No; true change is incremental and requires nourishing. It requires relinquishing some semblance of control. Though Bernie is still a diminutive douche, F1 can ironically be a positive vehicle for the betterment of Bahrainis. Will it happen? That's tough to say. The aftermath of 2011's debacle started a discussion that's going in the right direction. Each year, when F1 returns to Bahrain, journalists don't just document the race but capture context as well. Their eyes are open to the political and socio-economic realities. They search for signs of past trauma, examining concrete pours for a darker truth. F1 cannot escape the scrutiny, no matter how entertaining the race and how convincing the billboards are.

The UN, in its well of imbecility, selected Bahrain to serve of the Human Rights Council. Their term ended December 2021. Don't be too shocked. They also chose Cuba, China, Russia, Pakistan, and Venezuela to represent their respective regions. Heck, even everyone's favorite travel destination, Somalia, made the cut. What a joke! The next time some high-browed, faux intellectual bemoans the drift of American policies from UN norms, kindly tell them in every tongue spoken across the seven seas and seven continents to "go fuck themselves." The more people talk about caring for the "little guys" the more I'm convinced no one cares about doing for the "little guys."

The American military is equally affected. In 2015, Congress passed an annual defense bill requiring the Department of Defense to plan for the relocation of the 5th Fleet should political issues fail to improve. Naturally, Bahrain's leadership rebuffed suggestions that the 5th Fleet would ever be relocated, highlighting the nation's geopolitical significance. While it remains highly unlikely DOD would ever carry out this move, conversations of this nature are refreshing. Strategically, the relocation would embolden Iran and do little to improve Bahrain's treatment of opponents. Yet, power brokers are talking, and, more importantly, listening. That America has a foothold on Bahraini soil creates concerns that are impossible for the regime to fully avoid. The costs of an American exodus are immense. America's presence gives it leverage.

Bahrain's future is opaque. There's little doubt her path will follow one of prosperity in the short term. Interconnected and reliant, openness will continue to define future growth. It's inseparable. As gradual moderation takes root, cracks expose a rotting foundation stuck in two worlds. Pillars, driven deep in ancient oil sands and layered atop with reclaimed land, will buckle under the pressure of progress. The screams of the forgotten will reverberate louder and more powerfully than the whines of turbocharged engines rounding the bend.

DANGEROUS GROUND:
REEFS, SHOALS, & ROTTING HULLS

H istory is full of famous ships: *The Titanic*, "Old Ironsides", the "unsinkable" *Bismarck*, the "ironclad" *USS Monitor*, Japan's 65k ton behemoth *Yamato*, and, of course, the 1,122-foot-long *USS Enterprise* (the carrier, not the spaceship). Yet, there's one ship possibly more relevant than them all. A ship that's becoming less of a ship with each setting sun. Even in her heyday, this "ship" wasn't much to look at. Today, though, this ship's importance to geopolitics cannot be disputed. That ship is naturally the *BRP Sierra Madre (LT-57)*. Wait! You've never heard of it? How about the *USS LST-821*. Still nothing? Does *USS Harnett*

Country ring a bell? I'm guessing not. Despite its anonymity, this rotting hulk is a flashpoint in the Asia Pacific powder keg.

The former tank transport vessel has gone by many names under many flags. Tipping the scales at a meager 4k fully loaded long tons and measuring around 328 ft, the former *USS Harnett County*, is a ship with an interesting tale. Some ships are known for victories in combat or advanced weaponry. This vessel claims neither. At her height, she carried a crew of some 16 officers and just under 150 enlisted. Her armament is modest: A single 3-inch gun, 8x 40mm guns, and 12x 20mm guns. There aren't fancy missiles or air defense radars on this hulk. She must be super-sneaky fast then, right? Perhaps she was part of a special CIA program to test out a new magnetic drive. Nope. This vessel's crawls at a pathetic 14 knots. So why should we care about this vessel?

Let's take a trip down memory lane and talk about two things: The transfer of that crappy ship to the Philippines and a 1991 volcano eruption. These two events set into motion a chain that could destabilize a region that is the lifeblood of the global economy. Two events that could lead to a Third World War with China and America in each other's crosshairs. This is hardly an exaggeration. On the contrary, this situation is tense and very real. By now, many people are aware of China's military buildup in the South China Seas. China's real estate boom is far from limited to the mainland. Over the past decade, the mercurial state has been occupying artificially constructed islands – layering sand on reefs, rocks, and shoals. Truth is, China is not alone. Malaysia, the Philippines, Brunei, and others have grabbed shovels to partake insane spin on manifest destiny. Territorial disputes within the South China Seas are plentiful, pitting even our allies on opposite sides over scraps of submerged sovereignty and jutting parcels of property.

China has assumed the mantle as the unrepentant bully in these dangerous waters. They've taken the land grabs to a whole new level by militarizing these outposts, using threatening rhetoric against neighbors, marshaling their plentiful naval resources, and leveraging their economic position to coerce weaker nations into favorable agreements. China's aggressive actions – and the inability for all these Asia-Pacific neighbors to reconcile these disputes – are destabilizing a critical region. The real-world effects are palpable.

If you're not a hermit vegan living off your garden vegetables or a communal follower in a doomsday cult, you're probably the end user in the global trade system. Whether you loathe the World Trade Organization or globalization, you still rely on the fruits of an economic system based on capitalist principles. Andy George's YouTube channel, *"How to Make Everything,"* endeavoured to determine how much it would cost to make a sandwich without the benefits of trade networks. He grew his own veggies, pickled his own pickles, raised and slaughtered his own chicken, and even made salt from ocean water. The result was a sandwich that cost an impressive $1,500 and took 6 months to piece together before it could be devoured. It's doubtful the satisfaction of a savory, self-made sandwich proved a viable investment.

Trade is immensely important, and nowhere is that clearer than in the South China Seas. The United Nations estimates that roughly 80 percent of global trade by volume and 70 percent by value is transported by sea. Of that volume, 60 percent of maritime trade passes through Asia. The South China Sea carries an estimated one-third of global shipping. One-third! Disruption of this thoroughfare would send shockwaves through the economic system, crippling distribution and delivering consumers a serious case of sticker shock. Next time a dinner party drifts into the realm of anti-capitalist politics, kindly take the offender's plate away and tell him or her to make it themselves. You try to make pan-crusted

Mahi-mahi on a bed of risotto from scratch without the shackles of modern luxury! Get out of my affordable house with your nonsense.

Back to the tank transport and volcano. In September 1944, Missouri Valley Bridge and Iron Company – one of the many wartime converts to the arms industry – constructed LST-821 in Evansville, IN. By November, she earned her commission and entered the war effort. This diminutive tank transport was shipped off to the Pacific Theater to participate in the Battle of Okinawa – the largest amphibious assault in that theater. A bloody fight followed. From April 1, 1945, to June 22, a full 82 days, determined adversaries slugged it out. The brutality encountered later served as the basis for Truman's eventual decision to drop the atomic bomb on Hiroshima and Nagasaki. After the war, in March 1946, the vessel entered the Pacific Reserve Fleet. Alas, dreams of both world peace and a blissful slumber amongst other "ghost" ships were dashed when the United States once again found themselves locked in combat...This time in Vietnam (my favorite cluster).

In October 1970, the vessel was transferred to the South Vietnamese Navy, where it shed old glory" for three crimson stripes on a yellow field. Yes, this happens; American ships are sold off, leased, and otherwise transferred to other nations. The South Vietnamese rechristened her RVNS My Tho (HQ-800). Everyone knows the rest of the story. The unpopular war loses support, Saigon falls, and America concocts a false narrative that it didn't quite lose despite all evidence to the contrary. Following the Vietnam War, the ship took on another flag: The Philippines. How and why?

When Saigon fell, in April 1975, a flotilla of 35 South Vietnamese ships sailed to Subic Bay, Philippines. They successfully escaped capture by the Communist Viet Cong. Filipinos gladly took the dilapidated, antiquated transport and renamed her BRP

Sierra Madre (LT-57). Subsequently, the vessel disappeared from the public eye and combat. That is until 1999 when the Philippines Navy deliberately grounded her onto Second Thomas Shoal. Yes, a staunch ally of the United States ran a former American ship into a shallow sandbar about 100 nm west of Palawan, Philippines. You might be wondering why when it should've been designated a maritime target and blown to smithereens.

The answer involves a certain volcano eruption. U.S. Naval Base Subic Bay has a long, storied legacy. Built by Spain in 1885, the Spanish-American War not only handed stewardship of the Philippines to the U.S., but also that base. From 1899 to 1992 – apart from a brief hiccup from 1942-1945 when Japan occupied the country – Subic Bay served as an overseas bastion of American might. Ships participated in port visits, executed major repairs, and maintained regional security from this strategic outpost. At 262 square miles, it was America's largest overseas military installation. Its sheltered anchorages, deep waters, and natural beauty made it a highlight of the naval Sailor's, "Join the Navy, See the World" experience.

After WWII, a military bases agreement was signed granting the U.S. landlord status over this overseas (or, as others argue, "colonial") possession. However, in 1979 the agreement was amended to confer sovereignty back to the Filipino people. For years, drunken, horny sailors developed a habit of getting frisky with locals. There were alleged and actual rapes, vandalism, murders, fights and all the other things associated with young, reckless, and oftentimes disgruntled servicemen out on a binger. Throughout the 80s, a wave of anti-Americanism took hold in certain provinces. It shouldn't be surprising that such denouncements coincided with a struggling economy. Regardless, any slight, any mistake was magnified in this climate. Amidst this environment, both countries sought to renegotiate the 1979 terms. Negotiations dragged.

However, natural disasters determined the terms. Mount Pinatubo erupted on June 15, 1991, with a force eight times greater than Mount St. Helens. Ash plumes blotted out the sun while a typhoon relentlessly punched the region. When all was said and done, America's strategic holding lay buried beneath a foot of hard-packed, sandy ash. Entire buildings crumbled under the weight of Pinatubo's terror, as did part of a hospital. An estimated 60 people succumbed to the volcano's fury, including a nine-year-old American girl. The Philippines was in utter chaos and so was the American military. Water and electricity remained out with no recovery in sight. The dire situation prompted the U.S. military to evacuate the base of dependents (i.e., military family members). That decision – a correct one – would sow the seeds for what would follow. Thousands of men, women, and children were rushed onto navy warships and cargo planes in the hasty evacuation. Typhoon Yunya exacerbated the calamity. The ash-rain concoction forced follow-on evacuations of Filipinos from neighboring areas. Ashfalls devastated the base and outlying communities as rainwater remobilized earlier volcanic deposits. Rivers, water supplies, and infrastructure would take years to recover. All told, roughly 20,000 dependents were evacuated from the disaster area.

American service personnel and Filipinos rolled up their sleeves for cleanup work. Sure, they could salvage major portions of Subic Bay; however, Clark Air Base – much closer to Pinatubo – was deemed a complete loss. Tons of ash clobbered runways with debris and coated hangers like a winter lodge after an avalanche. But, by September, nearly all the evacuees had returned to Subic Bay. Yet, U.S. and Philippines negotiations regarding leasing costs were thrown into complete confusion.

Starting in 1988, both governments tried to forge an amenable deal to extend basing rights for Subic and Clark. The Filipinos wanted $825 million per year on a 7-year contract. The U.S. was dead-set on a $360 million for 10. It was akin to an NFL free agent contract in which both sides were not even in the same orbit on player value. In December, over six months after the eruption, the two governments again failed to agree on terms and a request to delay American withdrawal for up to three years was subsequently denied. The Filipino government intended to squeeze more money from their "colonizers."

The monumental recovery costs rankled Pentagon "bean counters," and a typically dysfunctional Congress remained typically dysfunctional. Thus, neither nation reached an accord. Now, there are many who cast blame on Bill Clinton just like we blame all Presidents for things they have nothing to do with. The narrative goes as follows:

Stupid, military-hating, draft dodger, dope-smoking, sexual pervert, Clinton, left the Philippines because of an innate disdain for the military and failure to understand America's role in maintaining peace and stability, apple pie, baseball, and the Ford Mustang...all that jazz. The truth is simple. Money may well be the root of all evil, but it's generally the root of everything else, too.

Capitalism won the Cold War and the heralded peace dividend was taking form. Finally, the world was going to stop killing itself and get to solving real problems. So, when Filipino President Corazon Aquino issued a formal notice directing the U.S. to leave by the end of 1992, America walked away. On 24 November 1992, the American flag was lowered at Subic Bay. Our quasi-colonial holding – a remnant of the Spanish-American War and symbol of the old world changed forever by the future's promise – was handed back to the Filipino people. For the first time since the Sixteenth Century, the Philippines was free of foreign forces.

In his fascinating book, *Pacific: Silicon Chips and Surfboards, Coral Reefs and Atom Bombs, Brutal Dictators, Fading Empires, and the Coming Collision of the World's Superpowers*, Simon Winchester discusses the fallout from Pinatubo's eruption and China's hegemonic rise. Throughout the rest of the 90s, the American military focused on containing Saddam Hussein, preventing genocide (doing so poorly), and navigating the icebergs of a Cold War's thaw. Consequently, the South China Seas was largely abandoned, and the Asia-Pacific became a secondary theater. The Middle East (i.e., an addiction to oil) mattered to a globalizing economy traveling at hyperspeed. Slowly, China began to garner attention in Pentagon circles as their expanding economy, due to the infusion of some free-market reforms, created two demands which could be secured with a sharpened spear.

Firstly, economic growth and state-controlled free-market implementation stirred protests. The intoxicating effects of economic growth whetted the public's appetite for more, bigger, and better. Soon, everyone wanted to climb their way up the rung into the cushy, middle class. Yet, China needed ditch diggers too, and dividends from China's meteoric rise were unevenly spread. A billion-plus people will cause that.

Demographics also caused trouble. As of 2020, China's fertility rate is 1.3 children per woman. This is far below what is needed to maintain a stable population. The one-child policy – conceived in the 70s – tilted gender ratios to an unhealthy imbalance. Think your dating scene sucks? Picture China where, as of 2014, there were 33-million more men than women. That's 117 men 0-14 years old per 100 women and 114 men 15-24 per 100 women. The U.S. is 105 and 104, respectively. Ever wonder why there are so many ads for Russian brides? Well, in "Mother Russia," women aged 25-54 exceed men with 104 for every 100. If you're single and not worried about losing your security clearance by marrying a potential spy, check Russia out. In China, you have serious competition. Whoever said everything was about sex, maybe Freud, was on to something.

Horny, disgruntled men are bad for social stability, which is a reason why China began a breakneck military expansion throughout the 90s. *A* reason, not the only one. China dramatically lowered recruitment standards. Military service gave Chinese men something to do other than bitch about not getting laid. Instead, these hard-luck men could bolster security to counter the increased frequency of protests, in part because government policies led to the gender imbalance that made them angry and horny in the first place (a vicious cycle is born). This isn't to suggest all protests stemmed from demographics, but there is a close correlation. The other solution a military buildup offered was to increase domestic support for the Communist Government through nationalist displays. This was when the then unknown Nine-Dash-Line gained popularity.

Any nationalist movement must have enemies. China's first was Taiwan, a basically independent country founded by separatists. Bringing Taiwan back into the fold is something sure to stoke nationalism. The other is more nuanced. The nine-dash-line is pure propaganda. It is a vaguely defined group of dashes denoting China's rightful territory. Running south of the Hainan Island, the dashes cover the entirety of the South China Seas, and, of course, includes Taiwan.

The nine-dash-line began as an eleven-dash-line published by the Republic of China in 1947 to justify claims over the South China Seas. When the communist government took over in 1949, the line was revised to nine dashes. But throughout the 70s and 80s, China remained weak. As a result, capturing these territories remained pure fantasy. This all changed in the 90s. America's exodus from the Philippines, Japan's lost decade (now pluralized to decades as the asset bubble collapsed and changing demographics damned the island to waning influence), and America's focus on oil market stability meant China could operate  freer in contested waters. A new dawn approached. No longer would China be carved up by imperialists. China would push forward with visions of dominion over all within the nine-dash-line. The beauty of the nine-dash-line is the vagueness of it all. China could lay claim to historic rights, citing a pattern of western imperialism and encroachment. Since China is presented as the eternal victim in this story, its citizens tend to respond with patriotic sympathy. It is both visionary and reactionary.

So, what about that ship? Throughout the 90s, China took her first steps to realize hegemonic ambitions. Previous attempts to seize control of the Spratly Islands and assert territorial claims sparked war with Vietnam, notably in 1988 during the Johnson South Reef Skirmish. Now, China had an ingenious plan for incremental dominion. In 1995, Chinese forces moved in and occupied Mischief Reef – located 130nm from the Philippines. Under International Law, this reef falls well within that country's Exclusive Economic Zone. The Philippines protested, prompting China to argue that the fortifications subsequently constructed were harmless fisherman shelters. The Philippines lodged a formal protest and did something else. Seeing an island-building arms race afoot with Malaysia, Vietnam, and others occupying reefs, rocks, and shoals, the Philippines did the unthinkable.

In 1999, they grounded the BRP Sierra Madre, that former American tank transport, onto Second Thomas Shoal. China was furious, but what could they do? The still commissioned warship became home to a handful of Filipino Marines operating under the protection of military service for 3-6 awful months in the middle of nowhere. Harassment or openly engaging these marines could spell trouble for China. Remember it happened before with Vietnam.

Greetings from
SECOND THOMAS SHOAL
Carefree living in the Spratly Islands

With International Law squarely behind the Philippines' rightful claim, China chose a policy of irritation. To this day, China regularly attempts to block resupply of this grounded vessel. Besides making the marines' shitty lives even shittier, risks of miscalculation have increased. Yet, irritation has proved a resounding success, forcing Filipinos to install a helipad onto the deck to conduct airborne provisioning. Undeterred, the Chinese still circle like sharks.

The Sierra Madre has had better days. The once-proud American warship is a rusting wreck. Since 1999, the Filipinos have reinforced the inside with concrete, adding creature comforts to make marines' lives less miserable (seriously, the post must be a nightmare). The reinforcement is a necessity as the ship is literally crumbling. The sight of the grounded ship is amazing. Brown rust cakes the vessel while what gray paint remains is dulled to a pinkish hue. In some spots, a skeletal form is visible. The keel's girders are exposed to the sea. Ever seen what the salty ocean does to metal over time? It has turned entire sections into a bark-like form that can be peeled away with ease. For the marines, there is no ground... just the rotting confines of Sierra Madre. In recent years, upgrades were made, giving the vessel its own electricity, running water, and meager entertainment options. Still, the marines mostly stand watch. Their watch, their task, is to be there. Be present. They exist as the Philippines' last line of defense against China's efforts to control areas within the nine-dash-line. The dichotomy couldn't be greater. A shark stalking a minnow.

To this day, China – the world's second-largest economy, a freakin' nuclear power - sends spectacular, billion-dollar warships to patrol the area. They threaten and antagonize Filipinos over an inhabitable shoal not off the coast of China, but in the Philippines backyard. Filipinos, unable to win a contest of arms, are forced to occupy the shoal in a dilapidated vessel they claim is still functional, just in distress. How can China be so serious about something so trivial? With all the turmoil in the world, is a shoal worth it? Better yet, is going against the entire world and international courts who all say you have no claim worth it? Respect is earned. Historically might has made right. However, we've come a long way since the days of Alexander the Great, Rome, Crusades, the Napoleonic Wars, and two world wars. Despite their limitations, International Agreements have emerged as a key tool to prevent conflict. Often, the true test of leadership is knowing when to walk away.

They call the South China Seas *Dangerous Ground* on account of all the islands, sandbars, and reefs. But the overlapping territorial disputes bring new meaning to the term. It is a hotspot. An unnerving situation echoing the entangling alliances that damned Europe's great powers in 1914. Consider that America has a defense treaty with the Philippines. Signed on August 30, 1951, "an armed attack in the Pacific Area on either of the parties would be dangerous to its own peace and safety and each party agrees that it will act to meet the common dangers in accordance with its constitutional processes." So, if China were to attack these poor marines, does that mean the U.S. would be compelled to join the conflict? Great question!

Everything depends on both how you read this treaty and who is pulling the levers of power. The answer is hardly clear. The point is that the situation poses a significant risk of escalating into a war. Were that to happen, other U.S. allies such as Thailand, Australia, Japan, and South Korea could find themselves involved as well. Taiwan, our close friend, also has claims to the area and a bone to pick with China.

The chain of events was laid out long ago and remains rooted in China's history of being exploited. Yet, that volcano created an opportunity that China seized. When deployed to the South China Seas in 2016, I discovered a region blanketed with Chinese warships and white hulls (coast guard-like vessels; they used to harass fishermen from neighboring nations). It appears we're too late. President Obama finally realized the risks of China's island building and open contempt for international standards. He summoned some semblance of political will and deployed a Carrier Strike Group to police the South China Seas. Near the end of his tenure, Obama announced an Asia-Pivot (later termed a rebalancing) designed to prioritize naval ships to the Asia-Pacific as opposed to the Middle East. He wasn't the only one; the previous administrations had been asleep at the wheel or otherwise preoccupied with occupation politics. In many ways, we awoke from the Global War on Terrorism only to realize a region long assumed safe and stable looked completely different. Subsequent Presidents continue replaying the realization game with little progress. Thus far, America's been more bark than bite.

China is here to stay, but how will China's rise fit with the interests of the United States and UN-backed policies? Will someone overreact? Will the Philippines get an itchy finger? What kind of damned irony would it be if the next global war takes place on a former American tank transport from the last one. Yes, a natural disaster and fiscal jurisprudence sprinkled with a dash of post-Cold War idealism prompted us to cede a crucial piece of the Asia-Pacific to an aspiring superpower. For the Philippines, a derelict American transport is the frontline unit in a lopsided battle of wills. Will anyone blink? Would America stand by its pledges? It's become increasingly apparent that the writing is on the wall. A spark may be minor, but it doesn't take much to set everything ablaze.

SLIMED! VAN RIPER'S KOBAYASHI MARU

Kobayashi Maru? What's that, a sushi dish? Well, if the name doesn't ring a bell, you aren't a "Trekkie." The Kobayashi Maru is a test in the Star Trek universe designed to evaluate how Starfleet Academy cadets approach a no-win scenario. When a gravitic mine disables the civilian vessel, *Kobayashi Maru*, only the best and brightest are charged with crafting a rescue strategy. Unfortunately, the stranded vessel is located smack dab in the middle of the Klingon neutral zone. Klingons, being the sworn enemies of the Federation, won't take kindly to the territorial infraction should the cadets enter, sparking an interstellar incident. This is not good. So, they can attempt the rescue or leave the crew to rot in space. Those are the choices. To confound matters, the simulation is rigged. Any incursion into the neutral zone will spawn a Klingon armada dead-set on vaporizing the cadets. Conversely, failure to render aid to the distressed ship constitutes a violation of Starfleet protocol. You're damned if you do, damned if you don't. Now, would you believe that there was another Kobayashi Maru far away from the realm of science fiction, nerds playing dress up, Klingons, and photon torpedoes? This simulation was a prelude to America's invasion of Iraq and pitted a grizzled Marine in an unwinnable situation. Designed to validate modern warfighting doctrine, it ended up exposing the hubris of a military industrial complex liquored up on its own advertising.

Star Trek's Kobayashi Maru backstory is a key element of Captain James T. Kirk's character arc, establishing his mythos. Now, in the real world the right to render aid for vessels in distress is protected so long as two conditions are met. First, transit must be expeditious. Second, the location of the vessel must be known. So, this test is a bit out to lunch; however, science fiction deserves a little creative license. Lacking expertise in the intricacies of Klingon – Federation foreign relations, one must press the "I believe" button that formal deliberations weren't an option. In the test's history, only one person ever passed: James T. Kirk. Yes, he won the unwinnable scenario and even earned acclaim for his original thinking. How'd he do it? Naturally, he rewrote the rules. By reprogramming the scenario, he avoided taking the coward's route, or death, to successfully rescue the crew. Did he cheat? Yes. But that's the beauty of it. In *Star Trek II: The Wrath of Kahn*, Lieutenant Saavik argues Kirk has never faced a no-win scenario. Kirk responds that's only because he doesn't believe in them. So, if the test is designed to assess ethical decision-making under stressful conditions, Kirk's approach was spot on. A never quit, never say die attitude. There's always a solution to every problem, even if it means bending or breaking cherished rules. Alas, the real life simulation earned its "cheater" no fanfare; instead, painstaking efforts were taken to bury the valuable lessons learned from an event that largely laid the groundwork for military operations during the subsequent Global War on Terrorism.

Millennium Challenge 2002, or MC02, was supposed to test futuristic concepts and serve as a building block for the military's transformation into a modern one. It harnessed technological breakthroughs brought on by the dawn of the information age. Let's back up. Explaining why this simulation happened requires a rudimentary understanding of the military in the 90s. The advent of desktop computers revolutionized day-to-day operations. Even the military, slow to adapt to the latest trends, wasn't immune to the power of computing. Mundane tasks were simplified and the Clinton era internet boom suddenly opened the floodgates of information sharing.

Yet the military was positioned to fight the last conflict. Politicians, taking advantage of the heralded "peace dividend," sharpened pencils and went to work hacking the defense budget. The Soviet Union's demise compelled fiscal hawks to make a deal with liberals, divesting outdated systems with the promise of concessions on the social program front. The trade-off was clear. Divest analog, embrace digital. A new military would be leaner, agile, and more lethal with cyber backbone. The Navy, for instance, experienced pains as it whittled down total ship numbers, sentencing many to purgatory in the "ghost fleets" sprinkled among America's coastlines. At the time, there were competing views regarding what truly mattered; the quantitative or qualitative. That battle rages today.

More recently, during the debate between Presidential hopeful Mitt Romney and Barack Obama, the discussion of ship numbers became a hot topic. The Republican argued that the Navy was the smallest since 1917. Obama countered that we also have fewer horses and bayonets now, making the case that quality is a force multiplier. The truth is more complicated and both candidates were right and wrong. More missions and requirements demand more ships. In essence, quantity has its own quality. Modern military assets still face the tyranny of geography. A ship can only be in one place at a time. But in the 90s, the numbers debate was a big deal in military circles. Yet, the discussion morphed as flashy slogans entered the arena. Force multipliers, revolution in military affairs, revolution in training, net-centric warfare, rapid decisive operations, and common operating pictures...yada, yada, yada.

Everyone drank the technology Kool-Aid flavored with superlatives imagined by think-tanks and consultants. Soon, like cultists attending a "We Love Jim" rally at Jonestown or a faux intellectual who snagged a copy of *Popular Science* magazine, everyone seemingly became convinced the nature of war could fundamentally change. Technology would allow the military to do more with less: locate enemies and conduct surgical strikes, all while keeping leadership in the know with real-time updates. Insert stealthy forces to cripple opposition defenses. Eavesdrop on enemy planning with sensitive antennas and overhead satellites. While this proved prescient in many ways, the belief that wars were

somehow different through technology spawned some dangerous opinions, policies, and awful military decisions that continue to haunt America. One needn't look further than the legacy of our escapades in Iraq and Afghanistan.

Enter Secretary of Defense, Donald Rumsfeld. He came to the Naval Academy when I was a Plebe, or Freshman, in layman's terms. I was dining in King Hall when he entered the gigantic mess hall that feeds around 4,000 shipmates, three times per day. To my surprise, he sat down at a table away from my squad and me. Ever the schmoozer, I raced over to introduce myself and snapped a blurry photo. He seemed nice. Ahhh, but beneath his outer layer of grins was an opportunist of the highest order. A man with doctrinal convictions that would clash with seasoned educators at the Naval War College and whose ego and penchant for bullying rankled the military establishment. In summation, he was a righteous prick. Too harsh? Well, MC02 might help explain the roots of disdain.

With the hopes of technology reducing war to a series of mouse-clicks, MC02 was born. At the heart of this part-live, part-simulated military exercise was testing new doctrine such as Rapid Decisive Operations (RDO) against a determined foe. RDO capitalizes on technology to compel the adversary to undertake certain actions or deny their ability to take actions that would be beneficial to their cause. Essentially, the concept rests on the idea that a highly deployable, lethal, agile force – properly supported – can rapidly defeat an enemy by crippling their operational and strategic centers of gravity. Say what?

Okay, let's handle this "Barney style." Instead of assembling huge divisions of army troops to invade or an armada of ships, the idea was to focus on and destroy the things that offer the enemy the tools to resist. If the enemy requires certain bridges to maneuver or power plants...Eliminate them. The concept involved overwhelming operations to shock and paralyze the adversary or destroy their ability to conduct offensive or defensive operations. The idea was to fragment enemy capabilities and ultimately prevent friendly loss of life. As opposed to occupation, this is decapitation. And, yes, it demanded technological superiority and rested on the assumption the U.S. could maintain it against that determined foe.

When Rumsfeld became the Secretary of Defense, he embraced this vision of a military that sought decapitation instead of occupation (yes, this is ironic). Millennium Challenge 2002 was funded, and he endorsed it, stating, "MC02...will help us create a force that is not only interoperable, responsive, agile, and lethal, but one that is capable of capitalizing on the information revolution and the advanced technologies that are available today." And was it ever costly? A full $250 million to explore RDO amongst other concepts. The most expensive ever! The largest, most elaborate concept-development exercise in U.S. military history. It included 13,500 service members participating from seventeen simulation sites and nine live training sites. Heralded as a tool to jump-start Pentagon efforts to incorporate "lead ahead" technologies. From July 24 to August 15, 2002, U.S. Joint Forces Command, or JFCOM, ran the seminal event. JFCOM, disestablished in 2011, was created in 1999, to lead the transformation of the U.S. military through experimentation and education. Prior to this, services regularly "stovepiped" their operations. This proved costly on the acquisition front, but also in times of war. JFCOM would serve a key role in teaching competing services, often with conflicting interests – Army, Navy, Air Force, Marines – to work better together. It is certainly more complicated than that, but let's just say JFCOM assumed traffic cop duties in the realm of combat and preparation for it.

The simulation took place in a high-end (meaning modern technology, not horses and bayonets), small-scale contingency with the potential to escalate into a major war. Its goals were to determine the U.S. military's ability to establish and maintain information superiority, set conditions for decisive operations, assure battlespace access, conduct effects-based operations, sustain synchronized operations, and improve joint fighting capabilities. Now, that gobbledygook probably makes little sense unless you've served. So really, this exercise was about knowing exactly what the enemy was doing, preventing them from knowing the reverse, having multiple separate operations working simultaneously or systematically to lay the groundwork for the enemies' defeat.

So, what you had were Blue Forces (the U.S.), and Red Forces or opposition forces (OPFOR), engaged in a potential combat scenario set five years in the future. This meant Blue Forces could use technology still in development but expected to be available five years ahead. Some of this technology, such as airborne lasers, still hasn't come to fruition. Red had a geography that even someone dumber than a bag of hammers could tell was modeled after Iraq or Iran. For their leader, they chose Lt. General (Retired) Paul Van Riper because he was considered a devious sorta guy. His task was to play the role of a wily General-turned dictator of a fictitious Muslim state.

Unfortunately, they chose the wrong man because Van Riper wasn't about to lay down to infidel imperialists. A warrior-scholar, Van Riper was intimately aware of the nature of war from antiquity to insurgent campaigns in the Twentieth Century. But he wasn't just a bookworm. He enlisted in the Marine Corps Reserve in 1956 but eventually earned an officer commission in 1963. Soon after, he'd deploy to Vietnam as an early advisor. He was wounded there in combat when attacking a machine gun nest in a rice paddy near Saigon. He'd go on to serve in other trouble spots such as Egypt and Lebanon, eventually commanding a battalion in South Vietnam in 1968. Continuously promoted, he became the Assistant Chief of

Staff, Command, Control, Communications, and Computer and Director of Intelligence before advancing to Lieutenant General. When he retired in 1997, he'd amassed forty-one years of Marine Corps service. So, when JFCOM needed an enemy, they looked no further than the retired General. He possessed the acumen to play the role of crafty tyrant to a "T."

But there was another reason he was chosen. During previous JFCOM experiments and wargames, Van Riper emerged as an outspoken critic of the scripted nature of wargames. Now, some scripting is necessary to put the pieces together to test certain things. However, without restraint, scripting can end up delivering results that only confirm assumptions and biases. This is a waste of money at best, downright dangerous at worst. During one wargame involving Van Riper, the Blue Team was tasked to eliminate the enemies' weapons of mass destruction (sound familiar?). To Van Riper's surprise, he received word from exercise control that the Red team's hidden ballistic missile sites were destroyed. How? Van Riper was furious since Blue never even figured out where they were located. Scripting assumed a future U.S. military would have real-time sensor and radar capabilities to find, localize, and destroy them. JFCOM promised Van Riper that MC02 would be different. A free-play, honest exercise that even the Red Team could win.

Leading up to hostilities in this fictional crisis, Blue issued an ultimatum: Surrender or face the wrath of the American arsenal. Van Riper knew the Bush Administration recently established the doctrine of preemption that was coined "the Bush Doctrine." This meant that the U.S. would and could unilaterally take military action should they feel an attack was imminent or, if left unchecked, would manifest itself into a future threat. Therefore, Van Riper decided to preempt the preempters. Facing a no-win situation, he invented a work-around. Taking latitude with the guidelines of the somewhat scripted wargame, he developed a plan that would send an entire battle group, an aircraft carrier, and thousands of Americans to the depths of the sea. His strategy was asymmetric. Hit the enemy with old, tried and true methods where they were weak while steering clear of their advantages. He knew these fanciful net-centric concepts guaranteed anything he said would be collected by advanced eavesdropping sensors. Remember, it was rigged. Thus, he simulated the use of motorcycle runners to relay orders to units. This effectively circumvented the technological advantage of Blue and left them with zero idea what he was up to. Meanwhile, he used civilian vessels to locate the Blue navy. Then he converted motor whaleboats and other craft into rocket-propelled grenade-wielding death boats to include suicide crafts laden with explosives. Radio communications were suspended. He operated his force in the shadows. He went so far as to transmit coded messages from mosque towers during the call to prayer. Sly, devious...Indeed!

As Blue's fleet approached his coast, he struck. Reports say he specifically attacked in the early morning since sophisticated radars have difficulty tracking when moisture is present. That day, a layer of fog blanketed the horizon, forcing radar operators to reduce sensitivity, decreasing Blue's ability to detect his murderous, small craft. At least not until they battered their targets with Van Riper's hellfire. His converted pleasure crafts saturated U.S. defenses, firing simulated salvo after simulated salvo. Blue, confused and shaken, received their own paralyzing dose of shock and awe. In less than ten minutes, it was all over. One aircraft carrier, ten cruisers, and about six amphibious ships were sunk. Done. As many as twenty thousand simulated souls went to Davy Jones and his locker. But it didn't end there. Van Riper's makeshift force launched adjacent attacks, performing mop-up work on unsuspecting forces with a fatal blend of missile and suicide attacks.

The good guys were at a loss, prompting their leader, LT. General Bell, to relay to JFCOM Commander, General Buck

Kernan, "Sir, Van Riper just slimed all of the ships." None can confirm if Bell was channelling his inner child with a Nickelodeon reference. Kernan wasn't prepared for that troubling phone call and JFCOM scrambled to salvage the costly wargame. Meanwhile, Van Riper and his band of guerrillas gazed, in a mixture of elation and horror, at their flawless pre-emptive strike. There was an eerie silence. Radio circuits rendered to static. In minutes, the symbol of American military dominance, the aircraft carrier, was crushed by a swarm of cheap boats employing outdated equipment. The JFCOM Commander Kernan was stunned: Van Riper had sunk his damn Navy.

If you're Kernan, what do you do? End the exercise? One that is fully funded. At the time, he had actual, live forces off the coast of San Diego and other spots awaiting orders to conduct forced entry operations. Do you call Donald Rumsfeld? What do you say? "Hey Donald, so bad news; our fleet is dead and we stopped the exercise. All those troops went back home." No, you don't do that. Remember, Rumsfeld is a dick (R.I.P.). Kernan magically respawned the fleet and pressed on. Van Riper was pissed. He won, or so he thought. Still, Van Riper would not go away without a fight.

He knew the forced entry portion meant that MV-22 Ospreys would bring Blue forces to the fight. The tilt rotor aircraft became his new target. He issued orders to light them up. That's when the White Cell leader, retired General Gary Luck, the architect of the event working directly for Kernan, changed the rules making attacks on the MV-22s unauthorized. The White Cell also directed Van Riper to position air defense assets in the open, making them sitting ducks. Despite the Blues failing to destroy all of them, he still had to sit and watch, helpless, as the "good guys" performed their own mop-up duties. Fuming, Van Riper asked the White Cell if he could deploy chemical weapons. This was denied. Awww, man, they wouldn't even let him let loose nerve agents. What a rip!

When Van Riper complained to Kernan, he was rebuked: "You're playing out of character. OPFOR would never have done what you did." And that was that. Van Riper shed the wily, tyrant character and decided to resign in frustration. Red became leaderless six days into the exercise meant as a free-play, winner-take-all wargame, showcasing future tech, and testing critical concepts. He opted to serve as a powerless advisor for the remaining seventeen days. The rest is as you might expect. Blue forces kicked the crap out of Red, crippled their naval and air forces, neutralized their WMD assets, and rendered Van Riper's proud, albeit fictitious, Middle Eastern state a shadow of its former self. A glowing report arrived on Rumsfeld's desk, lauding the transformative concepts proved and ready for implementation in the next conflict.

But they made the wrong enemy in Van Riper. He wrote his own report about the exercise's shortcomings, arguing "It could lead the Pentagon to have misplaced confidence in still un-tested military warfighting concepts....War-gaming is not normally corrupted, but this whole thing was prostituted; it was a sham intended to prove what they wanted to prove." Although his comments were leaked to the press, few noticed and fewer cared.

Douglas Smith, my professor at the Naval War College, taught me that prior to Pearl Harbor, Japanese war planners ran countless wargames against America. However, they all suffered from wishful thinking. The Japanese continually put Americans in situations that led to their demise to validate biased claims of Japanese naval superiority. Those decisions in simulated combat cost them in real combat. The enemy always has a vote.

History doesn't repeat, it rhymes. Soon after MC02, General Shinseki, then Army Chief of Staff, clashed publicly with Donald Rumsfeld. When asked during a Senate hearing how many troops were required to invade Iraq, he stated, "Something on the order of several hundred thousand soldiers." Far higher than Rumsfeld's estimate, he was lambasted by Rumsfeld and his Deputy Paul Wolfowitz. Low and behold, Shinseki retired. Many believe he was coerced into early retirement for his opinions. Years later, when the insurgency in Iraq took hold, the head of U.S. Central Command, General John Abizaid, confirmed that Shinseki had been right all along. To pour salt in the wounds, the challenges encountered by the "Coalition of the Willing" were mostly predicted during 1999's Desert Crossing War Game. That exercise, led by General Anthony Zinni, was designed to assess various outcomes concerning the removal of Saddam Hussein in Iraq and test OPLAN 1003-98. Remember everyone saying we didn't have a plan for post-invasion Iraq? They're mistaken. It was hidden, forgotten, or ignored. 1999's Desert Crossing After Action Report found:

The consensus was that the U.S. would not unilaterally intervene in Iraq except in response to WMD use or a humanitarian crisis, otherwise a coalition is required. ☑

A post-Saddam power vacuum will cause regional instability as rivals jockey for power. Anticipate fragmentation along religious / ethnic lines to include widespread violence. These problems will be stoked by surrounding countries with geopolitical motives in contrast to the U.S. and allies. ☑

The creation of a democratic government wasn't practical. Instead, nationalist leaders would be needed as a stabilizing force. Moreover, border security and restoring order will be the most pressing needs post-Saddam. A government that appears weak or subservient to foreign powers will increase the likelihood of civil war and tangle U.S. forces in an occupation absent an exit strategy. ☑

We knew the risks! Seasoned strategists had gone through painstaking efforts to characterize them. General Zinni recalls, "When it looked like we were going in, I called back down to CENTCOM and said, 'You need to dust off Desert Crossing.' They said, 'What's that? Never heard of it.'" But that wasn't all. He repeatedly expressed reservations suggesting, "God help us if we think this transition will occur easily." Zinni was also quick to point out that Desert Crossing (or OPLAN 1003-98) suggested about 385,000 troops and that border security and reconcentration would present the largest obstacles.

As for Van Riper, JFCOM eventually validated his criticism that the game was rigged. His emails, reports, and public comments had infuriated the military intelligentsia, but they ultimately relented. Sadly, Rumsfeld had little interest in Van Riper's critique. His protests only entrenched Rumsfeld and the Bush Administration views on the shifting nature of war and the empowering effects of new technology. We now can be honest with ourselves – Republican, Democrat, liberal, conservative, veteran, hawk, and pacifist – how that shitshow went.

When America went to war, it did so extolling concepts "validated" during MC02. Hubris convinced policymakers to learn the lessons they wanted to learn. What followed is well-documented: Not enough troops to maintain security early on, the rise of insurgent groups using the similar asymmetric tactics Van Riper adopted, and lost lives in a conflict rushed into with lofty ambitions. We didn't know the enemy or understand the culture. Technology proved less useful in urban combat where anyone could be an enemy. Even though technology changes, war will always be a terrible, uncertain, chaotic, bloody business. That will never change, despite the wishful thinking of technocrats. James Fallows describes it best:

"The American public and its political leadership will do anything for the military except take it seriously. The result is a chickenhawk nation in which careless spending and strategic folly combine to lure America into endless wars it can't win."

When it comes to fighting there will always be human factors that technology cannot surmount. Catchy slogans masquerading as ideas can lead overly optimistic leaders into making extremely poor decisions in matters of war and peace. When Iraq's invasion was still in an embryonic state, Van Riper proved that the enemy had a vote. He was the canary in a coal mine or the glitch in the matrix. He was right. Salvation wouldn't be found with microchips, processing power, and buzz words. No matter how rigged the scenario is, a crafty warfighter will find a way. See, no-win situations don't exist, especially against a determined adversary and student of history with a bloody-minded resolve to "Kobayashi Maru" the whole damned thing.

DENG XIAO: FROM CRIME TO CARRIER

It was April of 1997. Hong Kong frantically prepared for the United Kingdom's "handover" of the old Empire's last crown jewel to the People's Republic of China. Sunset arrived in "Britannia" along with their 99-year lease of Chinese territory. After the First Opium War (1839-1842), the British took Hong Kong Island and would further annex mainland China's Kowloon Peninsula in 1860. In 1898, the *Second Convention of Peking*, as it is commonly known, codified a lease agreement between the two powers. Few believed it would ever expire, nor could anyone imagine China's spectacular rise. Apart from a brief interruption, during Japanese occupation, the British maintained a steady presence in China's backyard. It wasn't as if the Qing Dynasty had a choice. They were too weak and fractured to stave off European ambitions. Chinese wooden junks splintered before steel armadas in a series of lopsided defeats. How times had changed. The British wouldn't just be handing back colonial property but one of the wealthiest, most capitalistic, and densely populated places in the world. A bustling financial, laissez faire titan: The anti-thesis of China's state-planned, one-rule government. Hong Kong was also the setting where Chinese military corruption made unlikely bedfellows in one of the weirdest arms deals in history. This deal, decades in the making, transformed a casino resort into China's first aircraft carrier. The stealthy operation is shrouded in mystery; especially since – other than the financial backer – the other co-conspirators are either dead or jailed.

Hong Kong's transfer ceremony represented the death knell of the British Empire and genesis of an Asia-Pacific hegemon. By 1997, China was on the move with a booming economy and determination to rectify past wrongs. Hong Kong was the first step towards fulfilling China's "Manifest Destiny" throughout the South China Seas. If only other countries would clear out. Moreover, it's only fitting reclaiming lost territory coincided with a quest for an aircraft carrier. Maritime deficiencies were what put China in a bind to begin with. But, like most things, power doesn't come easily or cheap. China's acquisition of their carrier was a saga fraught with danger and missteps. But why an aircraft carrier?

Carriers epitomize military *and* diplomatic muscle. Their mere presence demands respect. Have a dispute? Park a carrier off someone's coast and wait for them to piss themselves into compliance. Need to teach pesky terrorists a lesson? Park a carrier off the coast, launch fighters, and melt their faces with surgical strikes, or flatten them with 500-lb bombs. Carriers and embarked aircraft allow countries to control swaths of airspace and with, supporting ships, the waters beneath them.

WWII's Battle of Leyte Gulf is credited with the demise of the battleship. Until then, battleships and their heavyweight guns owned the seas. Yamato and Musashi were believed to be unsinkable, their punch unrivalled. The 18.1-inch gun shells weighed over 3,000 pounds and could be fired over twenty miles. Musashi sank courtesy of 17 bomb strikes and 19 torpedo hits from

American carrier-based aircraft. Yamato escaped but would later be deliberately grounded so its batteries could ward off attackers at Okinawa. Bombers and torpedo aircraft spotted her and went to work.

Currently, there are 22 fixed wing aircraft carriers in the entire world. 11 are American. The others are from UK (2), Italy (2), China (2), France (1), Russia (1), Spain (1), India (1), and Thailand (1). The U.S. also operates 9 amphibious assault ships that carry marines, landing equipment, and V/STOL aircraft such as the F-35B Lightning II and V-22 Osprey. You might recall the V/STOL AV8B Harrier from the film, True Lies. These non-carriers are far more capable than their foreign competition. Generally, foreign carriers are smaller, rely on "ski jumps" instead of sophisticated catapults, and are non-nuclear. U.S. Federal Law even mandates not less than 11 operational carriers.

Besides being expensive to build, carriers present technological hurdles from catapult designs to specially designed aircrafts themselves. These are engineering feats. Floating, regimented ecosystems packed with thousands of sailors carrying out vital daily tasks. Underway operations wreak havoc on weapon systems, sensors, and aircraft. Proper maintenance is paramount. Still, the hardest aspect operating carriers is training pilots and air crews in the onerous task of launch and recovery operations. Training a generation of carrier-based aviation pilots is a huge and costly undertaking...And mistakes always happen. Losses of life is to be avoided but comes with the territory. This isn't something taken lightly, which is why so few countries take the plunge, opting instead to develop coastal navies suited for presence patrols and anti-piracy.

So how did this whole deal happen? By picking the disease-ridden carcass of the Soviet Union of course! But it took one unlikely businessman to pull it off. That April, Xu Zengping, known for building a home modelled after Versailles, opened a quant office in Beijing's Grand Hotel overlooking the Forbidden City. Using a cover story of organizing a celebratory event; he coordinated an arms deal against the wishes of government officials (well, most of them). His task was to buy a two-thirds complete Soviet carrier rotting in Ukraine and deliver it to the People's Liberation Army – Navy (PLAN).

Why him, and better question, why didn't China just buy it? It's just a crappy unfinished ship! For starters, China worried antagonizing the United States. Carriers, being offensive weapons, risked being perceived as overly aggressive.

During the 70s and 80s Japanese xenophobia skyrocketed in the American consciousness. From automobiles to electronics, Japan decimated the competition. America's "Rust Belt," urban decay, and de-unionization were partly blamed on imbalanced trade relations with our former enemy. Japanese investors bought up prime real estate and businesses. Panicked Americans felt they'd been priced out of their own country. But cyberpunk's predictions of Japanese rule via omnipotent megacorporations didn't arrive. Japan entered a demographic death spiral and China became the new baddie. Every story needs a villain. China seems bent on deserving widespread scorn.

Meanwhile, prickly human rights situations complicated relations with the international community. From monks in Tibet to domestic turmoil, increasingly repressive tactics undermined China's "peaceful rise" narrative. The world remembered 1989's disaster, Tiananmen Square, memorialized by an image of an unarmed student staring down the barrel of a tank's mighty gun. The long-standing dispute between China and Taiwan was heating up as well. Yet, this was mostly about money. Tapping into the U.S.

market was far more vital to long-term security than a controversial carrier project. China had sent a delegation to Ukraine's Black Sea Shipyard back in 1992 and purchased a half-finished refuelling ship designed for aircraft carrier logistics support. However, by the mid-90s central leadership halted further progress in hopes of currying favor with the Clinton Administration.

China's carrier pursuit can be traced back to the Chairman Mao Zedong, "The Great Helmsman," who advocated for "railways on the high seas." He envisioned merchant ships dotting the horizon transiting under the protective shield of ever-vigilant aircraft carriers. Plans to procure one was shelved in the 1970s due to cost and, while obtaining a carrier regained popularity in the 80s, efforts stalled. Today, prosperity has opened the aperture on ambitions. It's a dream over a half-century in the making.

Absent formal support, snagging one fell to a rogue officer, Vice Admiral He Pengfei, and his merry band of crooks. Unfortunately, several Hong Kong moguls derided the mission as a fool's errand. With hope dissipating, one man stood up: Xu Zengping. He urged him saying, "It was a once in a century opportunity to buy a new carrier...Please do me a favor." Xu, a PLA veteran sympathetic to the noble cause, wasn't convinced it could be done. For nearly two years, from April 1996 – February 1998, the pair held clandestine meetings, Xu was invited to highly restricted military events, and probably enjoyed a vast array of illicit vices (c'mon, deals like these usually run afoul with moral decency). Midway through the courtship, Xu relented to secure the vessel, whatever the cost. It seems the Vice Admiral's willingness assume personal risks for national security was inspiring. Thus, Xu journeyed to Ukraine to negotiate a deal fully financed with his own sizable fortune.

Meanwhile, the cash-strapped Ukrainian Black Sea Shipyard had been trying to sell the skeleton of what was supposed to be the

Soviet carrier, *Varyag*. Ordered in 1983 and laid down in 1985, she was supposed tip the scales in the Cold War arms race. Instead, she languished 68% complete for over a decade. Without buyers or maintainers, salt spray caked the behemoth, rusting entire sections to a fine powder.

The shipyard proved eager to sell but not without a cover story. Xu told authorities in Kiev a convincing tale of glitz and glamour. See, this decrepit carrier would be a mesmerizing casino resort off Macau...Asia's Las Vegas. Sounds crazy but it wouldn't be the first time a carrier became a casino. China had done it before. That Xu learned the "casino" was not welcomed to berth off Macau was of trivial concern. Either Macau didn't have berths available, or the prospect of an unfinished,  rust-stained crapfest ruining the luxurious ambiance made them uncomfortable. Whatever the reason, it didn't matter. So, Xu bought the crapfest for a measly $20 million. The month before he'd nudged Ukrainian powerbrokers to look the other way with $2 million in cash and dozens of bottles of Chinese liquor. Macau should be comparatively easy, he must've reasoned.

Berthing rights were no issue that couldn't be fixed with the procurement of doctored casino-related documents from Macau authorities for about 6-million HKD. But getting the carrier across the finish line would take much more. Lacking sufficient collateral, he was forced to put up his palace designed to resemble Versailles. Yup, risking his palace for the king and country (err, Chinese Communist Party). Beyond the palace, he put everything else he owned up and secured multiple loans from business partners. But c'mon, it's a carrier! Right? He next hired several naval and shipbuilding experts and set up offices in Kiev for a shell company called, Agencia Turistica E Diversoes Chong Lot Limitada (or Chong Lot) headquartered in Macau. God, that name sounds fake. Coincidentally, Chong Lot was owned by Chin Luck Holdings and four of the group's six directors lived in Yantai where most of China's shipyards are located.

He did this all during the Asian financial crisis (i.e. he was screwed if this gamble failed). The purchase was finalized in March 1998. Around that time, Chinese premier Zhu Ronji formally rejected the carrier project. What did this mean? Nothing much other than lack of governmental support meant reimbursement was unlikely. Oh, it gets worse.

Everyone knows the last mile of the marathon is the hardest. In June 2000, the carrier exited the shipyard. Still operating under the casino cover, *Varyag* would be towed through the Bosporus Straits over to Macau for conversion into a $200-million floating resort and casino. The deal raised some eyebrows considering the shell company had no listed telephone number, wasn't at the listed address, and was run by former PLAN officers. Still, consensus in the intelligence realm was that the ship was far too crummy to ever be refurbished, let alone become an operational carrier. Before it left, about 40 tons of blueprints were shipped overland in eight trucks to China where they could be analyzed by top-level naval personnel in advance of the carrier's arrival.

That's when the mission hit a snag. 1936's *Montreux Convention Regarding the Regime of the Straits* grants Turkey control over access to the Black Sea through the Bosporus and Dardanelles Straits. During his rule, Josef Stalin felt the agreement held Russia by the throat. Subsequent Soviet leaders demanded major revisions and escalating tensions persuaded Turkey and Greece to abandon neutrality and join the NATO cause in 1952. Soviet gripes revolved around the stipulation that warships over

15,000 tonnes were restricted from passage except for designated capital ships of Black Sea States, including Russia and Ukraine. Under the terms, aircraft carriers were not considered capital ships; meaning their transit was unauthorized. Soviets did manage to bypass this legal matter by building the *Kuznetzov Class*.

The Soviets called the Kuznetzov Class "Heavy Aircraft Carrying Cruisers," and NOT aircraft carriers. To be more convincing, the Soviets armed them with an absurd number of missiles. So, if their jets didn't kill you, they'd shoot you in the face. The exercise in semantics worked! The Soviets could freely access the Mediterranean and Black Sea with their "aircraft carriers" while preventing the U.S. from using theirs. Turkey, leary that revised terms might reduce control, let the Soviets have their way.

The *Varyag* happened to be a member of the infamous *Kuznetsov Class*. However, when Xu tried to get his newly purchased hull through, he was operating under vastly different rules as he was not from a Black Sea State. Additionally, Turkey looked at the piece of junk being towed and was like, "you shall not pass;" fearing inclement weather or a collision could foul the straits and disrupt maritime commerce.

For nearly a year and a half the carrier burned circles in the Black Sea at an estimated daily cost of $8,500. Chinese authorities, experiencing a change of heart, came to the rescue, effectively bribing Turkey with tourism and trade concessions. In  November 2001, the ship passed the Bosphorus and Dardanelles with navigational charts set to Macau (err, China). It's said almost 30 escort vessels were employed, including 11 tugboats, and 16 highly trained navigational pilots were needed to safely transit the vessel.

Murphy's Law struck again. The tow cable snapped during a gale, leaving the carrier adrift and heading straight toward the Greek Island of Skyros. The crew was able to get the vessel back under tow; however, an unfortunate sailor lost his life in the process. It would get worse.

The plan was to tow the ship through the Suez Canal, except for one titanic problem. The Suez Canal forbade passage to "dead ships" without their own power source. Instead of the far shorter route, tugs towed the *Varyag* through the Straits of Gibraltar, around Africa's Cape of Good Hope, and through the Straits of Malacca...A 15k-plus nm journey at a tortuous 6-knots. The ship didn't arrive at Dalian Shipyard in Northwest China until February of 2002. When all was said and done, Xu believes he spent $120 million buying the carrier, setting up and operating offices, performing due diligence, and paying bribes, transit fees, and towing charges for the deal over 4-years in the making.

When the aircraft carrier finally arrived, it did so without fanfare, parades, galas, or dignitary visits. Xu was presented no plaque, though he has become an unofficial celebrity since sharing his tale to media outlets. Although Xu has spoken at length about his involvement in the deal, details of the transfer remain a mystery. Perhaps that's because Vice Admiral He Pengfei died from a heart attack in 2001. His co-conspirator, former PLA Intelligence Chief Major General Ji Shengde was jailed on corruption charges in 2000.

Ji Shengde is as slimy as they come. He's the son of the foreign minister, Ji Pengfei, who not only facilitated Nixon's 1972 visit, but also negotiated the return of Hong Kong. In 1999, Ji was demoted after being outed during congressional hearings *concerning illicit contributions to the Democratic National Committee. He paid DNC fund-raiser and another "piece of work," Johnny Chung, $300k to support President Clinton's reelection. Demotion didn't stop him from getting caught in a smuggling racket that earned him a suspended death sentence.*

In the end, Xu proved to be just the unlucky sap who "donated" an aircraft carrier to China. Never compensated, he's steadily paying off debts accrued during the four-year ordeal. His palace is long gone as is faith in restitution. Xu isn't bitter though. In fact, he's proud to have built his legacy on patriotism, not business ventures. Wholly ironic those two are intertwined regardless. His economic fortunes have recovered too and he's gained admirers for his contribution to China's "peaceful rise." *Week in China* ran a puff piece profiling Xu as a "naval hero."

Surveys of China's "Weibosphere" netizens indicate widespread praise for Xu. The daughter of a former PLAN commander revealed her father, who died in 2011, pledged to never close his eyes when he dies if China doesn't get a carrier. If you don't believe her story was written by propagandists, I have a ship to sell you in Ukraine. The consensus was that Xu's deception was justified it because "Our own country's interest is supreme." Several went on to recommend renaming the ship from Liaoning to Zengping as proper reward for his "donation." Authorities seem to have co-opted the narrative, replacing "rogue" with "patriot."

As for China, well, it's estimated buying Soviet leftovers saved roughly 15-years of scientific research. The blueprints were a godsend to the naval architects who turned the proposed floating casino into an operational carrier. China has since completed her first domestic carrier and plan to construct more. PLAN was also aided by the purchase of a former Australian carrier called the *HMAS Melbourne* which the Aussies sold to China for scrapping in 1985. Sure, China scrapped it but only after delaying the job to properly study the catapult system that the Australian navy allegedly failed to dismantle.

In November 2016, the re-christened *Liaoning*, was declared combat ready 14 years after reaching mainland China and over twenty years since the Soviet Union took its last gasp. The ranks of Chinese "naval heroes" are swelling too. Although details are sparse, dozens of pilots have already lost their lives getting  the carrier "combat ready." Engineering mishaps have added even more to the tally, though China is careful to downplay them. The point is that carrier-based aviation is not for the faint of heart or something one should rush into in order elevate themselves higher on the global totem pole.

They know this! They've studied their competition and are committed to bear the costs. As of 2021, China possesses roughly 60 more warships than the U.S., and about 70% are considered up to modern standards. If its Coast Guard and Maritime Militia is included, she has over 700 ships at her disposal. This is astonishing when considering the state of their maritime power when Xu brokered his deal. In twenty years, they've transformed a feckless coastal navy into a global juggernaut. PLAN intends these ships to comprise an anti-access/area-denial (A2/AD) force. This means deterring or delaying U.S. and allied intervention within the Nine-Dash Line (including Taiwan). It means suturing adversary defenses with overwhelming firepower. Originally PLAN prioritized numbers over capabilities to achieve this end. This has changed. PLAN naval development now seeks local parity with the

U.S.

In recent years, Australia, Japan, Thailand, India, the Philippines, have prioritized maritime security and naval modernization. These developments do not bode well for peace and tranquillity in a region so vital for global commerce, and rife with territorial disputes. But looks can be deceiving.

At one point I was assigned to the aircraft carrier, USS John C. Stennis, named after ardent segregationist (indeed it is). Onboard, I became a fanboy of the one and only "Party Boy." As the name suggested, he likes to have a good time, consequences be damned. A naval pilot and commander of a squadron, he was a cross between a chiselled Navy SEAL and 70s porn star, including a superbly quaffed Tom Selleck mustache. Our military, being run by geniuses, sent "Party Boy" to visit this mysterious casino-turned-carrier as part of a goodwill officer exchange. To put it mildly, he wasn't impressed with the ship claiming they'd merely "put lipstick on a pig." To him, it was all-show, no-go.

While true, China's first carrier won't be its last! Sure, *Liaoning* uses an inferior launch method called Short Take Off But Arrested Recovery (STOBAR) which limits aircraft range and payload. However, China is already developing Catapult-Assisted Take-Off But Arrested Recovery (CATOBAR) and, in most cases, outright copying U.S. designs. Which leads me to believe that China's commitment to a carrier-based navy will only strengthen... They've gotten a taste of the "big time."

The state-controlled China Global Television Network released a YouTube video showcasing PLAN flight operations from a once decrepit hull. I'd be lying if I said I wasn't impressed. Aside from the slight differences to the naked eye, one could mistake the exercise for a U.S. one. The flight deck crews wore the same color-coded outfits to distinguish roles. Forget the technology, the personnel acted with precision. Dual emotions gripped me: Scorn and pride. After all, imitation is the sincerest form of flattery, even if we one day end up in each other's crosshairs.

Let's assume these carriers turn out to be useful conducting deterrence patrols, flying nights missions, and intimidating neighboring countries. What then?

1967's film, "The Dirty Dozen," illustrates the realities of China's military aspirations. In it, a rag-tag group of military criminals sent by an OSS Major (played by Lee Marvin) on a suicide mission to storm a chateau swarming with Nazis. At one point the misfits arrive at a U.S. base under the pretence a General is in their cohort. They're greeted by U.S. platoon in formation and dressed to impress...A band also plays celebratory tunes. The base commander, a Colonel, confronts the OSS Major, assuming the General would want to inspect his troops. So, the OSS Major asks the criminals which one wants to play General stating that," all you need to do is walk slow and act dumb." Someone volunteers and, while he's slowly and dumbly inspecting a line of pristine soldiers, he brazenly states to the Colonel, "they sure are pretty... But can they fight?"

China's modern Navy sure is pretty, but can they fight? Now, I'm hoping we never have to find out but there's a big difference between talking combat and living it. While their ships may be flashy, modern warfare is less about fancy gadgets than knowing how to use them and keeping them operational. Logistics is the lifeblood of modern war, not weapons. You won't find "Rosie the Riveter" pumping out Stealth Bombers on an assembly line.

To quote a former boss, "Modern warfare means you run with whatchu brung." Fancy systems require state-of-the-art logistical solutions. Boring logistics means getting replacement parts yesterday for problems bound to happen tomorrow. Keeping systems operational means factoring in redundancies. It means proper maintenance and care. Refuelling at sea during inclement weather. It means lots of training. Technocrats can design marvellous tools for maritime carnage but they're have-finished hulks without a crew. Underestimated in a world of silver-bullets and buzzwords, people matter the most. They always have. People who think, take initiative, and are devoted to a cause. That can't be purchased. It must be ingrained in a culture of empowerment.

How long have the Chinese operated abroad and how many of those sailors have grown accustomed to sacrificing family for service? America's Navy has been doing this 24-7, 365. China is learning and growing. They're navigating further into the uncertain trappings of life at sea. It's a mistake to doubt them, or any adversary. Still, some perspective is warranted. Doom and gloom appraisals fail to appreciate how damned difficult it is mastering the seas. It's taken 200 years for us to get to this point, China's had 20. As for the American response, well one Admiral spoke my sentiments, "In my dreams the South China Seas are covered with Chinese aircraft carriers." The logic being a bunch of massive targets are far better than the current situation of hundreds of smaller ships packed to the gills with anti-ship cruise missiles ready to rain down hell on American battle groups.

SNAFU:
Developing Militaries
~~Fail to Develop~~

ormer Secretary of Defense, James "Mad Dog" Mattis, has a call sign problem. Despite the media's best efforts to paint him as one, the retired General was never a "Mad Dog." Perhaps that moniker produced better headlines along with his famous "Mattisisms," such as, "Be polite, be professional, but have a plan to kill everybody you meet." Maybe the nickname was concocted by critics as a form of derision, only to elevate his esteem ironically higher. Either way, he isn't buying what they were selling, especially when he already has a fitting one, "CHAOS." He earned this tongue-in-cheek nickname as a Colonel in the 1st

Marine Expeditionary Brigade. Sarcastically standing for "Colonel Has Another Outstanding Suggestion," CHAOS represents far more than his unique approach to problem-solving. See, chaos is at the heart of the American military's method of warfare, or doctrine. There's an old joke in which a Soviet, Nazi, and American are discussing the difficulty planning against American military doctrine. The Soviet suggests, "The trouble lies in the fact that Americans do not read their doctrine nor feel obligated to follow it." In response, the Nazi states, "The reason they perform so well is that war is chaos, and the Americans practice chaos on a daily basis." This prompts the American to offer, "If we don't know what we're doing, the enemy certainly can't anticipate our actions." Chaos, properly contextualized, explains American military prowess while exposing the weaknesses of developing militaries, mostly subscribing to the "Soviet Model." Predicated on individual initiative, America's approach can have a democratizing spillover-- That is, unless the great equalizer, hubris, gets its way.

Brian Chontosh strode methodically onto Naval Academy's Alumni Hall stage. His fearsome V-shaped frame crisply, purposefully presented itself to the crowd of awestruck Midshipmen. Silence swept the arena. He had a presence, a control. This Marine Captain was a badass built like a brick shithouse...an American Ivan Drago. Ignoring the pomp and circumstance and plethora of top brass attending the Naval Academy's Forrestal Lecture Series event, he paused just long enough to throw in a sizeable wad of Copenhagen. He then unapologetically asked the 3-Star Admiral overseeing the event, "I hope you don't mind but I think better with a dip in." No, this guy was the real deal and his nonchalant attitude hooked us. After a brief introduction powered by nicotine and just enough profanity to cause some butts to adjust, he began his heroic tale.

On March 25, 2003, his Combined Anti-Armor Weapons Company encountered an ambush from a heavily entrenched enemy. His actions that day earned him the coveted Navy Cross for gallantry and are encapsulated in his official citation. More elucidating than this description of events was his thought process. With rounds whizzing by, he told us he needed to act

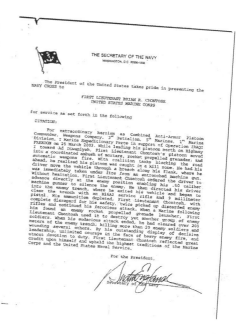

fast and being right or wrong didn't occur to him. Any delay, in his eloquent prose, "and we'd be fucked." He resolved to stop thinking and start doing.

America's military celebrates this as "taking the initiative." It's become the philosophical backbone of military operations. Executed through use of *Decentralization of Command* and *Command by Negation*, trusting service members to take actions commensurate with their training and informed judgment is a distinctively "Western" phenomenon. Long-dead kamikaze pilots may beg to differ; however, both go beyond suicide attacks or displays of selflessness in the heat of combat. It is worth noting that this is an educated generalization since the Viet Cong, Mujahideen, Islamic State, and countless South and Latin American insurgent campaigns utilized similar precepts, if only pursued out of necessity.

In its simplest form, *Decentralization of Command* shifts decision-making elements from higher echelons to give servicemen the freedom to achieve leadership's intended aims based on prevailing circumstances. Conversely, *Command by Negation* acts as a safety brake because it requires subordinates to report their intentions. This allows "the boss" to 'negate' actions when they object to proposed courses of action. Whether this is chaos or controlled chaos, trust is paramount. Therein lies the vital difference between "The West" and "The Rest." Trust gave Chontosh the flexibility to take decisive action and allowed Mattis to develop another "Outstanding Suggestion," much to the chagrin of his troops.

For the "The Rest," top-down, oppressive structures rule the roost... with damning consequences. Pejoratively coined the "Soviet Model," decisions are made at the top and secrecy is pervasive. As useful as this might be for rapid mobilization and preventing disclosures of plans, functionality collapses once the leader is out of the picture. The maxim "cut the head off the snake" is the proven tactic to deal with tyrants. This is done by severing communications lines, disrupting power grids, and flattening government buildings used for combat operations. Saddam Hussein, blinded by Tomahawk cruise missiles, could only wonder what his proud Republican Guard troops would do without his marching orders. The Answer: they gave up in droves.

This issue has beleaguered many developing nations but is pronounced in Arabic-speaking armies and African dictatorships. Even India's caste system impacts effective operations and reduces unit cohesion. Preference for this sub-optimal system is commonly the result of cultural traits and concerns over regime resiliency.

There's a story an American Lieutenant Colonel once wrote in Middle East Quarterly about how he was teaching Iraqis how to care for a mortar system they were supplying to security forces. Suddenly, an Iraqi Major showed up and confiscated the manuals, taking them to his tent. The American officer was perplexed. When the Major returned, he got everyone around in a circle to explain to HIS troops how to maintain the weapon. See, he'd studied the manual so he could be the expert.

While consulting the Royal Saudi Naval Forces on selecting the optimal missile for their new Multi-Mission Surface Combatant vessels, the Saudi officers couldn't understand the differences between various missile seeker types, amongst other things. They were obsessed with missile range despite range being only useful if the air search radar had appropriate coverage. For those in the field, this is basic knowledge. My efforts to educate them on the trade-offs of launch profiles, warhead size, and seeker types went on deaf ears. Vice betraying their ignorance, they picked the more expensive option with a head nod. Who cares? Saudis have the money.

Cultural norms may require the leader to save face. Instead of providing the tools (i.e., the manuals) the system is inculcated with a perverse reliance. This bestows undue gravitas and magnifies inherent power imbalances. On the surface, leaders becoming the experts may seem prudent; however, in practice, it perpetuates local paralysis. Those at the bottom are incapable and are discouraged from problem-solving. This is coupled with tribal rivalries, cronyism, and outright corruption... it shouldn't be surprising why developing militaries frequently fail to develop.

My ship was assigned Host Nation duties for a group of Chinese warships visiting San Diego. While providing tours to PLAN servicemen, our crew fielded multiple questions. We thought they'd try to trick us into revealing sensitive details about classified systems. Instead, their questions sought to comprehend the role of Non-Commissioned Officers, maintaining equipment, and damage control.

Non-Commissioned Officers (NCO) are the keystone of our armed forces. They carry out orders from officers but are expected to fix issues, manage the day-to-day, train and oversee the enlisted, and voice concerns up the chain of command. Most developing militaries have nothing resembling a functioning NCO system. We paint countries like China as ten feet tall, but war is about boring things – Maintenance, Logistics, Damage Control, and NCOs. At least China realizes her weaknesses.

Exercise Malabar is a trilateral exercise involving the U.S., Japan, and India, designed for participants to collaborate on an array of naval missions. In 2006, off the coast of Goa, representatives from the Indian Navy embarked on our vessel, USS MOBILE BAY (CG 52). There I witnessed the Indian Officer-Enlisted dynamic, which is best described as 'Serfdom.' Before our eyes, the officer berated his companion while he frantically tried to decrypt a message we'd already decrypted minutes before using better equipment. It was comical were it not so humiliating. I'd grown accustomed to the elitism of officers in the U.S. Navy... but this was otherworldly.

Beyond culture, over-centralization is a prominent feature. Most developing armies are a tool for regime stability. Citizens in stable, modern democracies, where external threats gain outsized influence, find this difficult to fully grasp. Despite propaganda to the contrary, authoritarian rule is continually beset by inner turmoil. Fearful of coups, dictators routinely cull the ranks of the unreliable, dislike individualism, and consolidate authority and decision-making within a trusted inner circle. Leaders walk a tightrope here. Though snakes at the top resist allowing the body to think for itself, once severed, the regime's military apparatus writhes and dies.

SNAFU is a cynical acronym suggesting that everything is messed up as it always is. Situation Normal All Fouled Up: it's always fouled up. This is wrong. Situation Normal (what is reported to the boss), All Fouled Up (what is actually happening) best describes typical reporting processes, especially in developing militaries. There is a tendency for junior officers to report incorrectly for fear of reprisal. Rather than frank discussions, leaders are given faulty information that pushes them to see the world through rose-tinted glasses.

The entire command structure is best represented by the meme with the dog sitting at a table, sipping at a cup of coffee while the kitchen around him burns, saying, "This is fine." When fear replaces initiative, "Yes Men" infiltrate. This is a recipe for disaster against hardened enemies.

Even for "the West," defeating asymmetric, or irregular forces, is a brutal business. As T.E Lawrence poetically lamented: "Making war upon insurgents is messy and slow, like eating soup with a knife." While technology and flexible command structures provide significant advantages over "The Rest," advanced weaponry requires a certain degree of democratization, in the form of trust in subordinates. Unfortunately, America's interventionism is all heartache and scar tissue in this regard.

Billions have been poured down a rat hole in Iraq, Afghanistan, and countless other war-ravaged hotspots in hopes of shaping modern militaries out of the primordial soup of post-colonial backwoods. Centermost in America's missteps is the optimism of technocrats, bankrolled by the military industrial complex and empowered by a political class more interested in placing an assembly line in their district than winning wars. Cluelessness is only surpassed by unbridled hubris. It shouldn't be surprising why developing militaries fail to develop.

While nations scramble to procure state-of-the-art weaponry blessed by "The West," their adversaries have grown comfortable repurposing inventions. Mark Twain put it best when he said, "Name the greatest of all inventors... Accident." History is full of them.

Sildenafil, going by the street name Viagra, was created when Pfizer scientists were looking to treat cardiovascular disorders. Instead, they discovered it perked up old peckers, helping our parents enjoy their twilight. Thanks, Pfizer!

An assistant professor reached into a pile of parts for a resistor to complete the circuit for a heart rhythm recording device. Despite grabbing the wrong resistor size, he noticed it produced intermittent electrical pulses. The pacemaker was born.

When a 3M scientist was trying to make a super-strong adhesive, his failure was repurposed. Bosses gained a tool to task employees without ever needing to speak to our face: Post-It Notes.

Botanist Arthur Galston synthesized triiodo benzoic acid, a hormone that sped up the flowering of soybeans, while defoliating them in higher concentrations. Imagine his horror when biowarfare scientists turned his wonderful, boring soybean breakthrough into Agent Orange. His discovery went on to level entire jungles and melt flesh during the super sweet Vietnam War.

However, history's most notorious repurposings might surprise you. Working in concert, they've killed more people than Alfred Noble's dynamite, Agent Orange, or the atomic bomb put together. Artillery and mortar fire can't compete with these ingenious weapons of mass carnage: The AK-47 and the Toyota Hilux pickups. Both "weapons" illustrate "The West's," at times, arrogant approach to interventionism.

The Avtomat Kalashnikova AK-47 is synonymous with misery. American servicemen have even been known to carry AK-47 cartridges since they're so prevalent on the battlefield and prove far more durable than M16s. Cheap, rugged, dependable, and simply good enough. Point to any conflict in the past fifty years and there's 100% certainty combatants are slinging AKs across their torsos. I dare you to find a picture of Osama Bin Laden without one! It's so common it has become a pop culture trope on par with villains smoking cigarettes.

In an era of breakneck advancements, how did the AK-47 become the preeminent weapon of modern warfare? Better yet, how did an aspiring poet and seventeenth child of nineteen from a peasant family from the middle of nowhere (Kurya, Russia) create a superbly minimalist and clever weapon?

Mikhail Kalashnikov spent his early childhood suffering various ailments, almost dying at age six (too bad, peaceniks packing the anti-gun lobby). Perseverance and toughness were ingrained while enduring severe, prolonged winters juxtaposed by unbearable summers. Yet, he possessed a softer side. Often finding solace in prose, he would write numerous poetry books during his life. Why is poetry common amongst so many would-be villains throughout history? Hunting was also a family affair when farming failed to make ends meet.

His early experiences made him fascinated by the mechanics of weapons, but Soviet conscription forever altered his life. In 1938, he joined the Red Army as a tank mechanic but was wounded at the Battle of Bryansk in October 1941. For about seven months, he lay in the hospital, hearing soldiers complain about the inferiority of Soviet arms. As a tank mechanic, he witnessed conscripts forced to share one rifle amongst three people. As soon as one died, the next man snatched it up in defense of the motherland.

Take a step back and imagine the horror of Eastern Front combat. Stalingrad, a battle over a besieged city that leveled it: 1.7 to 2-million dead, wounded, or missing. The city bearing the Soviet leader's name almost blotted from the map. Deaths on that front were staggering. While estimates differ, it is reasonable to assume the equivalent population of current-day New York City died at the hands of German invaders. Listening to his wounded comrades, Kalashnikov resolved to invent a new weapon.

Observing clear drawbacks in the typical infantry weapons, he prioritized ease of use. Soon after his release from the hospital, he completed his first submachine gun using the German Sturmgewehr along with the American M1 Garand as source material. Later in life, he would comment that he "felt no need to reinvent the wheel."

After an initial series of failures, steady refinements culminated in the Avtomat Kalashnikova Model 1947, or AK-47. In 1949, the AK-47 became the standard issue assault rifle for the entire Soviet Army. But it was the design, spartan and simplistic, that would propel his invention to dizzying highs. You must remember that Warsaw Pact, non-aligned communist countries, and post-colonial cesspools used conscripted, ill-trained forces. What Kalashnikov unknowingly did was make a weapon too easy to operate, too easy to maintain, and too easy to counterfeit.

For the next four decades of the Soviet Union, AK-47s reigned supreme in the arms trade. Why bother with more costly NATO arms when an AK did the trick? You could throw it, waterlog it, cover it in sand...nothing proved more resilient. The fall of the Soviet Union opened Pandora's box in the Third World. In the rush to make a buck, the Soviets before them and the Russians after made a killing licensing the production of AKs in other countries. Most of these would become hotbeds of civil war. But what made the AK-47 so ubiquitous? It was the design itself.

When Kalashnikov went to work, he built a weapon with looser tolerances than its counterparts, especially Western ones. The AK-47 used a mere eight moving parts. While this lack of complexity and loose tolerances made the weapon less accurate, it proved beneficial. Competing weapons with tighter tolerances were prone to malfunction should debris get caught in the small nooks and crannies. But the gaps in the AK-47 acted as a self-cleaning system of sorts. Get mud trapped inside...simply bang it out. Need to clean the barrel, lube up the lace of your boot and run it through a few times. That simplicity or inaccuracy from a manufacturing standpoint bolstered its success in the field. Nicholas Cage in *Lord of War* said it best:

Of all the weapons in the vast Soviet arsenal, nothing was more profitable than the Avtomat Kalashnikova model of 1947. More commonly known as the AK-47 or Kalashnikov, it's the world's most popular assault rifle. A weapon all fighters love. An elegantly simple 9-pound amalgamation of forged steel and plywood. It doesn't break, jam, or overheat. It'll shoot whether it's covered in mud or filled with sand. It's so easy, even a child can use it, and they do. The Soviets put the gun on a coin. Mozambique put it on their flag. Since the end of the Cold War, the Kalashnikov has become the Russian people's greatest export. After that comes vodka, caviar, and suicidal novelists. One thing is for sure, no one was lining up to buy their cars.

The Soviets cared little about intellectual property and patent laws. If you needed arms, they had warehouses full of them. If you wanted to produce your own, they'd provide technical drawings. In the U.S., companies weren't willing to hand over the keys to production. It wouldn't fly with the security-obsessed DOD either. The AK-47 could be had with no questions asked. After all, isn't perfection the enemy of good enough?

The immense success and proliferation of his creation came at a cost. Imagine the inventor's discomfort when the weapon designed to save his country from Nazi destruction was turned against them in the mountains of Afghanistan. Kalashnikov revealed his inner pain in a statement he made to *The Guardian*: "I'm proud of my invention, but I'm sad that it is used by terrorists...I would prefer to have invented a machine that people could use and that would help farmers with their work – for example a lawn mower." Before his death, while Russia was undergoing plans to erect a statue in his honor, he appealed to the Russian Orthodox Church for absolution.

The church absolved him and reaffirmed his patriotism and loyalty to the country. It even issued a firm declaration that when a weapon is used for defense of the motherland, the church supports its creators and the military that uses it. It's unknown if Kalashnikov's soul was eased by the approval of the church, but he died six months later. In truth, the AK-47 never fired a shot during WWII combat.

In 2017, Russia unveiled a statue memorializing Kalashnikov's invention. Standing upright at 25-ft tall, Kalashnikov carries his revered and reviled weapon. At the base, diagrams trace the evolution of his design work. However, one required replacement since the sculptor accidentally etched the blueprints of the German Sturmgewahr 44 instead of the first rendering of the AK-47. Perhaps that mistake was only fitting since Kalashnikov once commented, "Blame the Nazi Germans for making me a gun designer...all I ever wanted to do was construct agricultural machinery." If only he'd entered the lawnmower business instead of the arms one.

If AK-47s are the go-to firearm in the developing world, the Toyota Hilux pickup is the "War Chariot." At a fraction of the cost of tanks and armored personnel carriers, Toyota pickups or "Technicals" prove necessity is the mother of ingenuity. The term "Technical" originated during the 1990s in the Somali Civil War. Since Non-Governmental Organizations (NGO) were prohibited from contracting private security firms (cough, cough---Mercenaries), aid groups hired local gunmen for protection through a "technical assistance grant" racket. In layman's terms, NGOs required protection from warlords and their affiliates to deliver resources to starving refugees, since convoys were routinely hijacked by many of the same warlords they'd hire for protection in the first place. Who knows where the cycle began?

There's a high probability that the rusted-out Toyota Tacoma you drove in high school graduated to the frontlines. Known for their reliability, 4x4s are used and abused in "The West" to be repurposed for "The Rest." Eventually sold to overseas buyers, their treads make their impressions wherever blood is spilled. The benefits are obvious: they're cheap, fast, don't guzzle fuel like the alternatives, require no training, and can traverse rugged terrain. Whereas armored vehicles have huge logistical footprints, these don't. Parts are readily available. If one breaks down: fix it. If you can't: ditch it. Strap on a machine gun, artillery cannon, or missile launcher, and you have yourself a war rig Mad Max would be honored to scream across the badlands in.

From 1978-1987, irregular Chadian forces, backed by France, frustrated Muammar Gaddafi's annexation of northern Chad's Aouzou Strip. Reminiscent of David versus Goliath, Chadians stood down Libya's conventional army of T-62 tanks supported by artillery and air power. At a disadvantage, Chad improvised. Sporadic fighting reached its climax during the Battle of Fada. There, Chadians jury-rigged hundreds of Toyota pickups with machine guns, grenade launchers, and anti-tank missiles. Some 3,000 Chadians killed 784 and destroyed over 100 tanks and armored vehicles. Chadian losses amounted to 18 soldiers and 3 Technicals during the decisive battle of history's first Toyota War.

During the wars in Iraq and Afghanistan, the U.S. would regularly supply sophisticated weapons and "Humvee" trucks to security forces, only to discover months later it was all a waste. The operators couldn't or wouldn't maintain them. It took lots of time and money to figure out cultural differences in the realm of maintenance were real. To have sophisticated stuff, you need empowered individuals. At long last, the U.S. relented and provisioned allies with what they really needed - AK-47s and Toyotas.

In 2009, America linked a $181 million foreign military sales deal with Louisiana-based Swiftships Shipbuilders. The goal was to enhance oil infrastructure security by delivering up to fifteen Swift-Class Patrol Boats to the fledgling Iraqi Navy. Funds for the first six were paid through the Congressional appropriated FY 2007 war supplemental. The Iraqi Navy also awarded $109 million to procure two 60-meter Off-Shore Support Vessels. It's believed "Uncle Sam" kicked in $82 million of that total. Within months of initial delivery, headquarters dispatched our Chief Engineer to assess the material condition of Iraq's latest *toys*. He kept repeating, "Lack of ownership" over and over. Years later, when under "consideration" for an overseas individual augmented assignment, I learned the U.S. Navy was providing Iraq with engineering mentors. I breathed a sigh of relief that another "volunteer" took the bait. Ships are hell to maintain, absent a culture of ownership. Whatever. It's only American tax dollars.

It's no surprise developing militaries fail to develop. Initiative isn't easily taught. Flexible command structures are needed to promote local problem-solving. This requires trust and empowerment. Nor can initiative be bought. Fancy weaponry alone can't penetrate cultural barriers. They're just hunks of metal without training and care. Still, "The West" can learn a lot from "The Rest." In Afghanistan, American Special Forces faced significant logistical obstacles. Operators needed to scout remote, mountainous regions. Fuel was scarce, as were parts. They needed minimal logistics and were smart enough to steer clear of the bloated defense industry. So, what did the Special Forces do? They improvised and bought out entire Toyota showrooms to create Technicals of their own. Jury-rigged with roll cages, machine gun mounts, winches, and other trappings, these vehicles made believers out of the best "The West" had to offer. Stealthy and reliable, "The Rest" taught an important lesson about hubris. Oh, and American forces rode horses when the mission suited it. After all, horses are timeless.

TRIBES & TYRANNY: SEARCHING FOR BIG MEN

S addam Hussein was a kind man, lacking an angry bone in his body. I met him in 2009 while conducting the boardings of fishing dhows near Iraq's main oil terminals. I towered over his round-bellied, stocky frame. For what only could have been no more than thirty minutes, we bonded as closely as an American and Iraqi could-- which honestly, probably wasn't much. Of course, sharing his name with the infamous former leader of Iraq opened him up to quite a bit of ridicule. No, this was not the now-deceased dictator. This Saddam Hussein was the master of a fishing dhow. One day, beneath the blistering sun, backdropped by colossal oil terminals, his simple question exposed fundamental flaws in America's proclivity towards knee-jerk diplomacy. A non-threatening, uneducated fisherman made more sense than beltway wonks peddling institutionalist talking points.

Saddam's crew of about seven wore well-worn Adidas soccer jerseys and Navy issue brown camouflage shirts faded tan-gray from the years of salt-spray and hand washing. These were hard men, not in heart, but in how they lived; hands sliced raw from handling fishing lines, makeshift hooks, and the ever-present layering of salt into every crevice. Each dawn, hundreds of similar dhows, with similar masters, made their trek south to fish closer to the rich waters surrounding the Al Basrah (ABOT) and Khawr Al Amaya (KAAOT) Oil Terminals. Just as the fishing waters serve as the lifeblood for residents of the Al-Faw Peninsula, the massive terminals are strategically vital; the principal point of export for more than eighty percent of Iraq's gross domestic product.

The pockmarked terminals told the history of Iraq, both under Saddam Hussein and after him. Riddled with .50 caliber rounds from endless clashes, they stood erect but seemed to groan. They are one of today's frontlines in a test of wills between longtime adversaries whose tensions trace their ancestry to the Sunni-Shia schism. Yet, religion is a single dimension. Influence, ego, and commerce are the real stakes. Religion makes a great alibi...It always has.

While inefficient and antiquated, these facilities existed as Iraq's best hope for economic certainty, peace, and stability. Here, Americans worked with the young, inexperienced Iraqi Coastal Defense Force (ICDF) to patrol and defend the terminals from insurgent intrusions and their provocative Iranian neighbor. This resulted in a delicate balancing act as fishermen sought to inch closer and closer to exclusion zones. Because the best fishing spots lay inside these imaginary lines in the ocean, it was a daily battle to keep locals at bay while offering a necessary leniency.

Around the time we met, the fervor surrounding the Iranian elections hit full speed. A sense of dread permeated across the coastal waters of Iraq. Despite American dominance from a military standpoint, Iran's proclivity to bully loomed large. A few days earlier, Iranian Revolutionary Guard Corps Navy (IRGCN) boat crews boarded a dhow, ate some food, knelt in prayer, and fired shots into the pilothouse. I never fully grasped the rationale behind the kneeling in prayer portion, but then again, unloading rounds into an innocent fisherman's boat came off as excessive to say the least. Although no one was killed, a valuable point was made; zealots of the Iranian regime would not give in to democracy without a fight. Who knows? It was election season and perhaps lunacy moves the needle.

For weeks, we executed interaction patrols or IPATs. The main idea of the IPAT was for Visit, Board, Search and Seizure (VBSS) teams to traverse the waters around the terminals and either board fishing dhows, talk to locals, and gather information. My team, comprised of five other sailors from Patrol Coastal Crew INDIA, debarked our ship, the *USS Typhoon* by way of a rigid-hull inflatable boat (RHIB). *USS Typhoon*, being a Cyclone Class Patrol Ship or PC for short, is a 179-foot long, fast, agile ship, very suitable for coastal waters. Due to the small draft of roughly seven feet, it can navigate shallower waters than their larger counterparts, thus offering unique naval capabilities. In fact, the Navy SEALS originally used the PCs for clandestine transportation. When the Global War on Terrorism (GWOT) ramped up, the "big Navy" took advantage of PC capabilities and shifted them away from the special operations world.

Our team conducted roughly 40 boardings while deployed. This is not an amazing figure, but enough to gain some micro-level insights that could be understood and applied to our broader effort in the region. As in any endeavor, context is critical and my visit with Saddam finally helped me understand the many factors at play in the chaotic, oil-rich area. We had a young Intelligence Specialist (IS) with us. His job was interacting with fishermen to gather intelligence that might prove useful countering terrorism. What was done with this information was neither in my purview nor a major concern. For me, the overall goal was forming relationships and offering reassurance.

The IPAT routine was to get the boat in the water, drive around looking for dhows, and then board them. The whole effort wasn't very complicated, but still dangerous. On April 24, 2004, *USS Firebolt's* boarding team, then manned by Patrol Coastal Crew INDIA, attempted a boarding operation on a dhow approaching KAAOT. When the seven-man team pulled alongside, an explosion rocked both the RHIB and dhow. The list of casualties included 27-year-old U.S. Navy Petty Officer First Class Michael Pernaselli, 28-year-old Petty Officer Second Class Christopher Watts, and 24-year-old Coast Guardsman Petty Officer Third Class Nathan Bruckenthal. Three other sailors were injured in the blast, including 23-year-old Coast Guardsman BM3 Joseph Ruggiero. Although it occurred well before any of us joined the crews, this suicide attack offers a blunt reminder of the inherent dangers in this line of work. For the Coast Guard, this marked the first time one of their own died in action since the Vietnam War. As members of the INDIA crew, every day we wore hats inscribed with three stars and that horrific date to both honor and reinforce the lessons learned on that fateful day.

It was later discovered the attack was carried out by none other than the Jordanian, Abu-Musab al-Zarqawi. Many remember al-Zarqawi for his brutal series of attacks, bombings, and beheadings after he pledged allegiance to Al-Qaeda in 2004. Until his death on June 7, 2006, he led his Al-Qaeda in Iraq brand on a campaign of carnage and bloodshed. Although it took years and tremendous effort on the part of coalition forces, his life ended quite suddenly when two 500-pound bombs landed on his house. Yet, to me, his legacy will always be that attack on crew INDIA and the beheading of Nick Berg.

I first found out about Nick Berg when I graduated from the Naval Academy and moved to San Diego to assume the title of Ordnance Officer on the *USS Bunker Hill*. While looking for a place to live, I visited my brother's friend who had recently departed the same ship I'd be joining. Another Annapolis graduate, Todd was a carefree joker with a hard edge and a natural talent to lead people, despite irritating higher-ups. He was also a talker who spread ideas at a lightning pace like Vince Vaughn in the *Wedding Crashers*. When I met with this tall, handsome Pennsylvanian, he was deadly serious. "I need to show you something," he said almost as soon as I got through the door. "Everyone needs to see this video at least once," he remarked. The video clip was none other than Nick Berg being beheaded by al-Zarqawi.

Forgoing graphic details, what I'll say is that when movies like *Gladiator* or *The Last Samurai* depict a decapitation, it is clean, crisp, and almost conveys a sense of honor to a crude affair. What I saw was evil incarnate. A hacking. This was pure hatred packed in thirty seconds of footage. Now graduated from the pristine grounds of Annapolis, it was crystal clear that this is what us graduates were up against. Nick Berg, a Jewish-American businessman, went to Iraq to carry out contract work. Only 26 years old, he was now another lost youth to the plague al-Zarqawi unleashed. It is said that his death was in retaliation for the Abu Ghraib abuse scandal; however, a killing this horrific cannot be justified. For those who sought to shift responsibility or to seek a greater understanding of the violent act, beneath it all was a truth that there is an evil that exists which cannot be reconciled with words, appeasement, or disengagement. For them, 500-lb bombs do the trick.

Along with the IS was an interpreter. Like many folks supporting GWOT efforts, he was a contractor. We owned neither of them; rather, they were sent from the headquarters on ABOT to serve a supporting role. This contractor was an Arab who also spoke Farsi, the common language in Iran. We worked with him multiple times, but I never really got the opportunity to speak with him about anything other than the business. This had more to do with the fact that I had other concerns. When we spotted a dhow on the horizon, we immediately quickened the pace of the inboard-operated boat. A few minutes later, we made out the silhouettes of fishermen halting work to wave us on. Words weren't needed as we pulled alongside the dhow. Accustomed to frequent boardings, the master motioned us to join him on the deck of his weather-beaten fishing vessel.

In VBSS School, we are taught the textbook method for boarding a vessel. A considerable portion of the instruction involves the use of expensive caving ladders and a device called the hook and pole. Like many classroom inventions, this process is the less frequently used difficult approach. The dhows we boarded blessed us with ample access in the form of tractor and car tires, so it was relatively easy to find places for our hands and feet. Surrounding the port and starboard sides of the dhows, we easily, if not awkwardly, could climb quickly onto the decks to interact with locals. Where the caving ladder proves vital is in instances when a vessel either doesn't want to be boarded or lacks proper holds.

As far as boardings are concerned, my team and I were trained in non-compliant boardings. Non-compliant means exactly that. It can be situations where the vessel's crew have not assisted a team in the boarding process by not coming to a complete stop, or altering course against the team's wishes, or, in some cases, have used shards of broken glass and other obstacles to deny access. While trained to conduct these worst-case scenarios, our rules of engagement prevented us from carrying out those risky missions. Instead, skilled operators from the Special Forces and Marine Corps dealt with them.

When I gave the word, we grabbed onto the vessel's rubber façade and helped each other onto the wooden deck. The members of the fishing crew were already congregated at the stern. The day's scorching sun had left its mark. They were ragged, tired, and obviously malnourished. As members of our team finalized their status reports, I was struck by the sense of awe and wonder my team gave off. American servicemen can be intimidating. In the U.S., the average height of males is 5 foot 9 and a half; however, the average height of Middle Easterners hovers at around 5 foot 5. It is an understatement to say we simply towered over these men. At 210 pounds, I dwarfed the master by at least 60 pounds, perhaps even more. When television stations show video clips of returning servicemen cupping newborns in their arms, civilians see the softer side of the uniform; yet, on this dhow in the middle of the Northern Arabian Gulf, we must have come off as superhuman instruments of American greatness...Or imperialism.

Unlike most dhow crews who came from India and Pakistan, this crew was mostly of Iraqi descent. They came from Al-Faw, a tiny waterway next to Iran. Being disputed territory, living there gives true meaning to the phrase "rock and a hard place." The history of the residents on the Al-Faw Peninsula is one of pain and suffering. It saw armed conflict during WWI, but much of the devastation occurred during the eight-year Iran-Iraq war in the 80s and the Gulf War in the early 90s. Al-Faw, at the head of Shatt Al-Arab, is a strategic location viewed as important by Iraq, Iran, and the United States. In 1986 the Iranians led a sweeping surprise attack that culminated in the occupation of the region. With the use of roughly 100,000 Republican Guard troops, artillery, airstrikes, and chemical weapons, the Iraqis gradually rolled back

Iranian gains. Later celebrated by Saddam as a national holiday, the battles that took place in and around Al-Faw were nothing less than WWI-style scorched earth campaigns highlighted by bloody stalemates across unforgiving marshes. It is estimated that over 50,000 Iraqis perished in the First Battle of Al-Faw, while Iranian losses amounted to a mere fraction of that total. Violence returned during the Gulf War when the peninsula's defensive installations faced heavy bombing by Allied Forces. This time, fighting was not about territory but served as part of the broader Allied effort to close Iraqi export capabilities to bring Saddam's government to its knees and push out occupying forces from Kuwait. Once again, Al-Faw proved vital during Operation Iraqi Freedom (OIF) when Coalition Forces quickly removed enemy forces to secure the waterway and Iraq's oil-laden lifelines to the global marketplace.

While this crew lacked education from a Western point-of-view, they bore intellect from experiencing seeing seeds of hate sown, worn daily as wrinkled brows, exhausted faces, and beliefs turned cynical by perpetual disappointment. Despite this, they referred to me as "my friend." If you spend time in the Middle East, you'll quickly discover that everyone is everybody's friend.

We went down the list of required questions: Number and nationality of crew, last port, next port, etc. At one point, Saddam asked bluntly, "Why is oil so expensive?" No one was prepared for questions off the script. Thus, company lines flowed about how the Iraqi government was working with locals to provide low-cost oil for fishermen like himself and that some programs existed to help him. Typical silver-tongued bullshit. The master momentarily paused, and then, with a smirk, said, "But you have oil, you can give us oil too that you get from Iraq. Isn't that why you are here?" We told him that we don't get oil from Iraq, which was true. However, trying to explain the dynamics of international commodities markets is not easy. At the end of the day, oil is oil regardless of origin, and more of it means a lower price minus the speculation aspect. We chatted about democracy, capitalism, and how Iraqis are better without Saddam.

At this point, his smile widened. "Saddam was bad, yes, but he gave us oil. I didn't have to deal with Iranians. He gave fuel for free. I am glad that he is gone, but you Americans have all the power, money, and military. Why don't you give us fuel?" Falling back into coalition talking points, we reiterated that the Iraqi Government is in charge and working to fix issues. The master, now feeling ready to solve the world's problems, asked us if we wanted some tea. After initially refusing, not because I feared strychnine poisoning, but because it was 110 degrees outside, I acquiesced, but I don't think I drank but one sip. He alluded to the Iraqi Government lacking power and control, suggesting Americans were the only ones with true clout. The rest of the VBSS team looked on and held back agreement. One did chuckle a bit before heading to the bow for a cigarette.

We tried to reassure him that good things would happen; kind of like politicians do when they claim they're going to finally fix education or whatever crisis they created. I can't say I believed it, but I sure knew he didn't. For me, it was hard to speculate on the future. Is another insurgency going to topple the fragile democracy? Would violence subside enough to usher in stability? Can the Middle East ever accept modernity and capitalism? And if it did, would that solve anything? Speculations rest on hope, and to me, hope isn't a plan. Before we left, a member of Saddam's crew requested gloves that could help with handling fishing lines. We flipped him a pair and a pack of smokes. He beamed and gave us a thumbs-up. Just like prison, a pack of Marlboro Reds is better than a wad of fifties.

Returning to the ship, I rushed to the pilothouse to debrief our Commanding Officer (CO). The debrief was short and sweet. This was his second deployment with the PCs and his experience gave him a calmness. That's not to say he was immune to frustrations and bouts of doubt, but there was little that surprised him. When I told my CO the conversation, he shrugged. It was clear we hadn't broken new ground in American - Iraqi relations.

If experience makes us wiser, it can also leave us jaded or at least with lowered expectations. When I was a young boy, I looked at the world with wide eyes and wonderment. Now, my experience suggests that the world has far too much evil and not nearly enough good. I hope and pray this isn't true, but this perception slowly erodes idealism and leaves me desiring simple, realistic solutions.

I relayed my conversation with Saddam to the Chaplain and his response was far better than any textbook, *Foreign Affairs* article, or university lecture.

"Mark," he said, "one thing you have to understand is that the Middle East, in general, and Iraq, in particular, are tribal societies. They believe in the Big Man. The Big Man takes control and has all the wealth and power. Because of his strength, other members of the tribe must defer to him. In return, the Big Man bestows blessings on members of the tribe. He remains the true controller of the tribe until bested."

I was struck by both the simplicity and complexity of this message. On one level, the idea of a "Big Man" having power and Arabs looking to him for blessings doesn't come off as all that illuminating. Oh, thanks for telling me that the Middle East is tribal. I'm

sure I read that a thousand times. However, when taken in a broader context, the "Big Man" theory can explain a great deal. It seemed that American theory rested on the assumption that tribal sensibilities can and should give way to the natural desire for freedom and democracy. When things got bloody and insurgencies and sectarian violence sought to derail the Coalition's territorial, cultural, and societal gains, American efforts remained affixed to idealistic assumptions. Even in 2006, the narrative went like this: if we can keep the oil and water flowing, lights on, and reduce violence, then money will pour into Iraq and the people will be happy. Americans grew disappointed with what seemed to be a lazy society that couldn't care less about all the hard work the U.S. and Coalition Forces expended daily. The truth is that we went to war under naïve assumptions, using flawed evidence, and accepting overly optimistic appraisals concerning our ability to win. We wanted regime change without imagining a realistic outcome. We failed to understand the culture and what winning even meant.

Let's be clear - war is a learning process. Mistakes were made because our leaders are not infallible. Every conflict leads to new discoveries that are relevant to the war effort and can, in some instances, be applied to future ones. Throughout the Iraq War, countless pundits pointed fingers at the Bush Administration and war leaders in response to failures on the ground or meek gains coming at a high cost in human and financial capital. Just as war is a learning process, it is also complex and resides in the realm of uncertainty. Therefore, it is understandable that it would take time to identify the right approaches. That wasn't what many people wanted to hear. But, then again, I don't know how many of those people led a platoon, a company, commanded a vessel, or conducted night missions over enemy territory. Still, that doesn't excuse the failures from the start. Perhaps understanding the true challenge would've convinced decision-makers to select another tyrant to kick the piss out of. Maybe, cultural understanding would have developed an entirely different strategy should the temptation of war prove too difficult to resist.

As much as America chafed at the idea, we were the "Big Man" who provided the security, financing, gloves, and even Marlboros. Now, in our discussions with the master, we tried to assure him that the Iraqi Government was now the tribal leader. However, our presence, look, and demeanor told another story. What could the U.S. do to change this reality?

Early in the PC deployment on *USS Typhoon*, we began integrating efforts with Iraqi patrol boats from the ICDF. The Iraqis were expected to cover certain areas around the oil terminals. For instance, the U.S. might be tasked with the south, and Iraqis the north. The primary goal was to get their skin in the game. Until everyone feels the pain and success of a "joint" effort, real change is hard to visualize. If Iraqis were unwilling to take some ownership when they had the Americans playing the heavy, it's unlikely they ever would. One day, my ship was monitoring the eastern portion surrounding an oil terminal. As it frequently occurred, a small fishing dhow entered the Iraqi exclusion area. Headquarters sent word that the Iraqi boats needed to turn the vessel outbound. After about five minutes, they directed us to enter the Iraqi zone and complete the task for the Iraqis. The radio operator on ABOT alluded to an engineering casualty preventing both boats from executing the routine action. The math simply didn't add up. One casualty prevents one boat from accomplishing the task, not two. My boss was irate; "Why are they even here, we cannot keep doing their work for them. At some point this fuckin' baby-sitting needs to end." Within ten minutes, we pushed the vessel out and trekked back to our zone. This seemed to happen continuously over the next few weeks. Plus, whenever the weather got a bit choppy, the Iraqi boats would disappear back to their base.

Finally, a change occurred. Another fishing vessel entered the exclusion zone and the Iraqis responded just as they did in the past. But this time, we got no order to assist. Meanwhile, the dhow was having a nice time getting big catches closer to the terminals. Abruptly, the dhow's crew started frantically dragging in their nets and prepared to get underway. A thousand or so yards away, two bows pierced through the water giving off massive wakes. The Iraqis pushed their boats at max speed right at the dhow. Thinking a collision was a certainty, our crew readied to respond to the upcoming emergency. Yet, no emergency came. Instead, the dhow fired up its diesels and got out of Dodge. The Iraqis, feeling the adrenaline rush, gave chase until the dhow stopped looking back, should its crew be turned into pillars of salt. It was apparent that the Coalition had had enough; the Iraqis would take the torch. I'm sure that there were plenty of phone calls leading to this small victory for Iraqi self-sufficiency. Events like this renewed my hope for future success and gave the Iraqis a small triumph.

Every three weeks, barges brought workers from Al-Faw to the terminals. For security reasons, PC and U.S. Coast Guard crews used VBSS personnel to board and check these barges out prior to them entering the exclusion zones. My team accomplished a half-dozen of these boardings. Every time we would moor up to ABOT, meet with reservists, usually from Ohio, and conduct a safety brief. That day, the reservists brought three or four Iraqi Marines (IM) with them. Just like Saddam and his crew, these were tiny men only differing in their donning of bright orange Kapoks and mishandling of AK-47s. They almost looked like little kids in a pool with floaties waving a toy gun around. Making our transit to the barge, I soon grew wise to the fact that these guys couldn't even swim. Midway through the transit, all the IMs huddled together like homeless men around a barrel fire. Their AK-47s swung in all directions prompting my team members to offer some pointed corrections.

The reservists looked exasperated and almost defeated, but to their credit, they pressed on, explaining the error of the IMs ways. The IMs commenced verifying each worker's documents and searching every individual. The process was agonizingly slow, so we offered helping hands. A large reservist with massive arms clutching an outdated M-16 rifle and probably the biggest grenade launcher ever made stopped us; "They need to do this. We're going to let you guys go in a few minutes and we'll ride the barge to the terminal." There it was: let them do their job and truly learn, Americans take a back seat and enjoy the show.

In the latter months of my deployment, we began talking to fishermen about radio channels they could monitor to find out about weather and other issues that could help them stay safe. We always pushed the credit to the ICDF to demonstrate that a legitimate government and institutions stood ready to aid them. At first the fishermen gave a passing interest, but eventually, channels were monitored by locals. This marked an important, albeit small, transformation. It appeared that the Iraqi Government was taking its rightful place as the "Big Man" for its people.

In 2012, PBS aired a documentary, *World Peace...and Other 4th Grade Achievements*. The documentary follows schoolteacher John Hunter, and his classroom invention called the World Peace Game. The goal for these 4th grade participants is to achieve world peace. Realists might already deride this game as a foolish exercise in liberal idealism; however, watching the documentary, I came to see this as true learning. This was not about No Child Left Behind, test scores, or evaluation metrics, but rather tackling complex real-world problems. All aspects of this game were over the top. The entire geopolitical simulation was made of three physical levels. One level or board showed the territories in the game, another the air, and a third space. I cannot recall if an undersea portion was in the works, but the point is that this was visually complex.

In my favorite game, *Risk*, I never worried about rebellions, droughts, or economic downturns, just nabbing Siam. This game, though, had all that and more. Students drew responsibilities at the start of the game. For instance, one player might become president of a country and the other two ministers of the defense and the treasury. Another player leads the World Bank while another is a reviled arms dealer. Everyone has a unique role to carry out in this game. Truly exceptional is that Hunter assigns one of them to be something of a mayhem-creator. Just like the Mayhem insurance commercials, this student creates problems on the board. Selecting from a list of events, the mayhem-creator forces students to peacefully address complex problems. Just like in the real world, peace isn't always the byproduct. The documentary highlighted an instance a country chose to duke it out with another. A roll of the dice delivered a nasty blow to the invader. The country's leader was upset at the result and Hunter issued a punishment: Write a letter to the families of the dead soldiers. In this game, war is treated seriously. The rules aren't written to prevent that outcome; instead, students are taught to seek alternative solutions before marching gung-ho off to conflict.

I find it ironic that children, in their wide-eyed wonderment, can take more time to consider the costs of war than adults sometimes do. Our experience in leading us to seek realistic solutions usually translates into exercises of raw power. The seething demand for collective revenge after 9-11 was palpable. CNN's sensationalism and "Shock and Awe" captivated the nation. As the world's policemen, Americans have grown so accustomed to fighting everyone's battles that the human element is lost. Besides, with so few combatants fighting, what does the public risk in the rush to war? America is divorced from the realities of combat. Blowback hits those on the frontlines. People say, "support the troops" and "thank you for your service." Save the thanks and attempts to connect. Just hold politicians accountable. Instead of living in an ideological echo chamber, have the guts to vote out your preferred party's dimwit even if it means potentially losing control over Congress. Elect people who will ask tough questions and not treat soldiers like pieces on a *Risk* board. Vote the bastards out is a bipartisan solution we should get behind.

Still, there is no panacea; temporary peace rests on the shoulders of "Big Men." War flows through the arteries of history. However, that doesn't mean we can't demand better. Even if the Iraqi Government accumulates the strength it needs to provide for its people, there will always be a place for "Big Men." Across the globe, some leaders will take power and commit unspeakable acts. Left unchecked, humanity will pay the price for their ambitions. Thus, "Big Men" are needed to pursue justice and stand guard for the weak. The challenge is finding leaders with the moral character to make the tough calls on behalf of Americans and not special interests, self-aggrandizement, or party cohesion.

On one hazy day, we boarded a Kuwaiti dhow fishing near the terminals. With information gathered, I readied the team to depart. My gloved hand grasped the radio as I prepared to give a status report to my CO. Scanning the horizon, I spotted two Iranian speedboats off *USS Typhoon's* starboard bow and quarter. Before I could even fire a warning to my CO, he barked over the radio, "Get the hell back to the ship, now." All eight of us jumped into the boat and jetted back to safety. Our interpreter, being the only Farsi speaker, issued warnings over the bridge-to-bridge radio. Silence. We ordered him to issue a higher-level warning. Silence. Then the radio thundered, "Go fuck yourself." Hearing such a bold pronouncement sent chills up my spine. All I kept thinking to myself was how I didn't want to get rolled up like that British crew. My team locked and loaded stayed in the RHIB alongside the ship. Our CO, who'd already ordered general quarters, surveyed his gun crews hoping he was not about to start WWIII. The Mexican standoff continued for several minutes. Then our white horse arrived; *USS Chinook* at max speed drove straight at the speedboats. Like bullies do when confronted with a determined foe, the Iranians booked it outbound. We later determined that the Iranians sought to harass the Kuwaiti dhow as they had done countless times before. The dhow sat right next to us the entire time as if the crew knew we were their key to salvation.

You see, even if Iraq can become the "Big Man," they still need strong friends to help them handle the bullies of the world. When people talk about disengagement and isolationism, it's doubtful they contemplate the implications. If America isn't around to protect the vulnerable, who will? Where's the queue of volunteers? Europe? Don't make me laugh. America isn't perfect and makes plenty of foolish moves, but we do a lot of things right, too. There's an old naval maxim that states, "Rank has its privileges, rank has its responsibilities." As long as Americans want to be seen as great and mighty, we have to continue to maintain the kind of military that can keep the wolves at bay and stop "Big Men" from doing evil. Although many can claim America has abused its power, it's important to remember that leaders will always falter, mistakes will always occur, and power is not permanent. Responses to errors and failings are crucial to right the ship.

I wish it ended on that happy note. Yesterday's insurgents have become today's tyrants. Across the Fertile Crescent, the Islamic State (ISIS) captured swaths of territory. The results were grim. Tales of beheadings, firing squads, and general carnage gripped the headlines. Syria's civil war shows no signs of ever truly ending. Those who clamored for an American exit from "their unjust war" routinely rail against the plight of innocent refugees and besieged communities. Empathy compels them to seek American engagement to un-fuck the mess. The truth is that when a vacuum exists, something will fill it. A rushed drawdown and war-weary America provided a perfect avenue for marginalized and opportunistic factions to seize power. Maybe it would have happened anyway. Perhaps "The Surge" only delayed an inevitable un-civil war from Damascus to Baghdad.

While it'd be easier to believe America did all it could, I cannot help but consider all the lives lost delivering Iraqis a chance at something resembling freedom. What about the Army .50 cal gunner who deployed three times to "The Shit or Sandbox" as he calls it? If this was all inevitable, why'd he have to see his friends get mentally broken or blown up? What was the point? Hell, if we're to believe good can no longer best evil, then we've reached the end of the line for American greatness. I might be naïve, but I can't summon the level of cynicism to adopt that attitude. For the cynics, in the end, you might be right about all of it. Right about our not being able to change anything, fix anything, or help anything. Me, I'll hold firm to my childish opinion that the world still needs that "Big Man." Unless there are any other takers, the downtrodden will continue to seek out the stars and stripes as their best prospect for relief from hellish circumstances. Maligned people look to America. We must set an example.

The U.S.-Iraq relationship could have been a more symbiotic one. Sure, we taught them how to protect themselves, but neither one of us learned much from the other. As my naval adventures fade in memory, a whisper still asks what Americans learned. Despite public sentiment, some twenty years later, dramatically shifting in opposition to invading Iraq in the first place, I'm not surprised we gave politicians a pass. Liberal or conservative and Republican or Democrat, none faced repercussions.

Lack of accountability is a bipartisan issue too. Matters of war demand the highest standard. President Dwight D. Eisenhower, of course, knew this. In the aim of considering the serious costs of war and seeking the human element behind the war, he warned us that:

Every gun that is made, every warship launched, every rocket fired signifies, in the final sense, a theft from those who hunger and are not fed, those who are cold and are not clothed. This world in arms is not spending money alone. It is spending the sweat of its laborers, the genius of its scientists, the hopes of its children. This is not a way of life at all in any true sense. Under the clouds of war, it is humanity hanging on a cross of iron.

Dwight D. Eisenhower

Epilogue

As a former military officer, I've often been asked my opinion on the situation the nonsense swirling about in the insane realm of geopolitics. This book seeks to answer the mail. My sincere hope is that beyond a bevy of trivia you'll walk away with a few tools to sift through the oftentimes absurd situations humanity stumbles into. On the off chance these themes were buried beneath layers of bloviating and run-ons, I'll reinforce them:

Luck is fleeting. Though it aided Cold War adversaries in 1983, the risks of miscalculation are severe when mutual enmity stifles dialogue.

Snakes must be dealt with seriously and swiftly. Short-sighted approaches based on both arrogance and ignorance lead to ruin when others are playing chess in a world of checkers.

Isolation and ideology are nasty bedfellows. I haven't lived long enough to meet a hermit with a healthy worldview. In truth, they mostly creep me out.

Engagement matters. From cola to shows about oil barons, soft power has real power. Showing an alternative can create one. Even dreadful K-Pop can nudge the needle.

Differences needn't define us. Instead find unique ways to engage with the weirdos of the world. Besides, they probably think you're an oddity too.

When things are out of focus, keep perspective. It *really* could be worse.

When you travel outside your comfort zone you realize how grateful you should be. Bitterness and scorn replicates quicker than thankfulness. So be thankful.

Truth lies in the nuances. Nothing is as simple as the headlines make it. Understanding the backstory is the best route to the full one.

People who've been wronged have a long memory. For most, past traumas persist in the present. Therefore, understanding the historical context is vital.

We are all human beings, perfectly imperfect, and doing our best. Bullshit, buzzwords, pundits, and agendas are the real enemies.

References

LIVING ON THE EDGE: ABLE ARCHER 83

1983: The Brink of Apocalypse, a television documentary broadcast on Channel 5 (5 January 2008).

Andrew, C., & Gordievsky, O., eds. (1991). *Instructions from the Centre: Top Secret Files on KGB Foreign Operations, 1975-85*. London: Hodder & Stoughton.

Andrew, C., & Gordievsky, O. (1991). *KGB: The Inside Story of Its Foreign Operations from Lenin to Gorbachev*. New York, NY: Harper Perennial.

Arnav, M. (2009). *When truth is stranger than fiction: The Able Archer incident*. Cold War History, 9(1), 111-133.

Atomic Heritage Foundation. (2018, June 15). Nuclear Close Calls: Able Archer 83. From https://www.atomicheritage.org/history/nuclear-close-calls-able-archer-83.

Badham, J. (1983). WarGames. United Artists.

Bonderud, Doug. (2017, May 24). From Music to Missile Defense: The Very Interesting Life of Jeff Baxter. Now. From https://now.northropgrumman.com/from-music-to-missile-defense-the-very-interesting-life-of-jeff-baxter/

Cameron, J. (1984). The Terminator. Orion Pictures.

Fischer, B. (2012). Anglo-American Intelligence and the Soviet
War Scare: The Untold

Story. *Intelligence and National Security, 27*(1), 79.

Gordievsky, O. (1995). *Next Stop Execution.* London: Macmillan

Jones, N., & Scoblic, J. (2017, April 13). The Week the World
Almost Ended. Slate. From https://slate.com/news-and-
politics/2017/06/able-archer-almost-started-a-nuclear-
war-with-russia-in-1983.html

National Security Archive. Able Archer Sourcebook. From
https://nsarchive.gwu.edu/project/able-archer-83-
sourcebook

Olson, M. (2018, July 20). *Living on the edge: SDI, Able Archer
and America's Insurance Policy*. Missile Defense Review.
From https://missiledefensereview.org/2018/07/20/living-
on-the-edge-sdi-able-archer-and-americas-insurance-
policy/.

President's Foreign Intelligence Advisory Board (1990). The
Soviet "War Scare." From https://www.archives.gov/files/
declassification/iscap/pdf/2013-015-doc1.pdf

Reagan, R. (1990). *An American Life*. New York: Simon and
Schuster, 1990.

Rhodes, R. (2007). *Arsenals of Folly*. New York: Alfred A. Knopf.

Scott, L. (2011). Intelligence and the Risk of Nuclear War:
Able Archer-83 Revisited. *Intelligence and National
Security, 26*(6), 759-760.

CHECKMATE! RUSSIA'S ART OF THE LONG GAME

Beehner, L. (2005, July 26). *ASIA: U.S. Military Bases in Central Asia*. Council on Foreign Relations. https://www.cfr.org/backgrounder/asia-us-military-bases-central-asia.

Bodie, W. (1993, March 18). Moscow's "Near Abroad": Security Policy in Post-Soviet Europe. *National Defense University*, June 1993.

Boulegue, M., & Polyakova, A. (2021, January 29). *The Evolution of Russian Hybrid Warfare: Executive Summary*. Center for European Policy Analysis. From https://cepa.org/the-evolution-of-russian-hybrid-warfare-introduction/.

Chivvis, C. (2017, March 22). *Understanding Russian "Hybrid Warfare" And What Can Be Done About It*. RAND Corporation.

Ciochină, S., & Schwartz, R. (2015, December 1). *Transnistria's explosive inheritance from the Soviet era*. Deutsche Welle. From https://www.dw.com/en/transnistrias-explosive-inheritance-from-the-soviet-era/a-18886862.

Cojocaru, Natalia (2006). Nationalism and identity in Transnistria. *Innovation: The European Journal of Social Science Research*, 19(3-4), 261–272. From https://www.tandfonline.com/doi/abs/10.1080/13511610601029813.

Collective Security Treaty Organization. (2021, November 21). In *Wikipedia*. From https://en.wikipedia.org/wiki/Collective_Security_Treaty_Organization.

Commonwealth of Independent States. (2021, November 16). In *Wikipedia*. From https://en.wikipedia.org/wiki/Commonwealth_of_Independent_States.

Crowther, W. (1997). Moldova: caught between nation and empire. In I. Bremmer, R. Tara (Eds.), *New States, new politics: building the post-Soviet nations*. New York: Cambridge University Press.

CSTO Structure. (n.d.). Collective Security Treaty Organization. From https://en.odkb-csto.org/structure/.

Dulgher, Maria (2020, August 9). *The Russian ammunition depot from Cobasna discussed against the backdrop of the Beirut explosion*. Moldova.org. From https://www.moldova.org/en/the-russian-ammunition-depot-from-cobasna-discussed-against-the-backdrop-of-the-beirut-explosion/.

Edwards, J. (2018, January 23). *Garry Kasparov told us what it's like to live in fear of being assassinated by Putin*. Business Insider. From https://www.businessinsider.com/garry-kasparov-fear-of-being-assassinated-by-putin-2018-1.

Enlargement of NATO. (2021, November 21). In *Wikipedia*. From https://en.wikipedia.org/wiki/Enlargement_of_NATO.

Eurasian Economic Union. (2021, November 16). In *Wikipedia*. From https://en.wikipedia.org/wiki/Eurasian_Economic_Union.

Eurasian Economic Union to have common currency in 5-10 years. (2014, July 25). TASS Russian News Agency. From https://tass.com/economy/742323.

Europe: Frozen conflicts. (2008, November 19). The Economist. From https://www.economist.com/news/2008/11/19/ frozen-conflicts.

Farchy, J. (2014, December 23). *Eurasian unity under strain even as bloc expands.* The Financial Times.

Forbrig, J. (2014, February 28). *Will Ukraine's Crimea region be Europe's next 'frozen' conflict?* CNN.   From https:// edition.cnn.com/2014/02/27/opinion/ukraine-crimea- russia/.

Gogol, Nikolai. (2020). *The Overcoat and Other Stories.* Compass Circle.

Gracia, E., Mackey, W., Roscoe, J., & Welt, C. (2018, February 22). *Eurasian Economic Union.* Congressional Research Service.

Grove, T., & Strobel, W. (2014, July 29). *Special Report: Where Ukraine's separatists get their weapons.* Reuters. From https://www.reuters.com/article/us-ukraine-crisis-arms- specialreport/special-report-where-ukraines-separatists- get-their-weapons-idUSKBN0FY0UA20140729.

Haslett, C. (2019, February 26). *Mitt Romney finally gets credit years later for his warnings on Russia.* ABC News. From https://abcnews.go.com/Politics/years-mitt-romney- finally-credit-warnings-russia/story?id=61330530.

Hill, F. (2015, February 24). *This is what Putin really wants.* Brookings. Retrieved October 29, 2021, from https://www. brookings.edu/opinions/this-is-what-putin-really-wants/.

Hollis, D. (2008, January 6). *Cyberwar case study: Georgia 2008*. Cyberwar Case Study: Georgia 2008 | Small Wars Journal. Retrieved October 29, 2021, from https://smallwarsjournal.com/jrnl/art/cyberwar-case-study-georgia-2008.

How did chess become so popular in Russia?. (n.d.). Russian National Tourist Office. From https://www.visitrussia.org.uk/blog/How%20did%20chess%20become%20so%20popular%20in%20Russia%3F/.

Humphries, R. (2001, October 8). *Transnistria: relic of a bygone era*. The Japan Times.

Ingle, S. (2021, April 30). *Garry Kasparov: 'Why become a martyr? I can do much more outside Russia'*. The Guardian. From https://www.theguardian.com/sport/2021/apr/30/garry-kasparov-interview-chess-vladimir-putin-russia.

Kaminski, M. (2013, July 18). *Notable & Quotable: The Man Vladimir Putin Fears Most*. The Wallstreet Journal. From https://www.wsj.com/articles/SB10001424127887323309404578614210222799482.

Klein, M. (2019). *Russia's Military Policy in the Post-Soviet Space*. SWP Research Paper. From https://www.swp-berlin.org/10.18449/2019RP01/.

Kofman, M. (2016, March 11). *Russian Hybrid Warfare and Other Dar Arts*. War on the Rocks. From https://warontherocks.com/2016/03/russian-hybrid-warfare-and-other-dark-arts/.

Kofman, M. (2018, August 17). *The August War, Ten Years on: A retrospective on the Russo-Georgian War*. War on the Rocks. Retrieved October 29, 2021, from https://warontherocks.com/2018/08/the-august-war-ten-years-on-a-retrospective-on-the-russo-georgian-war/.

Kofman, M., Migacheva, K., Nichiporuk, B., Radin, A., Tkacheva, O., & Oberholtzer, J. (2017). *Lessons from Russia's Operations in Crimea and Eastern Ukraine.* Santa Monica: RAND Corporation.

Kubicek, P. (1999). Russian Foreign Policy and the West. *Political Science Quarterly, 114*(4), 547-568. From https://www.jstor.org/stable/2657783.

Kucera, J. (2014, June 17). *U.S. Formally Closes Its Kyrgyzstan Air Base.* Eurasianet. From https://eurasianet.org/us-formally-closes-its-kyrgyzstan-air-base.

LaGrone, S. (2019, March 18). *Russians use U.S. Navy's aegis ashore as excuse to deploy strategic bombers to Crimea.* USNI News. From https://news.usni.org/2019/03/18/russians-use-u-s-navys-aegis-ashore-excuse-deploy-strategic-bombers-crimea

Last U.S. plane leaves Uzbek base. (2005, November 21). BBC. From http://news.bbc.co.uk/2/hi/asia-pacific/4457844.stm.

Leprince-Ringuet, D. (2018, November 28). *How chess became a pawn in Russia's political war games.* WIRED UK. Retrieved October 29, 2021, from https://www.wired.co.uk/article/world-chess-championship-2018-london-carlsen-vs-caruana.

Lister, T., Ward, C., & Shukla, S. (2020, December 21). *Russian opposition leader Alexey Navalny dupes spy into revealing how he was poisoned.* CNN. From https://www.cnn.

com/2020/12/21/europe/russia-navalny-poisoning-underpants-ward/index.html.

"Little Green Men": a primer on Modern Russian Unconventional Warfare, Ukraine 2013-2014. The United States Army Special Operations Command. From https://www.jhuapl.edu/Content/documents/ARIS_LittleGreenMen.pdf.

Lowe, C., Tsvetkova, M., & Deutsch, A. (2018, March 14). *Secret trial shows risks of nerve agent theft in post-Soviet chaos: experts.* Reuters. From https://www.reuters.com/article/us-britain-russia-stockpiles/secret-trial-shows-risks-of-nerve-agent-theft-in-post-soviet-chaos-experts-idUSKCN1GQ2RH.

Mackinlay, J., & Cross, P. (2003). *Regional Peacekeepers, The Paradox of Russian Peacekeeping.* United Nations University Press: New York & Paris.

Mora, Antonio. (2014, March 3). *Interview with Mikheil Saakashvili.* Al Jazeera: Consider This. From http://america.aljazeera.com/watch/shows/consider-this/Consider-This-blog/2014/3/3/mikheilsaakashviliinterview.html.

Navalny 'poisoned': What are Novichok agents and what do they do? (2020, September 2). BBC News. From https://www.bbc.com/news/world-europe-43377698.

Necşuţu, M. (2020, August 18). *Beirut Blast Rattles Nerves in Moldova over Soviet-era Ammunition Depot.* Balkan Insight. From https://balkaninsight.com/2020/08/18/beirut-blast-rattles-nerves-in-moldova-over-soviet-era-ammunition-depot/.

Necşuţu, M. (2021, August 12). *Russia and Moldova agree to resume trade, destroy ammunition.* Balkan Insight. From https://balkaninsight.com/2021/08/12/russia-and-moldova-agree-to-resume-trade-destroy-ammunition/.

Neuman, S. (2018, May 24). *Yulia Skripal Says She And Father 'Lucky' To Survive Attack With Nerve Agent.* NPR. From https://www.npr.org/sections/thetwo-way/2018/05/24/613971900/yulia-skripal-says-she-and-father-lucky-to-survive-attack-with-nerve-agent.

Newman, J. (2021, September 12). *Socialist Realism: Stalin's Control of Art in the Soviet Union.* The Collector. From https://www.thecollector.com/soviet-realism-stalin-control/.

Nukus. (2021, November 21). In *Wikipedia.* From https://en.wikipedia.org/wiki/Nukus.

O'Reilly, K., & Higgins, N. (2008). The role of the Russian Federation in the Pridnestrovian conflict: an international humanitarian law perspective. *Irish Studies in International Affairs - Royal Irish Academy, 19,* 57-72.

Ramani, S. (2015, October 1). *Russia Offers to Support Tajikistan...But There's a Price.* The Diplomat. From https://thediplomat.com/2015/10/russia-supports-tajikistanfor-a-price/.

Rayfield, J. (2012, October 23). *Obama: The '80s called, they want their foreign policy back.* Salon. From https://www.salon.com/2012/10/23/obama_the_80s_called_they_want_their_foreign_policy_back/.

Republics of the Soviet Union. (2021, November 2). In *Wikipedia*. From https://en.wikipedia.org/wiki/Republics_of_the_Soviet_Union.

Russia defends "peacekeepers" the new Moldovan president wants out. (2020, December 7). Polygraph.info. https://www.polygraph.info/a/russia-defends-peacekeepers-the-new-moldovan-president-wants-out/30984597.html.

Russian arms depots in Transnistria most dangerous to Ukraine, Ambassador Pyrozhkov says. (2013, December 11). Ukrinform. From https://www.ukrinform.net/rubric-polytics/1574485-russian_arms_depots_in_transnistria_most_dangerous_to_ukraine_ambassador_pyrozhkov_says_312778.html.

Russian spy: What happened to Sergei and Yulia Skripal? (2018, September 27). CNN. From https://www.bbc.com/news/uk-43643025.

Russia responsible for Navalny poisoning, rights experts say. (2021, March 1). United Nations News. From https://news.un.org/en/story/2021/03/1086012.

Russia's "Hybrid Aggression" against Georgia: The Use of Local and External Tools. (2021, September 21). Center for Strategic and International Studies. From https://www.csis.org/analysis/russias-hybrid-aggression-against-georgia-use-local-and-external-tools.

Russia wants CSTO security alliance to boost cooperation over Afghanistan. (2021, August 28). Reuters. From https://www.reuters.com/world/russia-wants-csto-security-alliance-boost-cooperation-over-afghanistan-2021-08-28/.

Shaishmelashvili, G. (2021, March 2). *Russia's Permanent War against Georgia*. Foreign Policy Research Institute.From https://www.fpri.org/article/2021/03/russia-permanent-war-georgia/.

Smith, G. (1994). *The Baltic States: The National Self-determination of Estonia, Latvia, and Lithuania*. New York: St. Martin's Press.

Starr, F., & Cornell, S. (2005). *The Baku-Tbilisi-Ceyhan Pipeline: Oil Window to the West*. Central Asia-Caucasus Institute & Silk Road Studies Program. From https://www.silkroadstudies.org/resources/pdf/Monographs/2005_01_MONO_Starr-   Cornell_BTC-Pipeline.pdf.

Sukhankin, S. (2017, November 14). Russia Pours More Military Hardware into 'Fortress Crimea'. *Eurasia Daily Monitor, 14*(147). From https://jamestown.org/program/ russia-pours-military-hardware-fortress-crimea/.

Transit Center at Manas. (2021, October 11). In *Wikipedia*. From https://en.wikipedia.org/wiki/Transit_Center_at_Manas.

Tubman, Harriet. (n.d.) Brainy Quote. From https://www.brainyquote.com/quotes/harriet_tubman_135776.

US asked to leave Uzbek air base. (2005, July 30). BBC. From http://news.bbc.co.uk/2/hi/asia-pacific/4731411.stm.

Weitz, R. (2018). *Assessing the Collective Security Treaty Organization: Capabilities and Vulnerabilities*. U.S. Army War College: Strategic Studies Institute. From https://publications.armywarcollege.edu/pubs/3661.pdf.

Welt, C. (2019, October 17). *Georgia: Background and U.S. Policy*. United States Library of Congress, Congressional Research Service.

Zoria, Y. (2017, July 21). *Ukraine helps Moldova regain control over border in Transnistrian region*. Euromaidan Press. From http://euromaidanpress.com/2017/07/21/ ukraine-helps-moldova- regain-control- over-border-in- transnistria-region/.

Beasley, W. (1987). *Japanese Imperialism, 1894–1945*. Oxford: Oxford University Press.

Beasley, W. (1995). *The Rise of Modern Japan: Political, Economic and Social Change Since 1850*. New York: St. Martin's Press.

Beauchamp, Z. (2016, September 9). *The textbook definition of unstable: why North Korea's newest nuclear test is scary*. Vox. From http://www.vox.com/2016/9/9/12863700/north-korea-nuclear-test-five-bad.

Bolt, J., & Van Zenden, J-L. (2014). The Maddison Project: collaborative research on historical national accounts. The Economic History Review, 67(3), 627-651. From https://www.jstor.org/stable/42921771.

CFC announces start of key resolve and Foal Eagle 2016. (2016, March 6). United States Forces Korea. From https://www.usfk.mil/Media/Press-Releases/Article/686836/cfc-announces-start-of-key-resolve- and-foal-eagle-2016/.

Chase, A. (2019, September 6). *Harvard and the making of the unabomber*. The Atlantic. From http://www.theatlantic.com/magazine/archive/2000/06/harvard-and-the-making-of-the-unabomber/378239/.

Cumings, B. (2005). *Korea's place in the sun: A modern history*. New York: W.W. Norton.

Diamond, J. (2017, August 17). *Flashback: Unabomber Publishes His 'Manifesto'*. Rolling Stone. From https://www.rollingstone.com/culture/culture-news/flashback-unabomber-publishes-his-manifesto-125449/.

Dimitrov, M. (2013). *Why Communism Did Not Collapse: Understanding Authoritarian Regime Resilience in Asia and Europe*. Cambridge University Press.

Duus, P. (2008). *The Abacus and the Sword*. University of California Press.

Eunpyoung J. (2015, March 23). *Why North Korea is so freaked out by US-Rok Drills*. The Diplomat. From http://thediplomat.com/2015/03/why-north-korea-is-so-freaked-out-by-us-rok-drills/.

Fisherman, M. (2016, January 6). *The single most important fact for understanding North Korea*. Vox. From https://www.vox.com/2016/1/6/10724334/north-korea-history.

Fleming, S. (2021, May 7). The Unabomber and the origins of anti-tech radicalism. *Journal of Political Ideologies*, 1-19. From https://www.tandfonline.com/doi/full/10.1080/13569317.2021.1921940.

French, P. (2014). *North Korea: State of Paranoia*. Zed Books.

Friedman, T. L. (2005). *The World Is Flat: A Brief History of the twenty-First Century*. New York: Farrar, Straus and Giroux.

Gady, F-S. (2015, March 3). *North Korea fires 2 ballistic missiles into sea*. The Diplomat. From https://thediplomat.com/2015/03/north-korea-fires-2-ballistic-missiles-into-sea/.

Gady, F-S. (2016, March 8). *Largest Ever US-Korea Military Drill Focuses on Striking North Korea's Leadership*. The Diplomat. From http://thediplomat.com/2016/03/largest-ever-us-korea-military-drill-focuses-on-striking-north-koreas-leadership/.

Gittings, J. (1998, September 1). *North Korea Fires Missile over Japan*. The Guardian. From https://www.theguardian.com/world/1998/sep/01/northkorea.

Hawkins, K. (2017, August 1). *What Is The Unabomber Manifesto? The Document Helped End The 'Manhunt' For Ted Kaczynski*. Bustle. From https://www.bustle.com/p/what-is-the-unabomber- manifesto-the-document-helped-end-the-manhunt-for-ted-kaczynski-73651.

Helgesen, G. (1991). Political Revolution in a Cultural Continuum: Preliminary Observations on the North Korean "Juche" Ideology with its Intrinsic Cult of Personality. *Asian Perspectives, 15* (1).

Hunt, L., Martin, T., Rosenwein, B., Po-chia Hsia, R., & Smith, B. (2008). *The Making of the West: Peoples and Cultures*. Bedford/St. Martin's.

Iyenaga, T. (1912). Japan's Annexation of Korea. *The Journal of Race Development, 3*(2), 201-202.

Jansen, Marius B. (2000). *The Making of Modern Japan*. Cambridge: Harvard University Press.

Keene, D. (2002). *Emperor of Japan: Meiji and His World, 1852–1912*. New York: Columbia University Press.

Kihl, Y., & Kim, H-N. (2006). *North Korea: The Politics of Regime Survival*. M.E. Sharpe.

Klingner, B. (2016, September 10). *Why China fears North Korea (and it's not all about nuclear weapons).* The National Interest. From http://nationalinterest.org/blog/the-buzz/why-china-fears-north-korea-its-not-all-about-nuclear-17661.

Kwak, T-H. (2009). *North Korea's Foreign Policy Under Kim Jong Il: New Perspectives.* Ashgate Publishing.

Lynn, H-G. (2007). *Bipolar Orders: The Two Koreas Since 1989.* Halifax: Fernwood Pub.

Masterson, J. (2020, July). *Fact sheets & briefs.* Chronology of U.S.-North Korean Nuclear and Missile Diplomacy | Arms Control Association. From https://www.armscontrol.org/factsheets/dprkchron.

McMorrow-Hernandez, J. (2016, March 29). *Paper money - whatever happened to North Korean counterfeit U.S. $100 bills?* CoinWeek. From http://www.coinweek.com/people-in-the-news/crime-and-fraud/paper-money-whatever-happened-north-korean-counterfeit-u-s-100-bills/.

Medalia, J. (2005, March 11). *Nuclear Weapons: Comprehensive Test Ban Treaty.* Congressional Record Service.

Miller, J. (2016, January 7). *What can US do about North Korea? Six options after 'hydrogen bomb' test.* Fox News. From http://www.foxnews.com/opinion/2016/01/07/what-can-us-do-about-north-korea-six-options-after-hydrogen-bomb-test.html.

North Korea's 'biggest' export - giant statues. (2016, February 16). BBC News. From http://www.bbc.com/news/magazine-35569277.

North Korea Nuclear H-bomb claims met by scepticism. (2016, January 6). BBC News. From http://www.bbc.com/news/world-asia-35241686.

North Korea Profile - Timeline. BBC News. (2019, April 26). From http://www.bbc.com/news/world-asia-pacific-15278612.

Pike, J. (n.d.). Foal Eagle. Global Security. From http://www.globalsecurity.org/military/ops/foal-eagle.htm.

Pilkington, E. (2009, September 14). *My Brother, the Unabomber*. The Guardian. From https://www.theguardian.com/world/2009/sep/15/my-brother-the-unabomber.

Seth, M. (2019). *A Concise History of Modern Korea: From the Late Nineteenth Century to the Present*. Rowman & Littlefield.

Smith, R., & Chace, Z. (2011, August 11). *Drug dealing, counterfeiting, smuggling: How North Korea makes money.* NPR. From http://www.npr.org/sections/money/2011/08/11/139556457/drug-dealing-counterfeiting-smuggling-how-north-korea-makes-money.

Straelen, H. van. (1952) *Yoshida Shoin, Forerunner of the Meiji Restoration*. Leiden: E.J. Brill.

Suh, Jae-Jung, ed. (2012). *Origins of North Korea's Juche: Colonialism, War, and Development*. Lanham: Lexington Books.

Szczepanski, K. (2019, October 17). *The First Sino-Japanese War*. ThoughtCo. From https://www.thoughtco.com/first-sino-japanese-war-1894-95-195784.

Tashiro, K. (1982). Foreign Relations During the Edo Period: Sakoku Reexamined. *Journal of Japanese Studies, 8*(2).

The annexation of Korea. (2010, August 29). The Japan Times. From http://www.japantimes.co.jp/opinion/2010/08/29/editorials/the-annexation-of-korea/.

The Unabomber. (2008). *The Unabomber Manifesto: Industrial Society and Its Future.* WingSpan Classics.

Thuras, D. (2014, August 25). *Monument to African dictator Laurent Kabila.* Atlas Obscura. From http://www.atlasobscura.com/places/monument-to-african-dictator-laurent-kabila.

Zhu, W. (2015). *Rereading Modern Chinese History.* Brill.

SOCIABLE SYRUP: WHEN PEPSI RULED THE WAVES

Carlson, P. (2009). *K Blow Top: A Cold War Comic Interlude Starring Nikita Khrushchev, America's Most Unlikely Tourist*. New York: Public Affairs.

Ewbank. A. (2018, January 12). When the Soviet Union Paid Pepsi in Warships. Atlas Obscura. From https://www.atlasobscura.com/articles/soviet-union-pepsi-ships

Glinton, S. (2014, March 10). *What Pepsi Can Teach Us About Soft (Drink) Power in Russia*. NPR: All Things Considered. From https://www.npr.org/sections/thesalt/2014/03/10/288570744/what-pepsi-can-teach-us-about-soft-drink-power-in-russia

Hand, B. (2020, September 25). When Pepsi owned the sixth-largest submarine navy. Sun Journal. From https://www.newbernsj.com/story/lifestyle/2020/09/25/pepsico-had-its-own-soviet-submarine-navy-1989/3533419001/

History.com Editors. (2009, November 13). *Richard Nixon and Nikita Khrushchev have a "kitchen debate."* History. From https://www.history.com/this-day-in-history/nixon-and-khrushchev-have-a-kitchen-debate.

Kitchen debate transcript. (1959, July 24). www.foia.cia.gov

Knock, M. (2009). Khrushchev in Iowa. *Humanities, 30*(4). From https://www.neh.gov/humanities/2009/julyaugust/statement/khrushchev-in-iowa

Lewis, Flora. (1989, May 10). *Foreign Affairs; Soviets Buy American*. The New York Times. From http://www. nytimes.com/1989/05/10/opinion/foreign-affairs-soviets-buy-american.html?mcubz=0

Ramirez, A. (1990, April 9). International Report; Pepsi will be Bartered for Ships and Vodka in Deal with Soviets. The New York Times. From http://www.nytimes. com/1990/04/09/business/international-report-pepsi-will-be-bartered-for-ships-vodka-deal-with-soviets. html?mcubz=0

Safire, W. (2009, July 24). The Cold War's Hot Kitchen. The New York Times.

Sokolniki Park (n.d.). In Wikipedia. Retrieved October 20, 2017, from https://en.wikipedia.org/wiki/Sokolniki_Park

Shepherd, R. (1959, July 26). *Debate Goes on TV over Soviet Protest*. The New York Times.

Stenberg, M. (2020, November 11). *How the CEO of Pepsi, by bartering battleships and vodka, negotiated Cold War diplomacy and brought his soda to the Soviet Union*. Business Insider. From https://www.businessinsider.com/ceo-of-pepsi-brought-soda-to-the-soviet-union-2020-11

Taubman, W. (2003). Khrushchev: The Man and His Era. New York: W.W. Norton & Co.

Wolf, A. (2020, July 15). *The Cola Fleet: How Pepsi once controlled the world's sixth-largest navy*. War is Boring. From https://warisboring.com/the-cola-fleet-how-pepsi-once-controlled-the-worlds-sixth-largest-navy/

HOOKED: ROMANIA'S CULT OF PERSONALITY

Albert, D. (2018, December 27). Ceausescu still most beloved President of Romania. Transylvania Now. From https://transylvanianow.com/ceausescu-still-most-beloved-president-of-romania/.

Ballon, M. (1996, May 20). Who Shot JR - to Romania? 'Dallas' Fans Flock to Ranch. The Christian Science Monitor. From https://www.csmonitor.com/1996/0520/052096.intl.intl.6.html.

Behr, E. (1991). *Kiss the hand you cannot bite: the rise and fall of the Ceauşescus*. London: Hamish Hamilton.

Brian, P. (2020, January 21). The Last Days Of Nicolae And Elena Ceausescu. The American Conservative. From https://www.theamericanconservative.com/articles/the-last-days-of-nicolae-and-elena-ceausescu/

Deletant, D. (1995). *Ceausescu And The Securitate: Coercion And Dissent In Romania, 1965-1989*. New York: Routledge.

Gallagher, T. (2008). *Modern Romania: The End of Communism, the Failure of Democratic Reform, and the Theft of a Nation*. New York: NYU Press.

Handlery, G. (2013, February 18). *Can tyranny survive capitalism?*. The Brussels Journal. From http://www.brusselsjournal.com/node/5039.

How I brought down Ceausescu: Larry Hagman, who played Texas oil baron J R Ewing, claims Romania's decision to screen Dallas toppled Communist rulers. (2011, May 20). Daily Mail. From https://www.dailymail.co.uk/news/article-1388776/Larry-Hagman-claims-Romanias-decision-screen-Dallas-toppled-communist-rulers.html

Mackinnon, A. (2019, May 16). What Actually Happens When a Country Bans Abortion. Foreign Policy. From https://foreignpolicy.com/2019/05/16/what-actually-happens-when-a-country-bans-abortion-romania-alabama/

Matula, T. (2010). *The Pony Excess*. ESPN 30 for 30.

Mazaud, E. (2019, August 29). *Treated like Trash: How Roma in Romania are Forced to Live by City Dumps*. META from the European Environmental Bureau. From https://meta.eeb.org/2019/08/29/treated-like-trash-how-roma-in-romania-are-forced-to-live-by-city-dumps/.

Nita, R. (2019, October 7). World's First Southfork Rank Replica: Hermes Slobozia. World Record Academy. From https://www.worldrecordacademy.org/architecture/worlds-first-soutfork-ranch-replica-hermes-slobozia-219377

Odobescu, V. (2015, December 28). *Half a million kids survived Romania's 'slaughterhouses of souls.' Now they want justice*. The World. From https://theworld.org/stories/2015-12-28/half-million-kids-survived-romanias-slaughterhouses-souls-now-they-want-justice

Orwell, G. (2004). *Animal Farm*. New York: Penguin Books.

Roxborough, S. (2016, February 15). Berlin Hidden Gems: How TV's 'Dallas' Toppled Romanian Communism. The Hollywood Reporter. From https://www. hollywoodreporter.com/movies/movie- news/hotel-dallas-shows-how-tv-865438/

Sebetsyen, V. (2009). *Revolution 1989: The Fall of the Soviet Empire*. New York: Pantheon Books.

Steavenson, W. (2014, December 10). *Ceausescu's Children*. The Guardian. From https://www.theguardian.com/ news/2014/dec/10/-sp-ceausescus-children.

Stone, Oliver. (1987). *Wallstreet*. 20th Century Fox.

Whitley, V. (2016, April 14). Film Shows How Dallas Gave Romania A Glimpse Of Life In The West. Art and Seek. From https://artandseek.org/2016/04/14/film-shows-how-dallas-gave-romania-a-glimpse-of- life-in-the-west/.

Friends Like These: Sinking the Rainbow Warrior

Alexander, D. (2012, September 20). *U.S. lifts 26-year-old ban on New Zealand warship visits to U.S. bases.* Chicago Tribune.

Armstrong, J. (2005, July 1). *Reality behind the Rainbow Warrior outrage.* NZ Herald. From https://www.nzherald.co.nz/nz/reality-behind-the-rainbow-warrior-outrage/5U2NIK3HXRVQYUS3CHW6HF6YUI/.

Brand, H. (2020, March 15). Texas roads are among the nation's most beautiful, by design. Texas Highways. From https://texashighways.com/wildflowers/texas-roads-are-among-the-nations-most-beautiful-by-design/.

Bremner, C. (2005, July 11). *Mitterrand ordered bombing of Rainbow Warrior, spy chief says. The Times.* London.

Carson, R. (2002). *Silent spring.* Boston: Houghton Mifflin.

Case Concerning the Differences Between New Zealand and France Arising from the Rainbow Warrior Affair. (1986). United Nations, International Arbitral Awards, Vol. XIX, pp. 199-221. From http://large.stanford.edu/courses/2017/ph241/perry1/docs/un-rainbow-jul86.pdf.

Catalinac, A. (2010). Why New Zealand took itself out of ANZUS: observing "opposition for autonomy" in asymmetric alliances. *Foreign Policy Analysis,* 6, 317-338.

Greenpeace International. (2015, May 20). The Boat and the Bomb [Video]. YouTube. https://www.youtube.com/watch?v=2uw8tg9_BU4.

Journeyman TV. (2016, September 8). The Rainbow Warrior Bomber Breaks His Silence (2015) [Video]. YouTube. https://www.youtube.com/watch?v=cSDELHN-JGw.

Kahn, H. (2007). *On Thermonuclear War*. New York: Routledge.

King, M. (1987). *Death of the Rainbow Warrior*. New York: Penguin.

Lange, David (1991). *Nuclear Free: The New Zealand Way*. New York: Penguin.

Le Zotte, J. (2015, May 21). *How the Summer of Atomic Bomb Testing Turned the Bikini Into a Phenomenon*. Smithsonian Magazine. From https://www.smithsonianmag.com/smithsonian-institution/how-wake-testing-atomic-bomb-bikini-became-thing-180955346/.

McClure, T., Spence, R. (2006). *Don't Mess with Texas: The Story Behind the Legend*. Idea City Press.

Mcwilliam, D. (2004, June 6). 'Don't mess' with this Texas slogan. Associated Press. From https://www.nbcnews.com/id/wbna5151681.

Medalia, J. (2005). *Nuclear Weapons: Comprehensive Test Ban Treaty*. Congressional Record Service.

Morgan, J.G. Jr. (2006, February 3). *Release of Information on Nuclear Weapons and on Nuclear Capabilities of U.S. Forces*. Washington, DC: Department of the Navy – Office of the Chief of Naval Operations.

Nodjimbadem, K. (2017, March 10). *The Trashy Beginnings of "Don't Mess With Texas" A true story of the defining phrase of the Lone Star state. Smithsonian Magazine.* From https://www.smithsonianmag.com/history/trashy-beginnings-dont-mess-texas-180962490/

Page, C., & Templeton, I. (1985, September 24). *French inquiry into Rainbow Warrior bombing.* The Guardian.

Paihia Dive. From https://divenz.com/trips/rainbow-warrior/.

Rainbow Warrior spy Christine Cabon breaks 32-year silence. (2017, July 8). NZ Herald. From https://www.nzherald.co.nz/nz/rainbow-warrior-spy-christine-cabon-breaks-32-year-silence/RLQVRBD2N5O4XM6MVE5VZLADWA/.

Robie, D. (2007). *The Rainbow Warrior Bombers, the Media and the Judiciary.* Pacific Media Center: Auckland University of Technology.

Robie, D. (2016). Eyes of Fire: The Last Voyage of the Rainbow Warrior. New Zealand: Little Island Press.

Shabecoff, P. (1987, October 3). *France Must Pay Greenpeace $8 Million in Sinking of Ship.* The New York Times.

Sunday Times of London Insight Team. (1986). *Rainbow Warrior: The French Attempt to Sink Greenpeace.* Hutchinson, 1986.

Szabo, M., & Grace, R. (1994). Wreck to reef-the transfiguration of the Rainbow Warrior. New Zealand Geographic 23, Jul-Sep 1994. From https://www.nzgeo.com/stories/wreck-to-reef-the-transfiguration-of-the-rainbow-warrior/.

Thakur, R. (1986). A Dispute of Many Colours: France, New Zealand, and the Rainbow Warrior Affair. *The World Today, 42*(12), 209.

The Australia, New Zealand and United States Security Treaty (ANZUS Treaty), 1951. Department of State – Office of the Historian. From https://history.state.gov/milestones/1945-1952/anzus.

Truver, S. (1986). Maritime Terrorism, 1985. *Proceedings.* United States Naval Institute. *112* (5).

Vaughn, B. (2013, March 8). *New Zealand: U.S. Security Cooperation and the U.S. Rebalancing to Asia   Strategy.* Congressional Research Service.

Watkins, T., & Maude, S. (2016, November 15). *Earthquake: International flotilla and aircraft drafted in to   help with humanitarian relief in Kaikoura.* Stuff. From https://www.stuff.co.nz/national/86479193/us-warship-may-help-rescue-stranded-kaikoura-tourists.

Weingroff, R. (2017, June 27). *Lady Bird Johnson's I-95 Landscape-Landmark Tour - Highway History – FHWA.* U.S. Department of Transportation Federal Highway Administration. From   https://www.fhwa.dot.gov/infrastructure/ladybird.cfm.

Willsher, K. (2015, September 6). *French spy who sank Greenpeace ship apologises for lethal bombing.* The Guardian. From https://www.theguardian.com/environment/2015/sep/06/french-spy-who-sunk-greenpeace-ship-apologises-for-lethal-bombing.

COMING TOGETHER: THE BRITISH IGNITION

Allen, D. (2007). Feelin' Bad This Morning: Why the British Blues. *Popular Music, 26*(11). From https://www.jstor.org/stable/4500305.

Baime, A.J. (2010). *Go Like Hell: Ford, Ferrari, and Their Battle for Speed and Glory at Le Mans.* New York: Mariner Books.

Bertram, C. (2019, November 13). The True Story Behind 'Ford v Ferrari.' Biography. From https://www.biography.com/news/ford-v-ferrari-true-story.

Binder, S. (1964). *T.A.M.I. Show.* AIP.

Gertstenzang, P. (2014, August 26). 14 Things You Didn't Know About Epic Rock Doc *The T.A.M.I. Show.* Esquire. From https://www.esquire.com/entertainment/music/a29785/tami-show-facts/.

Hellmann, J. (1973). 'I'm a Monkey': The Influence of the Black American Blues Argot on the Rolling Stones. *The Journal of American Folklore. 86* (342).

Mangold, J. (2019). *Ford v Ferrari.* 20th Century Fox.

Miles, M. (2010, August 13). 'The T.A.M.I. Show': A Groundbreaking '60s Concert. Fresh Air – NPR. From https://www.npr.org/templates/story/story.php?storyId=125599928.

Mills, R. (2014). *Carroll Shelby.* Minneapolis: Motorbooks.

Nelson, M. (2010). *The Rolling Stones: A Musical Biography*. Santa Barbara, CA: Greenwood Publishing Group.

Peeno, J. *The biggest mistake the Rolling Stones ever made*. Far Out Magazine. From https://faroutmagazine.co.uk/the-rolling-stones-biggest-mistake/.

Perone, J. (2004). *Music of the Counterculture Era*. London: Greenwood Publishing Group.

Puterbaugh, P. (1988, July 14). *The British Invasion: From the Beatles to the Stones, The Sixties Belonged to Britain*. Rolling Stone. From https://www.rollingstone.com/feature/the-british-invasion-from-the-beatles-to-the-stones-the-sixties-belonged-to-britain-244870/.

Robbins, I. The Invasion (music). Britannica Online. From https://www.britannica.com/event/British-Invasion.

Symons, R. (2002). *The Snake and the Stallion*. Spirit Level Film.

Tannert, C. (2019, November 14). Ford vs. Ferrari: The Real Story Behind The Most Bitter Rivalry In Auto Racing. Forbes. From https://www.forbes.com/wheels/news/ford-vs-ferrari-the-real-story-behind-the-most-bitter-rivalry-in-auto-racing/.

KOREAN WAVES, BUTTER BATTLES, & BS

A Fake Village and a Colossal Flagpole: North Korea's Bizarre Propaganda Methods. (2013, October 14). Atlas Obscura. From http://www.slate.com/blogs/atlas_obscura/2013/10/14/a_fake_village_and_a_colossal_flagpole_north_koreas_bizarre_propaganda.html.

Altman, A., & Fitzpatrick, A. (2014, December 17). *Everything We Know About Sony, 'The Interview' and North Korea.* Time. From https://time.com/3639275/the-interview-sony-hack-north-korea/.

Aykroyd, L. (2019, September 27). *Book: Unified Korean hockey team showed impact of sport on global issues.* Global Sport Matters. From https://globalsportmatters.com/culture/2019/09/27/book-unified-korean-hockey-team-showed-impact-of-sport-on-global-issues/.

Beauchamp, Z. (2016, September 9). *"the textbook definition of unstable": Why North Korea's newest nuclear test is scary.* Vox. From http://www.vox.com/2016/9/9/12863700/north-korea-nuclear-test-five-bad.

Berkman, Seth. (2019). *A Team of Their Own: How an International Sisterhood Made Olympic History.* New York: Hanover Square Press.

Collins, L. *25 Years of Negotiations and Provocations: North Korea and the United States*. Beyond Parallel. From https://beyondparallel.csis.org/25-years-of-negotiations-provocations/.

De Souza, N. (2021, June 29). *K-drama takes a dark turn*. The Interpreter. From https://www.lowyinstitute.org/the-interpreter/k-drama-takes-dark-turn.

Dr. Suess. (1984). *The Butter Battle Book*. New York: Random House.

Flexible Deterrent Options (FDO). (n.d.). Global Security. From https://www.globalsecurity.org/military/ops/fdo.htm.

Harden, B. (2013). *Escape from Camp 14: One Man's Remarkable Odyssey from North Korea to Freedom in the West*. New York: Penguin Books.

Havely, J. (2002, February 20). *Korea's DMZ: 'Scariest place on Earth'*. CNN. From http://edition.cnn.com/2002/WORLD/asiapcf/east/02/19/koreas.dmz/.

Joint Chiefs of Staff. (2018). *JP 3-0: Joint Operations*. From https://www.jcs.mil/Portals/36/Documents/Doctrine/pubs/jp3_0ch1.pdf.

Joint Chiefs of Staff. (2020). *JP 5-0: Joint Planning*. From https://irp.fas.org/doddir/dod/jp5_0.pdf.

Kim, H-K. (2018, February 8). *In small interactions before Olympics, Korean unity emerges*. Associated Press. From https://apnews.com/article/winter-olympics-north-korea-sports-asia-international-news-sports-96a042a0c0df4f93b9313ea5422e508f.

Korea Demilitarized Zone Incidents. (n.d.). Global Security. From http://www.globalsecurity.org/military/ops/dmz.htm.

Koreas switch off loudspeakers. (2004, June 15). BBC News. From http://news.bbc.co.uk/2/hi/asia- pacific/3807409. stm.

Lee-Lassiter, S. (2019, December 28). *The All-Female Korean Hockey Team That Won the World's Heart*. Pass Blue. From https://www.passblue.com/2019/12/28/the-all-female-korean-hockey-team-that-won-the-worlds-heart/.

Lewis, A. (2019, February 7). *When sports and politics collide – what happened when North and South Korea unified on the ice*. CNN. From https://www.cnn.com/2019/02/07/sport/south-korea-north-korea-unified-ice-hockey-team-winter-olympics-2018-spt-intl/index.html.

McMorrow-Hernandez, J. (2016, March 29). *Paper money - whatever happened to North Korean counterfeit U.S. $100 bills?* CoinWeek. From http://www.coinweek.com/people-in-the-news/crime-and-fraud/paper-money-whatever-happened-north-korean-counterfeit-u-s-100-bills/.

Ministry of Foreign Affairs (Japan). (2021, August 6). *Abductions of Japanese citizens by North Korea*. From https://www.mofa.go.jp/region/asiapaci/n_korea/abduction/index.html

Moore, M. (2009, May 26). *Inside North Korea's Third Tunnel of Aggression*. The Daily Telegraph. From http://blogs.telegraph.co.uk/news/malcolmmoore/9902611/Inside_North_Koreas_Third_Tunnel_of_Aggression/.

North Korea's 'biggest' export - giant statues. (2016, February 16). BBC News. From https://www.bbc.com/news/magazine-35569277.

North Korea Nuclear H-bomb claims met by scepticism. (2016, January 6). BBC News. From http://www.bbc.com/news/world-asia-35241686.

North Korea Profile - Timeline. (2019, April 26). BBC News. From http://www.bbc.com/news/world-asia-pacific-15278612.

Paterson, S. (2016, January 12). *Korean loudspeakers: What are the north and south shouting about?* BBC News. From https://www.bbc.com/news/world-asia-35278451.

Potts, R. (1999, February 3). *Korea's no-man's-land.* Salon. From https://www.salon.com/1999/02/03/feature_115/.

Roblin, S. (2019, October 19). *Attack from Underground: North Korea Has a Secret Tunnel Network Ready for the Next War.* National Interest. From https://nationalinterest.org/blog/buzz/attack-underground-north-korea-has-secret-tunnel-network-ready-next-war-84831.

Smith, R., & Chace, Z. (2011, August 11). *Drug dealing, counterfeiting, smuggling: How North Korea makes money.* NPR. From http://www.npr.org/sections/money/2011/08/11/139556457/drug-dealing-counterfeiting-smuggling-how-north-korea-makes-money.

Stone, D. (2014, February 27). *North Korea's isolation is visible in new satellite photos that show the energy-bankrupt country at night.* National Geographic. From https://www.nationalgeographic.com/pages/article/140226-north-korea-satellite-photos-darkness-energy.

The annexation of Korea. The Japan Times. (2014, March 28). From http://www.japantimes.co.jp/opinion/2010/08/29/editorials/the-annexation-of-korea/.

The female coach behind the unified Korean ice hockey team, a symbol of peace and hope. (2019, March 8). Olympics.com. From https://olympics.com/en/news/the-female-coach-behind-the-unified-korean-ice-hockey-team-a-symbol-of-peace-and.

Thuras, D. (2014, August 25). *Monument to African dictator Laurent Kabila.* Atlas Obscura. From http://www.atlasobscura.com/places/monument-to-african-dictator-laurent-kabila.

Tran, M. (2008, June 6). *Travelling into Korea's demilitarised zone: Run DMZ.* The Guardian. London.

U.S. Committee for Human Rights in North Korea. *Taken! North Korea's Criminal Abduction of Citizens of Other Countries.*

Wilmes, J. (2018, July 30). *Dr. Seuss' forgotten anti-war book made him an enemy of the right.* The Outline.

Wilson, G. (1970, September 2). *North Koreans Caught Building Another Tunnel.* The Washington Post. From https://www.washingtonpost.com/archive/politics/1979/09/02/north-koreans-caught-building-another-tunnel/0839b28e-afe7-41fe-be4b-2eb0ccb5e19d/.

Yeung, J., & Seo, Yoonjung. (2021, July 23). Why North Korea is so afraid of K-pop. CNN. From https://www.cnn.com/2021/07/23/asia/north-korea-culture-war-kpop-intl-hnk-dst/index.html.

VeNi Vidi ViCi: Cod Wars & MiNerva ReeFs

Anand, R.P. (1976). The "Cod War" Between UK And Iceland. *India Quarterly*, 32(2), 215-220. From https://www.jstor.org/stable/45070410.

Cod Wars. (2021, October 26). In *Wikipedia*. https://en.wikipedia.org/wiki/Cod_Wars.

Field, M. (2011, June 12). *Bainimarama silent on looming clash*. Stuff. From http://www.stuff.co.nz/world/5133527/Bainimarama-silent-on-looming-clash.

Michael, M. (2011, May 16). *Fiji, Tonga war over Minerva Reef*. Stuff.

Fiji and Tonga govts continue talks on reef dispute. (2011, February 8). Radio New Zealand International.

Frost, N. (2018, June 21). *How Iceland Beat the British in the Four Cod Wars*. Atlas Obscura. From https://www.atlasobscura.com/articles/what-were-cod-wars.

Hellmann, G., & Herborth, B. (2008, July 1). Fishing in the mild West: democratic peace and militarised interstate disputes in the transatlantic community. *Review of International Studies, 34*(3), 481–506.

Jónsson, H. (1982). *Friends in conflict: the Anglo-Icelandic cod wars and the Law of the Sea.* London: C. Hurst.

Middleton, N. (2015). *An Atlas of Countries That Don't Exist: A Compendium of Fifty Unrecognized and Largely Unnoticed States.* London: Macmillan.

Minerva Reefs. (2021, October 21). In *Wikipedia.* https://en.wikipedia.org/wiki/Minerva_Reefs.

Principality of Sealand. (2021, November 12). In *Wikipedia.* https://en.wikipedia.org/wiki/Principality_of_Sealand.

Republic of Minerva. (2021, October 21). In *Wikipedia.* *https://en.wikipedia.org/wiki/Republic_of_Minerva.*

Ruhen, O. (1963). *Minerva Reef.* Sydney: Halstead Press.

Showdown between Tonga and Fiji looms. (2011, June 11). ONE News. From http://tvnz.co.nz/world-news/showdown-between-tonga-and-fiji-looms-4221560.

South Sea Reef Proclaimed a Republic by 3 Americans. (1972, January 30). The New York Times.

South Seas: The Minerva Ploy. (1972, October 23). Newsweek.

Strauss, E. (1984). *How to Start Your Own Country.* Port Townsend, WA: Breakout Productions.

The United Nations Convention on the Law of the Sea (A historical perspective). (1998). United Nations Division for Ocean Affairs and the Law of the Sea. From https://www.un.org/Depts/los/convention_agreements/convention_historical_perspective.htm.

United Nations Convention on the Law of the Sea. United Nations Treaty Collection. From https://treaties.un.org/pages/ViewDetailsIII.aspx?src=TREATY&mtdsg_no=XXI-6&chapter=21&Temp=mtdsg3&clang=_en.

Menefee, S. (1994). 'Republics of the Reefs': Nation-Building on the Continental Shelf and in the World's Oceans. *California Western International Law Journal, 25*(1).

Prostitution & Spearmint: Everyone's A Weirdo

Allison, G. (2015, March 28). *Lee Kuan Yew: Lessons for leaders from Asia's 'Grand Master'*. CNN.

Avakian, T. (2015, August 4). *16 odd things that are illegal in Singapore*. Business Insider. From https://www.businessinsider.com/things-that-are-illegal-in-singapore-2015-7.

Bailey, T. (2015, July 16). *How Singapore married dictatorship with a market economy*. World Finance. From https://www.worldfinance.com/special-reports/how-singapore-married-dictatorship-with-a-market-economy.

Bischoff, E. (2006). *Controversy Creates Cash*. New York: Simon and Schuster.

Coleridge, S. T., & Sarason, H. M. (1956). *Kubla Khan*. Los Angeles: Place of publication not identified.

DeVeyra, D-M. (2021, October 22). *Singapore: Laws To Know Before You Go*. Go Abroad. From https://www.goabroad.com/articles/study-abroad/singapore-laws-to-know-before-you-go.

Evans, G. (2018). *NITRO: The Incredible Rise and Inevitable Collapse of Ted Turner's WCW*. WCWNitroBook.com.

Fournier, R. (1994, April 14). Clinton Decries Planned Singapore Flogging of American. Associated Press. From https://apnews.com/article/074a9b219ed656421af7c01425cc56c3.

Ghesquière, H. (2007). *Singapore's success: engineering economic growth*. Thompson Learning.

Gibson, W. (1993, April 1). *Disneyland with the Death Penalty*. Wired. From https://www.wired.com/1993/04/gibson-2/.

Graffiti man faces Singapore caning. (2010, June 25). BBC News. June 25, 2010.

Heng, C-K. (2016). *50 Years of Urban Planning in Singapore*. Singapore: WSPC.

Hill, M., & Kwen, F-L. (1995). *The Politics of Nation Building and Citizenship in Singapore*. New York: *Routledge*.

King, R. (2008). *The Singapore Miracle, Myth and Reality*. Western Australia: Insight Press.

Lingle, C. (1996, July 1). *Singapore's Authoritarian Capitalism: Asian Values, Free Market Illusions, and Political Dependency*. Foreign Affairs.

Loverro, T. (May 22, 2007). <u>The Rise & Fall of ECW: Extreme Championship Wrestling</u>. Simon and Schuster.

Mauzy, D., Milne, R-S. (2002). *Singapore Politics: Under the People's Action Party*. New York: Routledge.

Reuters. (1994, June 27). *Teen-Ager Caned in Singapore Tells of the Blood and the Scars*. The New York Times. From https://www.nytimes.com/1994/06/27/us/teen-ager-caned-in-singapore-tells-of-the-blood-and-the-scars.html.

Reynolds, R. D. (2004). *The Death of WCW*. Ontario, Canada: ECW Press Ltd.

Richardson, M. (1994, May 5). *Responding to Clinton's Plea, Singapore Cuts 6 Lashes to 4*. The New York Times.

Sandhu, K-S., Wheatley, P. (1989). Management of Success: The Moulding of Modern Singapore. *Institute of Southeast Asian Studies*. From https://books.google.com/books?id=ldKwPQ2PyBAC.

Sim, S-F. (2001, January 1). Asian Values, Authoritarianism and Capitalism in Singapore. *Javnost - the Public, 8*(2). From https://doi.org/10.1080/13183222.2001.11008771.

Singapore: The death penalty: A hidden toll of executions. (2004). Amnesty International. From https://web.archive.org/web/20080111225751/http:/www.amnesty.org/en/alfresco_asset/aad0c6f3-a509-11dc-a92d-271514ed133d/asa360012004en.html.

Spare the Rod, Spoil the Child: Michael Fay's Caning in Singapore. (2015, August 20). HuffPost. From https://www.huffpost.com/entry/spare-the-rod-spoil-the-c_b_8012770.

Tan, C. (2015, March 23). *Lee Kuan Yew leaves a legacy of authoritarian pragmatism*. The Guardian. From https://www.theguardian.com/world/2015/mar/23/lee-kuan-yews-legacy-of-authoritarian-pragmatism-will-serve-singapore-well.

The 98 Rock. (n.d.) Atlas Obscura. From https://www.atlasobscura.com/places/the-98-rock-united-states-minor-outlying-islands.

Shaw, E. (n.d.) *14 singapore laws you should know before you go*. Explore Shaw. From https://www.exploreshaw.com/14-crazy-singapore-laws-to-know-before/.

The Sandman (wrestler). (2021, November 15). In *Wikipedia*. From https://en.wikipedia.org/wiki/The_Sandman_(wrestler).

Top 10 Busiest Ports In The World. (2021, October 19). Marine Insight. From https://www.marineinsight.com/ports/top-10-busiest-ports-in-the-world/.

Trocki, C. (2009). *Singapore: Wealth, Power and the Culture of Control*. Routledge.

Yew, L-K. (2000). *From Third World To First: The Singapore Story: 1965–2000*. New York: HarperCollins.

UNIFiED:
The Drive Towards Moderation

Abdulhadi, K. (1987). The elusive quest for gulf security. *MERIP Middle East Report, 148*. From https://merip.org/1987/09/the-elusive-quest-for-gulf-security/.

Bahrain activists in 'Day of Rage'. (2011, February 14). Al Jazeera. From https://www.aljazeera.com/news/2011/2/14/bahrain-activists-in-day-of-rage.

Bahrain bristles at threat to move 5th Fleet. (2015, May 19). US News. From https://www.usnews.com/news/articles/2015/05/19/bahrain-bristles-at-threat-to-move-5th-fleet.

Bahraini Despot Wages Demographic War. (2009, February 17). Voice of Bahrain. From https://web.archive.org/web/20110928051031/http://www.vob.org/en/index.php?show=news&action=article&id=390.

Bahrain doles out money to Families. (2011, February 12). Al Jazeera. From http://www.aljazeera.com/news/middleeast/2011/02/20112125185485792.html.

Barrett, R. (2011, February 15). *Bahrain emerging as flashpoint in Middle East unrest*. The Christian Science Monitor.

Bassiouni, M., Rodley, N., Al-Awadhi, B., Kirsch, P., & Arsanjani, M. (2011, November 23). *Report of the Bahrain Independent Commission of Inquiry*. From http://www.bici.org.bh/BICIreportEN.pdf.

Beer, M. (2011, June 4). *Webber critical of Bahrain Decision*. Autosport. From http://www.autosport.com/news/report.php/id/91981.

Bew, G. (2009, February 15). 40 *sailors who face black flag face suspension*. Defense PK. From http://archives.gdnonline.com/NewsDetails.aspx?date=04/07/2015&storyid=243067

Chulov, M. (2011, March 18). *Bahrain destroys Pearl roundabout*. The Guardian. From https://www.theguardian.com/world/2011/mar/18/bahrain-destroys-pearl-roundabout.

Cohen, B. (2011, May 25). Bahrain: The Missing 'A' Word. HuffPost. From https://www.huffpost.com/entry/bahrain-the-missing-a-wor_b_824309.

Donaghy, R. (2015, May 30). *Uprising strong, economy dire in Bahrain, say activists*. Middle East Eye. From https://www.middleeasteye.net/news/uprising-strong-economy-dire-bahrain-say-activists.

Fleishman, J. (2011, May 11). *After crushed protests, Bahrain is accused of increased oppression of Shiites*. Los Angeles Times. From https://www.latimes.com/world/la-xpm-2011-may-11-la-fg-bahrain-shiites-20110502-story.html.

Ghosh, B. (5 March 2007). *Behind the Sunni-Shi'ite Divide*. Time. From http://www.time.com/time/magazine/article/0,9171,1592849-2,00.html.

Handlery, G. (2013, February 18). *Can tyranny survive capitalism?*. The Brussels Journal. From http://www.brusselsjournal.com/node/5039.

Huang, C. (2011, June 5). *Facebook and Twitter key to Arab Spring uprisings: Report*. The National. From https://www.thenationalnews.com/uae/facebook-and-twitter-key-to-arab-spring-uprisings-report-1.428773.

Katwala, A. (2015, March 12). *Bernie Ecclestone: Is he formula 1's saviour, or the man driving the sport into a dead end?* talkSPORT. From https://talksport.com/sport/motorsport/252649/bernie-ecclestone-he-formula-1s-saviour-or-man-driving-sport-dead-end-150312139508/.

Khalaf, A. (2013, February 28). *The Many Afterlives of Lulu: The Story of Bahrain's Pearl Roundabout*. Ibraaz. From https://www.ibraaz.org/essays/56.

Kristof, N. (2011, February 22). *Is This Apartheid in Bahrain?*. The New York Times. From https://kristof.blogs.nytimes.com/2011/02/22/is-this-apartheid-in-bahrain/?mtrref=wwwwwgooglecom&gwh=0F8085A05410AF183053F33CC05ACC5E&gwt=regi&assetType=REGIWALL.

Law, B. (2013, April 16). Bahrain GP: The BBC explains the background to the protests. BBC News. From http://www.bbc.com/news/world-middle-east-22122792.

Madani, A. (2011, April 27). *Arabian Spring: The Hidden Tragedy of Bahrain*. HuffPost. From https://www.huffpost.com/entry/bahrain-arab-spring_b_854191.

Mapping the Global Muslim Population: A Report on the Size and Distribution of the World's Muslim Population. (2009, October 7). Pew Research Center. October 7, 2009. *From* https://www.pewforum.org/2009/10/07/mapping-the-global-muslim-population/.

Marlowe, J. (2012, October 22). *Women Join Bahrain's Uprising.* Witness Bahrain. From https://witnessbahrain.com/tag/pearl-roundabout/.

Newman, A. J. (2021, October 3). *Battle of Karbala.* Encyclopædia Britannica. From https://www.britannica.com/event/Battle-of-Karbala.

Raban, J. (1979). *Arabia Through the Looking Glass.* William Collins, Sons.

Richter, F. (2010, June 9). *Bahraini sex shop thrives in Conservative Gulf.* Reuters. From https://www.reuters.com/article/us-bahrain-sexshop-odd-idUSTRE6573QT20100609.

Shaheen, K. (2011, March 15). *Defensive shield for the Gulf created in 1982.* The National. From http://www.thenational.ae/news/uae-news/defensive-shield-for-the-gulf-since-1982.

Ten years on, Bahrain paralysed by legacy of Arab Spring. (2021, December 2). France 24. From https://www.france24.com/en/live-news/20210212-ten-years-on-bahrain-paralysed-by-legacy-of- arab-spring.

The Concorde Agreement. (27 September 2013). Federation Internationale de l'Automobile http://www.fia.com/news/concorde-agreement.

World Report 2011: Rights trends in Bahrain. (n.d.). Human Rights Watch. From https://www.hrw.org/world-report/2011/country-chapters/bahrain.

World Report 2021: Rights trends in Bahrain. (2021, January 14). Human Rights Watch. From https://www.hrw.org/world-report/2021/country-chapters/bahrain.

Zunes, S. (2013). Bahrain's Arrested Revolution. *Arab Studies Quarterly, 35*(2), 149-164.

DANGEROUS GROUND: REEFS, SHOALS, & ROTTING HULLS

A Cooperative Strategy for 21st Century Seapower. (2015). U.S. Navy.

Bateman, S., Ho, J., & Chan, J. (2009, April 1). Good Order at Sea in Southeast Asia. S. Rajaratnam *School of International Studies*, 11-14. From https://www.jstor.org/stable/resrep05941.7.

Beckman, R., Townsend-Gault, I., Schofield, C., Davenport, T., & Bernard, L. (2013). *Beyond Territorial Disputes in the South China Sea: Legal Frameworks*. Edward Elgar Publishing.

Beech, H. (2016, July 11). China's Global Reputation Hinges on Upcoming South China Sea Court Decision. TIME. From http://time.com/4400671/philippines-south-china-sea-arbitration-case/?xid=homepage.

Branigin, W. (1992, November 24). *U.S. Military Ends Role in Philippines*. Washington Post. From https://www.washingtonpost.com/archive/politics/1992/11/24/us-military-ends-role-in-philippines/a1be8c14-0681-44ab-b869-a6ee439727b7/.

BRP Sierra Madre. (2021, November 23). In *Wikipedia*. https://en.wikipedia.org/wiki/BRP_Sierra_Madre.

Campbell, E. (2014, May 20). *Reef Madness. ABC News. From* http://www.abc.net.au/foreign/content/2014/s4008035. htm.

Chan, M. (2021, May 30). *Chinese military faces challenge from falling fertility rate.* South China Morning Post. From https://www.scmp.com/news/china/military/ article/3135342/chinese-military-faces-challenge-falling-fertility-rate.

China building 'great wall of sand' in South China Sea. (2015, April 1). BBC. From https://www.bbc.com/news/world-asia-32126840.

de Castro, E., & Ng, R. (March 31, 2014*). Philippine ship dodges China blockade to reach South China Sea outpost.* Reuters.

Declaration by the High Representative on behalf of the EU on the Award rendered in the Arbitration between *the Republic of the Philippines and the People's Republic of China [Press Release].* (2016, July 15). Council of the European Union. From https://web.archive.org/ web/20180209060419/https:/www.consilium.europa. eu/en/press/press-releases/2016/07/15/south-china-sea-arbitration/.

Dee, L. (2016, May 31). *Politics, Pinatubo and the Pentagon: The Closure of Subic Bay.* Association for Diplomatic Studies and Training. From https://thediplomat.com/2014/08/the-nine-dashed-line-engraved-in-our-hearts/.

Etzler, T. (2017, July). *Wrecks, rats and roaches: Standoff in the South China Sea.* CNN. From https://www.cnn.com/ interactive/2014/07/world/south-china-sea-dispute/.

Ezrati, M. (2021, March 14). *China's Great Challenge Isn't America, But a Baby Bust.* The National Interest. From https://nationalinterest.org/blog/buzz/chinas-great-challenge-isnt-america-baby-bust-180192.

Gao, Z., & Jia, B-B. (2013). *The nine-dash line in the South China Sea: history, status, and implications.* American Journal of International Law, *107*(98).

Gomez, J. (2014, March 29). *Philippine supply ship evades Chinese blockade.* Associated Press.

Green, M., Hicks, K., Cooper, Z., Schaus, J., & Douglas, J. (2017, June9). *Counter-Coercion Series: Second Thomas Shoal Incident.* Asia Maritime Transparency Initiative. From https://amti.csis.org/counter-co-2nd-thomas-shoal/.

Himmelman, J. (2013, October 27). *A Game of Shark And Minnow.* The New York Times Magazine. From https://www.nytimes.com/newsgraphics/2013/10/27/south-china-sea/index.html.

Hutchison, C., & Vijayan, R. (2010). What are the Spratly Islands? *Journal of Asian Earth Sciences, 39*, 371-385).

Kaplan, R. (2007, October). *The Navy's New Flat-Earth Strategy.* The Atlantic. From https://www.theatlantic.com/doc/200710u/kaplan-navy.

McDevitt, M. (2020). *China as a Twenty-First-Century Naval Power: Theory Practice and Implications.* Naval Institute Press.

Mogato, M. (2014, February 13). *U.S. admiral assures Philippines of help in disputed sea.* Reuters. From https://www.reuters.com/article/us-philippines-usa-southchinasea-idUSBREA1C0LV20140213.

Mogato, M. (2015, July 13). *Exclusive: Philippines reinforcing rusting ship on Spratly reef outpost - sources. Reuters.* From https://www.reuters.com/article/us-southchinasea-philippines-shoal-exclu-idUSKCN0PN2HN20150714.

1991 Eruption of Mount Pinatubo. (2021, November 21). In *Wikipedia.* From https://en.wikipedia.org/wiki/1991_eruption_of_Mount_Pinatubo.

Philippines drops food to troops after China 'blockade'. (2014, March 13). Channel News Asia. From http://www.channelnewsasia.com/news/asiapacific/philippines-drops-food-to/1033960.html.

Press Release: The South China Sea Arbitration (The Republic of the Philippines v. The People's Republic of China). (2016, July 12). Permanent Court of Arbitration "The Hague." From https://web.archive.org/web/20160712201412/https:/pca-cpa.org/wp-content/uploads sites/175/2016/07/PH-CN-20160712-Press-Release-No-11-English.pdf.

Riegl, M., Landovský, J., Valko, I., eds. (2014). *Strategic Regions in 21st Century Power Politics.* Cambridge Scholars Publishing.

Sanger, D. (1991, December 28). *Philippines Orders U.S. to Leave Strategic Navy Base at Subic Bay.* The New York Times. From https://www.nytimes.com/1991/12/28/world/philippines-orders-us-to-leave-strategic-navy-base-at-subic-bay.html.

South China Sea: Tribunal backs case against China brought by Philippines. (2016, July 12). BBC News. From https://www.bbc.co.uk/news/world-asia-china-36771749.

Strangio, S. (2020, September 17). *Former US Bases in the Philippines Prompt Mixed Feelings.* The Diplomat. From https://thediplomat.com/2020/09/former-us-bases-in-the-philippines-prompt- mixed-feelings/.

US Navy carries out third FONOP in South China Sea. (2016, May 10). The Interpreter - Lowy Institute for International Policy. From http://www.lowyinterpreter.org/post/2016/05/10/US-Navy- carries-out-third-FONOP-in-South-China-Sea.aspx.

Valente, C. (2021, November 20). *PH won't 'abandon' shoal despite Ayungin incident.* The Manila Times. From https://www.manilatimes.net/2021/11/20/news/national/ph-wont-abandon-shoal-despite-ayungin-incident/1822960.

Wendel, J., & Kumar, M. (2016, June 9). *Pinatubo 25 Years Later: Eight Ways the Eruption Broke Ground.* Eos. From https://eos.org/articles/pinatubo-25-years-later-eight-ways-the-eruption-broke-ground.

Westby, E., & Phillips, D. (2016, June 13). *Remembering Mount Pinatubo 25 Years Ago: Mitigating a Crisis.* USGS. From https://www.usgs.gov/news/remembering-mount-pinatubo-25-years-ago-mitigating-crisis.

Why is the Strait of Malacca so Important to the World's Economy & Military [Video]. (2021, June 13). The Maritime Post. From https://themaritimepost.com/2021/06/13/why-is-the-strait-of-malacca-so-important-to-the-worlds-economy-military/.

Wilkins, V. (2015, September 16). *Man Spends 6 Months and $1,500 to Make a Sandwich From Scratch*. ABC News. From https://abcnews.go.com/Lifestyle/man-spends-months-1500-make-sandwich-scratch/story?id=33802231.

Winchester, S. (2016). *Pacific: Silicon Chips and Surfboards, Coral Reefs and Atom Bombs, Brutal Dictators and Fading Empires*. New York: Harper Perennial.

Wong, E. (2011, March 30). *China Hedges Over Whether South China Sea Is a 'Core Interest' Worth War*. The New York Times. From https://www.nytimes.com/2011/03/31/world/asia/31beijing.html.

Yoshihara, T., & Holmes, J. (2013). *Red Star over the Pacific*. Naval Institute Press.

SLIMED! VAN RIPER'S KOBAYASHI MARU

Borger, J. (2002, September 6). *Wake-up Call*. The Guardian. From https://www.theguardian.com/world/2002/sep/06/usa.iraq.

Brecher, G. (2002, December 11). *U Sank My Carrier!* The Exile. From http://www.exile.ru/articles/detail.php?ARTICLE_ID=6779&IBLOCK_ID=35.

Devil's Advocate. (2021, August 2). In *Wikipedia*. https://en.wikipedia.org/wiki/Devil%27s_advocate.

Fallows, J. (2008, December 6). *Karmic justice: Gen. Eric Shinseki*. The Atlantic. From https://www.theatlantic.com/technology/archive/2008/12/karmic-justice-gen-eric-shinseki/9162/.

Fallows, J. *The Tragedy of the American Military*. The Atlantic. January/February 2015. From https://www.theatlantic.com/magazine/archive/2015/01/the-tragedy-of-the-american-military/383516/.

Forster, M. (2013). *World War Z*. Skydance Productions.

Galloway, J. (2006, April 26). *Rumsfeld's War Games*. Military.com. From http://www.military.com/opinion/0,15202,95496,00.html.

Gladwell, M. (2005). *Blink: The Power of Thinking Without Thinking*. New York: Little, Brown and Co.

Glatt, E. (2013). The Unanimous Verdict According to the Talmud: Ancient Law Providing Insight into Modern Legal Theory. *Pace International Law Review Online*, Winter 2013. From https://digitalcommons.pace.edu/cgi/viewcontent.cgi?article=1034&context=pilronline.

Glueck, K. (2012, October 22). *Sharp reaction to Obama's 'bayonet.'* Politico. From https://www.politico.com/story/2012/10/sharp-reaction-to-obamas-bayonet-082730.

Grossman, E. (2006, May 29). *Millennium Challenge '02 lessons left unresolved*. Inside the Army, 18(21), 13-15. From https://www.jstor.org/stable/24823089.

Horton, F. (2019, November 6). *The lost lesson of Millennium Challenge 2002, the Pentagon's embarrassing post-9/11 war game*. Task and Purpose. From https://taskandpurpose.com/opinion/millenium-challenge-2002-stacked-deck/.

Kaplan, F. (2003, March 28). *The Officer Who Predicted Saddam's Moves*. Slate. From https://slate.com/news-and-politics/2003/03/the-officer-who-predicted-saddam-s-moves.html.

Kaplan, W. (2017). *Why Dissent Matters: Because Some People See Things the Rest of Us Miss*. McGill- Queen's University Press.

Kobayashi Maru. (2021, August 25). In *Wikipedia*. https://en.wikipedia.org/wiki/Kobayashi_Maru.

Meyer, C. *The Tenth Man Rule: How to Take Devil's Advocacy to Another Level*. The Mind Collection. From https://themindcollection.com/the-tenth-man-rule-devils-advocacy/#:~:text=In%20the%20film%2C%20the%20Tenth,example%20of%20the%20learning%20ocurve.&text=Well%2C%20there's%20more%20to%20the%20principle%20than%20just%20cinematic%20effect.

Meyer, N. (1982). *Star Trek II: The Wrath of Khan*. Paramount Pictures.

Mizokami, K. (2020, January 3). *The U.S. Lost a (Fictional) War With Iran 18 Years Ago*. Popular Mechanics. From https://www.popularmechanics.com/military/a30392654/millennium-challenge-qassem-soleimani/.

Naylor, S. (2002, August 26). *War games rigged? General says Millennium Challenge 02 'was almost entirely scripted.'* Army Times.

O'Hanlon, M. (2005, January 1). Iraq Without a Plan. Brookings. From https://www.brookings.edu/articles/iraq-without-a-plan/.

Paul Van Riper, interview by Scott Willis, "Battle Plan Under Fire." Nova Online, December 17, 2003, https://www.pbs.org/wgbh/nova/wartech/nature.html.

Post-Saddam Iraq: The War Game. (2006, November 4). National Security Archive Electronic Briefing Book No. 207. From https://nsarchive2.gwu.edu/NSAEBB/NSAEBB207/index.htm.

Ricks, T. (2007). *Fiasco: The American Military Adventure in Iraq, 2003 to 2005*. New York: Penguin Books.

Rosen, N. (2010). *Aftermath: Following the Bloodshed of America's Wars in the Muslim World*. New York: Nation Books.

Rumsfeld, D. (2011). *Known and Unknown*. New York: Penguin Group USA.

Shanker, T. (2008, January 12). *Iran Encounter Grimley Echoes '02 War Game.'* The New York Times. From https://www.nytimes.com/2008/01/12/washington/12navy.html.

Stemwedel, J. (2015, August 23). The Philosophy of Star Trek: The Kobayashi Maru, No-Win Scenarios, And Ethical Leadership. Forbes. From https://www.forbes.com/sites/janetstemwedel/2015/08/23/the-philosophy-of-star-trek-the-kobayashi-maru-no-win-scenarios-and-ethical-leadership/?sh=6f8094305f48.

Stilwell, B. (2021, June 15). *That time a Marine general led a fictional Iran against the US military – and won*. We Are The Mighty. From https://www.wearethemighty.com/mighty-trending/that-time-a-marine-general-led-a-fictional-iran-against-the-us-military-and-won/.

Ukman, J. (2011, August 4). *U.S. Joint Forces Command formally dissolved*. The Washington Post. From https://www.washingtonpost.com/blogs/checkpoint-washington/post/us-joint-forces-command-formally-dissolved/2011/08/04/gIQAQbzBuI_blog.html.

U.S. Joint Forces Command Millennium Challenge 2020: Experiment Report. USJFCOM. From https://www.esd.whs.mil/Portals/54/Documents/FOID/Reading%20Room/Joint_Staff/12-F-0344-Millennium-Challenge-2002-Experiment-Report.pdf.

Woods, K. M. (2006). *Iraqi perspectives project: A view of operation iraqi freedom from Saddam's senior leadership.* United States Joint Forces Command, Joint Center for Operational Analysis.

Zengerle, P. (2012, October 23). *"Horses and bayonets" becomes latest debate catchphrase.* Reuters. From https://www.reuters.com/article/us-usa-campaign-horses/horses-and-bayonets-becomes-latest-debate-catchphrase-idUSBRE89M08F20121023.

Zenko, M (2015, November 5). *Millennium Challenge: The Real Story of a Corrupted Military Exercise and its Legacy.* War on the Rocks. From https://warontherocks.com/2015/11/millennium-challenge-the-real-story-of-a-corrupted-military-exercise-and-its-legacy/.

Zenko, M. (2015). *Red Team: How to Succeed By Thinking Like the Enemy.* New York: Basic Books.

DON LAO MAGAL: FROM CASINO TO CARRIER

Aldrich, R. (1967). The Dirty Dozen. Metro-Goldwyn-Mayer

Anderson, J. (2001, July 22). *Turks Keep Ship Going Round in Circles*. Washington Post. From https://www.washingtonpost.com/archive/politics/2001/07/22/turks-keep-ship-going-round-in-circles/4ae7af0c-3004-43ad-9998-ae2941c01497/

CBC. (1998, November 10). Soviet killing machine heads for Macau. From https://www.cbc.ca/news/world/soviet-killing-machine-heads-for-macau-1.166118

Chan, M. (2015, April 29). 'Unlucky guy' tasked with buying China's aircraft carrier: Xu Zengping. South China Morning Post. From https://www.scmp.com/news/china/diplomacy-defence/article/1779703/unlucky-guy-tasked-buying-chinas-aircraft-carrier-xu

China Global Television Network (CGTN). "Chinese Aircraft Carrier Liaoning Celebrates China's National Day." *YouTube*, YouTube, 2 Oct. 2021, https://www.youtube.com/watch?v=h_m5ZvnqZEE.

Chu, H., & Mann, J. (1999 July 3). *Chinese Reassign Intelligence Chief Implicated in Fund-Raising Scandal*. Los Angeles Times. From https://www.latimes.com/archives/la-xpm-1999-jul-03-mn-52579- story.html

Erickson, A. (2021). A Guide to China's Unprecedented Naval Shipbuilding Drive. *The Maritime Executive*.

Erickson, A. (2017). Chinese Naval Shipbuilding: An Ambitious and Uncertain Course (Studies in Chinese Maritime Development). Naval Institute Press.

Harnett, D. (2014, October 8). *The Father of the Modern Chinese Navy–Liu Huaqing*. Center for International Maritime Security.

Larson, D. (1989). *Origins of Containment: A Psychological Explanation*. New Jersey: Princeton University Press.

MDAA. (2018, August 24). China's Anti-Access Area Denial. Missile Defense Advocacy Alliance. From https://missiledefenseadvocacy.org/missile-threat-and-proliferation/todays-missile-threat/china/china-anti-access-area-denial/

Muller, D. (1983). *China as a Maritime Power: The Formative Years: 1945–1983*. Boulder, CO: Westview Press.

Mustaksubhedar. (2021, July 4). *How deception was incorporated into China's first aircraft carrier*. India News Republic. From https://indianewsrepublic.com/how-deception-was-incorporated-into-chinas-first-aircraft-carrier/364547/

O'Rourke, R. (2021). *China Naval Modernization: Implications for U.S. Navy Capabilities—Background and Issues for Congress*. Congressional Research Service. From RL33153.

Reuters Staff. *Factbox: China's aircraft carrier ambitions.* Reuters. From https://www.reuters.com/article/us-china-defence-carriers-factbox/factbox-chinas-aircraft-carrier-ambitions-idUSTRE6BM0YG20101223.

Rielage, D. (2018). The Chinese Navy's Missing Years. *Naval History Magazine.* 32(6).

Roblin, S. (2017, May 6). The Super Sneaky Way China Got Its Hands On Its First Aircraft Carrier. National Interest. From https://nationalinterest.org/blog/the-buzz/the- super-sneaky-way-china-got-its-hands-its-first-aircraft-20528

Roblin, S. (2021. July 15). How China's navy went rogue to get its first carrier. Business Insider: From https://www. businessinsider.com/how-chinese-navy-went-rogue-to-get-first-aircraft-carrier-2021-7

Schloss, G. (1998, March 19). Mystery Macau company buys aircraft carrier. South China Morning Post. From https://www.scmp.com/article/233887/mystery-macau-company-buys-aircraft-carrier

Smith, Douglas. (2013). Carrier Battles: Command and Decision in Harm's Way. Naval Institute Press.

The Straits Times. (2015, January 20). China never paid businessman who bought aircraft carrier from Ukraine: Report. From https://www.straitstimes.com/asia/east- asia/china-never-paid- businessman-who-bought-aircraft-carrier-from-ukraine-report

Vines, Stephen. (1997, January 3). A lease no one thought would run out. Independent. From https://www.independent.co.uk/news/world/a-lease-no-one-thought-would-run-out-1281384.html

WIC. (2014, August 29). *A naval hero: Meet the man who bought an aircraft carrier and gave it to China.* Week in China. From https://www.weekinchina.com/2014/08/a-naval-hero/

Yoshihara, T., & Holmes, J. (2018). *Red Star over the Pacific: China's Rise and the Challenge to U.S. Maritime Strategy.* Naval Institute Press.

SNAFU:
Developing Militaries
~~Fail to Develop~~

Russia unveils statue of AK-47 inventor Kalashnikov. (2017, September 19). The Guardian. From https://guardian.ng/news/russia-unveils-statue-of-ak-47-inventor-kalashnikov/.

AK-47 rifle inventor Mikhail Kalashnikov wrote letter saying he regretted creating weapon. (2014, January 13. ABC News. From https://www.abc.net.au/news/2014-01-13/ak-47-rifle-inventor-mikhail-kalashnikov-regrets-creating-weapon/5198396.

Biddle, S. (2015, February 13). Crazily Brilliant Libyan Rebels Weld Tank Turret to Truck (And It Works!). Gizmodo. From https://gizmodo.com/crazily-brilliant-libyan-rebels-weld-tank-turret-to-tru-5811364.

Brian Chontosh. (2020, December 22). In *Wikipedia.* https://en.wikipedia.org/wiki/Brian_Chontosh.

Chivers, C.J. (2011). *The Gun.* New York: Simon & Schuster.

De Atkine, N. (1999). Why Arabs Lose Wars. *Middle East Quarterly.* 6(4). From https://www.meforum.org/441/why-arabs-lose-wars

Elkin, F. (1946). The Soldier's Language. *American Journal of Sociology, 51*(5), 414-422. From https://www.jstor.org/stable/2771105.

Foley, K. (2017, September 10). *Viagra's famously surprising origin story is actually a pretty common way to find new drugs.* Quartz. From https://qz.com/1070732/viagras-famously-surprising-origin-story-is-actually-a-pretty-common-way-to-find-new-drugs/

Gunderman, R. (2019, November 8). *World's deadliest inventor: Mikhail Kalashnikov and his AK-47.* The Conversation. From https://theconversation.com/worlds-deadliest-inventor-mikhail-kalashnikov-and-his-ak-47-126253.

Ingersoll, G. (2014, January 13). AK-47 Inventor In Letter To Church: 'My Spiritual Pain Is Unbearable.' Business Insider. From https://www.businessinsider.com/ak-47-inventer-wrote-to-church-2014-1.

In Memoriam: Arthur Galston, Plant Biologist, Fought Use of Agent Orange. (2008, July 18). Yale News. From https://news.yale.edu/2008/07/18/memoriam-arthur-galston-plant-biologist-fought-use-agent-orange.

Kalashnikov felt guilt for AK-47 victims. (2014, January 13). Al Jazeera. From *https://www.aljazeera.com/news/2014/1/13/kalashnikov-felt-guilt-for-ak-47-victims*.

Larson, C. (2020, May 29). *Fact: Why Toyota (Yes, Toyota) Dominates Today's Battlefields.* The National Interest. From https://nationalinterest.org/blog/buzz/fact-why-toyota-yes-toyota-dominates-today%E2%80%99s-battlefields-158581.

Mattis, J., & West, B. (2019). *Call Sign Chaos: Learning to Lead.* New York: Random House.

Milzarski, E. (2021, August 25). *The Interesting Backstories to Each of Gen. Jim Mattis' Nicknames. We Are The Mighty.* From https://www.military.com/off-duty/2021/08/25/interesting-backstories- each-of-gen-jim-mattis-nicknames.html.

Mizokami, K. (2018, April 5). *How U.S. Special Forces Get Their Vehicles.* Popular Mechanics. From https://www.popularmechanics.com/military/a19694154/how-us-special-forces-get-their- armored-pickups/.

Mizokami, K. (2013, November 7). *The Toyota Pickup Truck Is the War Chariot of the Third World.* War is Boring. From https://warisboring.com/the-toyota-pickup-truck-is-the-war-chariot-of-the-third-world/.

Monument to designer of AK-47 rifle scarred by sculptor's lapse. (2017, September 22). Reuters. From https://www.reuters.com/article/us-russia-kalashnikov-monument/monument-to-designer-of-ak-47-rifle-scarred-by-sculptors-lapse-idUSKCN1BX2O6.

Nagl, J. (2005). *Learning to Eat Soup with a Knife: Counterinsurgency Lessons from Malaya and   Vietnam.* University of Chicago Press.

Neville, L, & Dennis, P. (2018). *Technicals: Non-Standard Tactical Vehicles from the Great Toyota War to modern Special Forces.* New Vanguard.

Niccol, A. (2005). *Lord of War.* Lions Gate Films.

Nolutshungu, S. (1995). *Limits of Anarchy: Intervention and State Formation in Chad.* University of Virginia Press.

Pollack, K. (2002). Arabs at War: Military Effectiveness, 1948-1991. University of Nebraska Press.

Reuters. (2017, September 22). Kalashnikov statue changed because of German weapon. BBC. From https://www.bbc.com/news/world-europe-41367394.

Schneider, B. (2003) Agent Orange: A deadly member of the rainbow. *Yale Scientific, 77*(2). From https://web.archive.org/web/20090125154522/http:/research.yale.edu/ysm/article.jsp?articleID=48.

Simon, Sam. (2020, July 21). *The Great Toyota War. History of Yesterday.* From https://historyofyesterday.com/the-great-toyota-war-52a22751b2c1.

Somaiya, R. (2020, October 14). *Why Rebel Groups Love the Toyota Hilux.* Newsweek. From https://www.newsweek.com/why-rebel-groups-love-toyota-hilux-74195.

Stanton, D. (2010). *Horse Soldiers: The Extraordinary Story of a Band of US Soldiers Who Rode to Victory in Afghanistan.* New York: Scribner.

Swiftships Shipbuilders To Be Awarded Iraqi Patrol Boat Contract. (2009, July 30). DDN. From https://www.defensedaily.com/swiftships-shipbuilders-to-be-awarded-iraqi-patrol-boat-contract-2/international/.

Tatum, S. (2017, January 12). *Mattis: 'Mad Dog' was a nickname given by the press.* CNN. From https://www.cnn.com/2017/01/12/politics/james-mattis-mad-dog-nickname/index.html.

The Technical, How a Pickup Truck Influences Modern Warfare. (2021, June 20). de faakto. From https://defaakto.com/2021/06/20/the-technical-how-a-pickup-truck-influences-modern-warfare/.

U.S. Navy and Swiftships Deliver Two 35m Patrol Boats to Iraq. (2013, February 22). Offshore Energy. https://www.offshore-energy.biz/u-s-navy-and-swiftships-deliver-two-35m-patrol-boats-to-iraq/.

TRIBES & TYRANNY: SEARCHING FOR BIG MEN

Al-Faw peninsula. (2021, November 7). In *Wikipedia*. https:// en.wikipedia.org/wiki/Al-Faw_peninsula.

Coalition forces kill Abu Musab al-Zarqawi. (2006, June 8). Air Force. From https://www.af.mil/News/Article-Display/Article/130779/coalition-forces-kill-abu-musab-al-zarqawi/.

Eisenhower, D. D. (2020, April 11). *Address to the American Society of Newspaper Editors*. American Rhetoric. From https://www.americanrhetoric.com/speeches/dwighteisenhowercrossofiron.htm.

Filkins, D. (2004, May 12). *Iraq Videotape Shows Decapitation of an American*. The New York Times. From https://www.nytimes.com/2004/05/12/international/middleeast/iraq-videotape-shows-the-decapitation-of-an.html.

FM 3-24 MCWP 3-33.5 Insurgencies and Countering Insurgencies. (2014, May). Headquarters, Department of the Army. From https://irp.fas.org/doddir/army/fm3-24.pdf.

Heinatz, S. *Suicide Attack Killed Local Sailors*. (2004, April 27). Daily Press. From https://www.dailypress.com/news/dp-xpm-20040427-2004-04-27-0404270122-story.html.

Helmer, K. (2004, April 27). *Suicide bombing attack claims first Coast Guardsman since Vietnam War*. Stripes. From https://www.stripes.com/news/suicide-bombing-attack-claims-first-coast-guardsman-since-vietnam-war-1.19271.

Hunter, J. (2011, March). *Teaching with the World Peace Game*. TED. From https://www.ted.com/talks/john_hunter_teaching_with_the_world_peace_game?language=en.

Iranian Naval Forces: A Tale of Two Navies. (February 2017). Office of Naval Intelligence. From https://www.oni.navy.mil/Portals/12/Intel%20agencies/iran/Iran%20022217SP.pdf.

Iraq Crude Oil Export Expansion Project. (2012, January 7). Unaoil. From https://web.archive.org/web/20120107072200/http://www.unaoil.com/activities.html.

Iraq terrorist leader Zarqawi 'eliminated.' (2006, June 8). *The Guardian*. From https://www.theguardian.com/world/2006/jun/08/iraq.alqaida.

Montgomery, D. (2009, September 10). *U.S. Sailors, Coast Guard Protect Iraq's Economy*. American Forces Press Service. U.S. Department of Defense. From https://web.archive.org/web/20120414083508/http://www.defense.gov/News/NewsArticle.aspx?ID=55782.

Nadimi, F. (2020). Iran's Evolving Approach to Asymmetric Naval Warfare: Strategy and Capabilities in the Persian Gulf. *The Washington Institute for Near East Policy (Policy Focus)*, 164. From https://www.washingtoninstitute.org/media/591?disposition=inline.

Remarks by President Bush: Justice Delivered to the Most Want-ed Terrorist in Iraq. (2006, June 8). U.S. Department of State. From https://2001-2009.state.gov/p/nea/rls/67696.htm.

Roth, D. (2019, April 24). *NSA Bahrain Honors Fallen Firebolt Shipmates.* U.S. Naval Forces Central Command. From https://www.cusnc.navy.mil/Media/News/Display/Article/1822351/nsa-bahrain-honors-fallen-firebolt-shipmates/.

Simmons, K. (2009, April 29). *Iraq assumes control of offshore oil terminal.* U.S. Naval Forces Central Command. From https://www.centcom.mil/MEDIA/NEWS-ARTICLES/News-Article-View/Article/883841/iraq-assumes-control-of-offshore-oil-terminal/.

Starr, B. (2008, January 7). *Iranian boats 'harass' U.S. Navy, officials say.* CNN. From http://edition.cnn.com/2008/WORLD/meast/01/07/iran.us.navy/index.html.

Sutherland, J.J. (2009, June 20). *Aging Oil Terminal Vital To Iraq's Economy (Audio).* NPR – Weekend Edition Saturday. From https://www.npr.org/templates/story/story.php?storyId=105670955.

UK sailors captured at gunpoint. (2007, March 23). BBC News. From http://news.bbc.co.uk/2/hi/uk_news/6484279.stm.

Whitaker, B., & Harding, L. (2004, May 12). *American beheaded in revenge for torture.* The Guardian. From https://www.theguardian.com/world/2004/may/12/iraq.alqaida.

Woods, K. M. (2006). *Iraqi perspectives project: A view of operation iraqi freedom from Saddam's senior leadership.* United States Joint Forces Command, Joint Center for Operational Analysis.

World Peace Game Foundation. (2018, November 14). From https://worldpeacegame.org/.

'Zarqawi' beheaded US man in Iraq. (2004, May 13). BBC News. From http://news.bbc.co.uk/2/hi/middle_east/3712421.stm.